## More Praise for This Book

"*Conscious Accountability* presents a profound concept, ～～～～～ ～
If you want to be a better leader or have a better life, read this book to gain
timeless wisdom uniquely positioned to help with today's challenges."
—**Amy C. Edmondson**, Professor, Harvard Business School; Author,
*The Fearless Organization*

"This insightful book offers a fresh look at accountability. It will help
any leader in any organization deepen relationships and improve team
performance."
—**Daniel H. Pink**, *New York Times* Bestselling Author, *The Power of Regret*,
*Drive*, and *When*

"In this important new work, the authors explain why accountability is about
more than efficiency—it's at the core of healthy relationships. Conscious
accountability is not a way of checking boxes, but a way of being human."
—**Douglas Stone**, Co-Author, *Difficult Conversations* and *Thanks for the Feedback*

"We don't often think of happiness and accountability as complementary
terms. But *Conscious Accountability* makes an artful case for reimagining
accountability so that it works not only in achieving our goals but also
in strengthening the bonds with our colleagues and communities."
—**Emma Seppälä**, Author, *The Happiness Track*; Lecturer, Yale University

"*Conscious Accountability* is a brilliantly written, must-read for any professional.
The ultimate how-to guide for accelerating valuable outcomes, this book
offers a highly practical framework for moving to the next level of influence,
no matter your level of experience. The authors also illustrate how practicing
conscious accountability can create a positive force for change in the world."
—**Geetu Bharwaney**, Founder and CEO, Ei World

"*Conscious Accountability* is a must-read for any CEO or leader. To turn dreams into a successful business you have to create an outstanding work culture—which means getting accountability right. Relatable anecdotes make it easy to read this book and absorb the concepts, plus it's packed with actionable tips and exercises. A fantastic resource!"

—Julia Pimsleur, Founder and CEO, Million Dollar Women; Author, *Million Dollar Women* and *Go Big Now*

"*Conscious Accountability* helps us be more aware of ourselves, reminds us of the power we harness when we are thoughtful about our relationships, and gives us critical tools to accomplish our goals. I encourage anyone who wants to inspire, connect, and deliver positive results, for the benefit of your professional and personal life, to read this book."

—Justin Elicker, Mayor, New Haven, Connecticut

"*Conscious Accountability* makes a tremendous contribution by showing us how accountability can be an inclusive practice—one that connects us to people, missions, and organizations. As we wrestle with new forms of work, political turmoil, and the uncertainties of a global pandemic, chapter-by-chapter this book frames awareness, intention, and the practice of accountability as tools we can use to incentivize ourselves and our teams to do our best work."

—Kerwin Charles, Dean, Yale School of Management

"Perhaps more than ever, all organizations need to embrace a new way of considering accountability—one that elevates the power and importance of relationships in ensuring a sustained and successful way forward. *Conscious Accountability* moves beyond a transactional, product-driven approach by showing us how to build self-reflective, humanistic skills into our leadership practices. Every leader needs the lessons this book has to offer."

—Linda Mayes, Arnold Gesell Professor of Child Psychiatry, Pediatrics, and Psychology; Director, Yale Child Study Center

"Build the team, communication style, and efficiency you've dreamed of for your company with *Conscious Accountability!* As experts in leadership development, David, Marianne, and Daryn will teach you step-by-step how to create cultures where accountability to your work and team can thrive."

—**Marshall Goldsmith**, Thinkers50 #1 Executive Coach; *New York Times* bestselling author, *Triggers, Mojo,* and *What Got You Here Won't Get You There*

"The COVID-19 pandemic created unprecedented disruption in communities, organizations, and the lives of countless people. *Conscious Accountability* offers engaging and clearly written guidance for getting back on our feet and for creating a new era of productivity and work satisfaction."

—**Robert M. Kaplan**, Clinical Excellence Research Center, Stanford University School of Medicine

"*Conscious Accountability* offers a way of thinking and acting in our relationships—with colleagues, family, friends, and self—that promises to help us accomplish meaningful things together and build better relationships. The authors use stories, illustrations, and exercises to share practical wisdom and wise practices for experiencing accountability, not as a means of control or being controlled, but as a humane exchange in which we help one another live up to our aspirations."

—**Ruth Wageman**, Founder, 6 Team Conditions

"*Conscious Accountability* is a powerful must-read for anyone wanting to take their management, leadership, or organizational effectiveness to the highest level. The book offers a practical framework for applying a proactive approach to accountability in the complex, evolving leadership landscape."

—**Scott Drozd**, CEO, FCP Euro

# CONSCIOUS ACCOUNTABILITY
## Deepen Connections, Elevate Results

DAVID C. TATE | MARIANNE S. PANTALON | DARYN H.DAVID

PRESS

Alexandria, VA

ATD Press is an internationally renowned source of insightful and practical information on talent development, training, and professional development.

**ATD Press**
1640 King Street
Alexandria, VA 22314 USA

Ordering information: Books published by ATD Press can be purchased by visiting ATD's website at td.org/books or by calling 800.628.2783 or 703.683.8100.

Library of Congress Control Number: 2022935221

ISBN-10: 1-950496-71-6
ISBN-13: 978-1-950496-71-6
e-ISBN: 978-1-950496-72-3

**ATD Press Editorial Staff**
Director: Sarah Halgas
Manager: Melissa Jones
Content Manager, Management: Kimberly McAvoy
Developmental Editor: Jack Harlow
Production Editor: Hannah Sternberg
Text Design: Shirley E.M. Raybuck
Cover Design: Darrin Raaum

Printed by BR Printers, San Jose, CA

*To Jimmy and Jude—two of my greatest teachers—
who continually show me the way to becoming
more conscious and more accountable.*
—DCT

*To my husband Michael, the most
committed and accountable person I know.
To Matt who reminds me to slow down and notice.
To Nick who inspires me to keep trying.*
—MSP

*To Jeffrey—your kindness and steady support,
your compassionate wisdom and your sense of integrity
provided the light that guided me to the shore.*
—DHD

# Contents

# Introduction

*The price of greatness is responsibility.*
WINSTON CHURCHILL

Have you ever worked with someone who was really good at accountability? Someone who helped get the job done while also raising their game along the way? Someone you would never dream of letting down? The type of person who always brings the best out of everyone around them? What qualities come to mind that would describe this person?

Kendra Curtis is one of those people. A Canadian with a creative spirit and engineering mind, Kendra has been enjoying building furniture during her early retirement after a successful career as a software engineer. She began managing teams at Google when the organization was less than a decade old, an experience that formed her approach to leadership and accountability after she moved on.

As an engineering manager at a different high growth tech company, Kendra was tasked with leading a multidisciplinary team in the development of a cloud-based application of a database. The project had a hard deadline and not enough engineers on staff. To be accountable to delivering the product on time, Kendra knew she would need more hands on deck. Therefore, she was charged with building the team and the product at the same time.

She dove in with a commitment to clarity. In fact, Kendra shared that *clarity* is the first word that comes to mind when she thinks of accountability. And not just clarity about the task and who owns what, but clarity about why they are doing the task, and if they have the right people for it.

As Kendra started to assemble the right people, she organized them into groups she called "Feature Pods." The pods included all the people who had skin in the game: the engineers, the user-interface designer, the person who would write the user documents, and anyone else who was developing that feature. They met on a weekly basis.

Getting the teams engaged posed some challenges. People had a lot of questions. They wondered, "What are we supposed to do in these Feature Pod meetings? What is the purpose? I don't get it." So she laid out the aims of the pods: to keep an open line of communication and to make sure they were all on the same page regarding the feature, the goals, and how they were getting there. To make their weekly meeting not feel like a performance review, she organized the discussions around a very simple framework with three main questions:

- What is the progress you have made?
- What are the problems?
- What is your plan?

To encourage buy-in and commitment, she invited people to come on a journey with her. "Do one feature like this with me," she said. "I know you don't experiment. I'm just asking you to try it once with me, and then we will evolve it." That took humility and vulnerability on her part, which she hoped her team members would reciprocate throughout the process.

Between their meetings, the team relied on written communication, which Kendra knew could be easily misunderstood and misinterpreted. Her aim was to coach the team to expect miscommunications and realize the need for several attempts to get to clarity. During one-on-one meetings she would demonstrate this using an email that one of her direct reports had written. She would share her interpretation of it, which was intentionally different from the intended message of the writer, to show how easily miscommunication could occur. Often, it was a watershed moment for the writer.

To create an atmosphere that encouraged experimentation and risk taking and to set the stage for deep engagement to occur, Kendra made a habit of sharing her own failures. At her first job as an engineer, her team was making some of the first wireless networking equipment and she was making a chip driver. She had to put these little probes on this small chip, but she shorted out two of the pins with the little probe. As she likes to retell it, "I let the magic smoke out. Literally, smoke started coming out of the chip and the chip stopped working."

She was so upset that it took her a week to work up the courage to tell her boss. When she finally showed him the chip and the melted probe, he laughed and said, "Oh yeah, something bad happened," and then he gave her a new board, saying, "Here you go, and now when you break that one, you come and tell me."

By sharing her own mishaps and struggles, she communicated that she has been there, she has messed up, and she knows what that is like. Not only did she anticipate that team members would break things, like she did, but she also considered it a critical rite of passage for people to be celebrated at the moment they became a full-fledged member of the team.

When people would join her team, especially new engineers, she would say, "You're not an engineer until you break something. I want you to come and tell me when you have broken something because I want to give you a high five and welcome you into the group of true engineers." This encouraged team members to embody the grit to work through these failures and the grace to accept that things sometimes just go wrong.

She also built a culture of constructive feedback, baking it in as a standard occurrence and always leading with what was going well. During a team's first after-action review, Kendra shared, "I would start with a little speech about how this is not about pointing fingers or assigning blame.

We're all human. Mistakes are always going to happen. And the only time I'll be upset is if we keep repeatedly making the same mistake. But if you make a mistake, that's OK. And next time we're going to find a much more creative and interesting way to make a mistake—because we're going to be in this room again." This was all about noticing with compassion, and sharing and receiving feedback without judgment, so they could respond effectively, learn from it, and move forward.

The structure and process of the Feature Pods also had a powerful impact on team dynamics and on elevating a culture where relationships were central. The pods created more empathy and better understanding among a cross-functional team. Members were able to see the perspectives of the other roles because they needed to work together to make a successful feature. The engineer could build the most successful feature ever, but if the documentation person did not understand it and could not write user documentation for it, the feature would just languish. They would understand why the project manager was pushing so hard to know when a piece of technology would be delivered. This all led to deeper conversations and improved communication, enabling the team to become more accountable to one another.

As can be expected, there were bumps in the road and setbacks as they developed the product. Some challenges were people related; others were more task focused. When Kendra had a problem with a tech lead who did not buy into the process, she attempted numerous times to coach the individual. Eventually, she had to make the difficult decision to remove this person as tech lead because they were not a good fit. At other times, setbacks occurred around product development. For example, the team would come to the conclusion that the feature they were attempting to build out did not make sense and they would need to go back to the drawing board.

This individuals were enabled to thrive by teams with a clear goal; guidelines for communication, feedback, and iteration; and a culture that viewed failure as progress. The conditions were set for ideas and empathy to freely flow, and they were able to flexibly adapt both their work process and the product development. As a result, they became more accountable to themselves and to the team in a way that led to transformative results. The rollout of their product was so successful that any time a new project was put forth, people immediately started asking about the Feature Pods.

Kendra's openness to try, learn, and try again allowed this project and process to launch. She exemplified a growth mindset with regard to both the development of the teams and the product. Things will go wrong, stuff will break, some people won't be the right fit. We just don't know all that we will get. However, a commitment to being open, to look deeper for what is not obvious, and to keep trying are the bricks that can form the path for a journey of continuously improved accountability.

## Why Does Accountability Matter?

You do not have to look very far to see why accountability is so important. It is everywhere—in our workplaces, in our marriages and families, in our friendships, and in our communities. It exists with the person we see each morning in the mirror and with strangers we will never meet. Accountability matters because it lies at the core of healthy and productive human relationships. It functions as the invisible thread that connect us to other people and enables more effective interactions with others in fundamental ways. Its presence or absence can mean the difference between success or failure, between the extraordinary or the mediocre, and even between life or death. Consider these examples:

- We often have some goal for ourselves, or some way in which we want to grow, change, or improve. We want to eat healthier or exercise more. We want to learn a new language, or write a book, or spend more time with loved ones. But how many times do we say or initiate some new activity or endeavor, and then fail to follow through? Accountability can make the difference between reaching the goal or not.
- Now more than ever, many of us are juggling our professional and personal lives. In a single day, we try to serve our clients, customers, or superiors; support our colleagues; meet deadlines; and respond to

countless emails. And in that same day, we also may need to ensure that children get fed and off to school, to remember what our spouse asked us to do, to bring our relative to a doctor's appointment, to call back the friend who really needs a listening ear, or to make room for some kind of self-care or personal development. Accountability makes the difference between delivering on our promises or dropping the ball and letting people and ourselves down.

- The realities of modern work life add complexity to the process of getting things done and people's experience of each other in that process. More of us are working from home or in offices dispersed around the globe. We rely on technology to connect with others through email, texting, and video calls. And organizations need to do more with fewer resources. Communication and building relationships under these conditions can be much more challenging. Accountability makes the difference between teams aligning and winning together or becoming disjointed and flailing.

- Finally, consider the problems associated with the Boeing 737-MAX aircraft, which went into operation in 2017 but was grounded in March 2019 after two crashes, killing 346 people. Investigations found that multiple parties failed to do what they were supposed to do, including company engineers, managers, and government regulators (Schaper 2020). In cases like this one, accountability makes the difference between life and death.

Accountability is the powerful but often elusive "secret sauce" that makes a profound difference in our results. But what does it really mean to be accountable? And what are the risks when we are not accountable?

Earlier, we saw the excellent example of Kendra engaging in the practices of conscious accountability, leading to the development of a tight team and stellar results. Conversely, neglecting these practices puts you at risk of a whole host of problems. Have you ever worked with someone or on a team that was really bad at accountability? Where it was really difficult to bring your A game? A time when you felt let down and could not help but let others down too?

Perhaps people seemed to be in their silos, discussions were challenging, the atmosphere was tense, and there was a lack of trust. Maybe people were apathetic and just phoning it in. Chances are this experience left you feeling uninspired, demoralized, resentful, angry, frustrated, confused, or disconnected. Whatever your experience, when we are not accountable to ourselves and each other, we feel bad and our work and relationships suffer. Conscious accountability offers a new way forward.

## What Is Conscious Accountability?

In this book, we will describe our notion of accountability at its best—what we call *conscious accountability*. We define it as expanding awareness to create deliberate intentions, take informed actions, and be responsible for our impact. Let's break that down a bit further. By *awareness*, we mean awareness of ourselves, awareness of other people, and awareness of the interdependence between self and others. *Deliberate intentions* refers to having preconceived ideas about what it is we want to do, and about the desired effects we want to have on others. *Informed actions* are actions that are both informed by our awareness and are consistent with our intentions. Finally, *being responsible for our impact* means acknowledging that our actions (and inactions) affect other people, and that we are willing to own the results that follow.

We believe that conscious awareness is the thing that helps us become more accountable. How does that work? When we are more aware of ourselves (what we need, want, and value), we can communicate our expectations more clearly. When we are more aware of others (what they need and want, and the context in which they are operating), we can better understand them, honor their expectations of us, and respond to them with empathy. When we are more aware of the interdependence between ourselves and others, we are in a better position to generate win-win scenarios. When we are aware of our impact on others, we can better adjust and become more committed to behaviors that support the kind of influence on others that we hope to have. Taken together, the result of greater consciousness is both better task outcomes (things get done well) and improved human relationships (more understanding and an enhanced sense of our connection to others). In this way, conscious accountability goes beyond something that is transactional in nature—you do your part, and I will do mine. It becomes more transformational, which makes more meaning, joy, fulfillment, and excellence possible.

So, how do you actually create conscious accountability? The simple answer is, through practice. To help develop your personal capacity to create conscious accountability with other people, this book offers seven practices, which we call the CONNECT framework. Here's a quick summary:

1. **Creating clarity.** This practice is all about establishing a clear vision and shared goals and expectations. It requires strong, crisp communication in which people can negotiate the terms of interacting together, so that they can identify and iron out any areas of potential disagreement or misalignment. For example, at the outset of every meeting, Nancy, an elementary school principal, establishes both the desired outcomes ("What do we want to walk away with?"), as well as the desired process for reaching the outcomes ("How do we need to work together to reach our goals?").

2. **Opening up engagement.** This practice is about creating the conditions in which people feel safe and free to express themselves and feel committed to working together to complete the tasks at hand. Engineering manager Peter helps establish safety by emphasizing the importance of learning (especially learning through trial and error), which helps his team feel more comfortable admitting and discussing the times when things do not go as planned. Peter also takes the time to explain the purpose and the reasoning for any decisions, helping the team see why their work matters. This helps foster greater commitment among team members.

3. **Nailing it.** This practice means doing what you say you will do and ensuring that others are doing the same. It often involves managing competing priorities so that balls do not get dropped and helping others organize toward task completion. For important deadlines, Rajeed sits down with team members and helps them figure out

how to make space for the necessary actions, ensuring there is a plan in place for dealing with anything that could pull the team's focus elsewhere.

4. **Noticing.** In this practice, people pay attention to what they are seeing outwardly and experiencing internally, actively checking in with others to share any of their observations and ensure the other person is doing OK with their part. This includes noticing when actions are veering off from previously agreed-on intentions. Maria, a nurse manager, walks the hospital floor to get a sense of the general mood and, based on what she sees, will check in with her staff. After she delegates a project, she will touch base to see how it is going and ensure her staff have what they need to make progress.

5. **Exchanging feedback.** This practice involves soliciting, receiving, and giving feedback to help oneself and others expand awareness, learn what is or is not working, and make any necessary course corrections. Joe and Elaine, who have been married for 15 years, have a date night every week. Part of their weekly ritual is to ask each other how they did at attending to important things that matter to each of them, which they have discussed previously. Then each person shares one appreciation of what went well and one wish for how things could go better for the coming week.

6. **Claiming it.** This practice is all about taking ownership and responsibility for the results—both the successes and the failures—and consolidating the learning without blaming others. Scott, the CEO of a manufacturing company, has a sign outside his office that says, "The buck stops here." When the company is successful, he recognizes the individuals and teams that made it happen. When they fail, he takes responsibility for making sure that measures are taken so it never happens again.

7. **Trying again.** This practice is about taking what you have learned from an experience and applying it in the next situation. It is crucial for creating a cycle of continuous improvement. Iris, who runs a

small consulting firm, sits down with her team after every client engagement wraps up. They review what happened, determining what they learned and how to implement any new insights in the next project.

Now think back to the beginning of this introduction and the descriptors that you associated with someone who is really good at accountability. How many of those ideas are related to these seven practices? Did clear expectations or clarity make your list? What about safety and commitment? Or doing what you say you will do? How about noticing and checking in with others? Or exchanging feedback and taking responsibility? That is what it means to embody conscious accountability.

## What Will This Book Offer You?

This book is a resource for anyone who wants to improve their own effectiveness, both at getting things done and optimizing relationships. But it is especially helpful for people who are responsible for getting work done with and through others, whose work focuses on and supports the well-being of others, and for anyone focused on building organizational culture (for example, leaders and managers). This book is for people who want to become masterful at holding high expectations while also holding themselves and others in full humanity.

To bring these concepts to life, we draw from the rich experiences of our lives and those of our clients. Across the book, we will share our own stories and present real, fictional, and hybrid accounts that cover a range of different industries (healthcare, academia, finance, and technology) and business types (startups, nonprofits, family run, private equity, Fortune 1000), based on our work coaching and consulting with practitioners, leaders, and teams. In presenting these cases, we have worked hard to anonymize any features that could identify the people on whom such stories may be based. We hope they will bring to life the successes and setbacks that can occur when accountability is involved.

This book will invite you to think about yourself and others in your life more completely and to try out new ways of thinking and acting. Specifically, you will have the opportunity to explore the skills and mindsets of the seven practices of conscious accountability. Through the CONNECT framework, we will give you the tools you need to better relate to everyone in your professional and personal life—to raise your understanding and awareness of basic human needs like autonomy, mastery, and belonging; to put people in a position to succeed and inspire excellence everywhere you turn; to enjoy more meaningful relationships; and to absolutely, positively crush your goals. With this book, you will discover how to create a culture of accountability for yourself and others around you.

You will do this, first, by developing your capacity for self-reflection. Reflection is a crucial means of increasing conscious awareness of self and others, which will allow you to operate with greater intentionality and, ultimately, to become more accountable. Throughout this book we will invite you to reflect upon both your internal and external experiences. Second, you will also be invited to take actions by engaging in specific practices that will increase your personal, interpersonal, and team effectiveness over time. You will not be perfect at this. Neither will we. In fact, no one will ever be. You will have good days and bad days, successful and failed attempts. The important thing is to be in it for the learning—which is always available, if you are open to finding it.

## Who We Are in This Work

We, the authors, come to the work around conscious accountability in a number of ways. We are psychologists who bring theoretical and practical expertise on human behavior change. We are executive coaches who have walked alongside people through their journeys to greater personal satisfaction and team performance. We are also educators who teach strategies for greater personal and leadership effectiveness to graduate students, faculty members, healthcare professionals, executives, and leaders from around the world. But primarily, we come to this work as fellow human beings who strive to "walk the talk" every day in our professional and personal lives. And, like you, we experience the challenges associated with work, life, and relationships, complete with all of the ups and downs.

The time during which we wrote this book—from late 2019 through late 2021—was a particularly turbulent moment in modern history. We have watched a global pandemic wreak havoc on people's lives and livelihoods. We have witnessed the rightful struggles for greater equity, justice, and inclusion for marginalized people in the United States. We have seen the global political and social order shaken. We have experienced the stress of civic polarization and have been saddened by the divides that have emerged in the US, in our communities, and in our own families.

All of these things have increased our own need to live the practices we discuss in these pages. We have had to be clearer with spouses about family members' needs and expectations that come along with working and schooling from home. We have thought deeply about our clients and students, including how we may best anticipate their needs and foster their capacity to work to high standards of excellence amid the psychological and physical burdens of increased social distancing, fears about physical safety, and the unique demands created by remote work, or in some cases, direct patient contact in healthcare, all during a global pandemic.

We have considered what our own role is in creating safe spaces that allow people with different lived experiences and beliefs to find common ground and build something productive from there. We have had to adjust our writing process and be more specific and clear with each other in what we can do, and by when, as schedules shift and circumstances change. We have experienced what it is like to practice conscious accountability, with some successes, some failures, and lots of learning along the way.

So, as we are engaged in striving each day to embody the practices of conscious accountability, we are here to support, encourage, and challenge you to do the same as you embark on your own voyage to a more aware, centered, connected, and effective version of yourself.

## Our Call to Read Further

In the pages ahead, we will guide you through the ideas, reflections, and actions designed to help you unlock your potential and have a better impact on everyone around you.

In part 1, we define what conscious accountability means and explain why you should rethink traditional notions of accountability. We also explain how conscious awareness is a key differentiator between traditional notions of accountability and conscious accountability, and how conscious accountability is different from transactional ideas about accountability. In part 2, we describe each of the seven practices in detail, including why they are important, barriers that may block your progress, and mindsets and behaviors that allow you to embody each practice. We also illustrate each practice with examples and offer practice exercises for you to try. In part 3, we offer additional tips and inspiration for implementing conscious accountability and encourage you to think about how the world would be different if more people practiced it.

We invite you to make your practice of conscious accountability a part of your life and to make the most of the opportunity that this book offers. We are thrilled to have you along for this journey! Ready? Let's begin.

# PART 1
## A Different Approach
## to Accountability

# CHAPTER 1

# Rethinking Accountability

*Life doesn't make any sense without interdependence. We need each other, and the sooner we learn that, the better for us all.*

ERIK H. ERIKSON

Josh Hudson was the CEO of his family's manufacturing business, Integrated Solutions Incorporated (ISI). He was an intelligent, capable leader with a gifted capacity to envision the future. He could be very charismatic and persuasive, which helped him negotiate incredible opportunities for the company. After a devastating financial recession, ISI struggled to get back on its feet, plagued by issues of product quality and slow delivery. Josh saw that his team was not working well together. Different departments blamed one another for problems instead of working together to find solutions, and employees and mid-level managers were reluctant to make decisions. As a result, decisions were pushed upward, creating bottlenecks and sluggish response times.

Frustrated by these seemingly intractable problems, Josh recognized that ISI's culture needed to change. He hired a consultant to help the senior management team embrace a new way of working together. During an intensive retreat, the team began to prepare to embark on this culture change initiative. On the last day of the retreat, Josh did not appear. He left a message for one of the other team members, saying that he needed to fly to Chicago to jump on an important opportunity that he was just made aware of and to go on without him. Josh further reasoned that the team seemed to be working well and was learning the concepts that he had already mastered. And that's when everything unraveled.

In Josh's absence, the team shared with one another how angry, frustrated, and fed up they were with his leadership. They saw this "no-show" behavior as emblematic of how he operated—he did what he thought was best, with no consideration, consultation, or discussion with the team. He was a stickler for following prescribed processes but was the first to break process when it did not suit his immediate objectives. He would frequently override his managers' decisions if he disagreed with them, but sharply berated them or sent scathing emails if they dared to question or challenge his ideas publicly. He also played favorites, leading to resentment and divisions within the company. On one hand, hearing each other's experiences with Josh was very validating for the team. However, they struggled with what to do next. Ultimately, they decided to bring their concerns to Josh directly.

The next week when the team got together for their Monday morning meeting, Josh energetically described his success in pitching a project to the important new customer in Chicago. Then, Martha, the vice president of finance and Josh's cousin, spoke up. She shared the team's disappointment and frustration with Josh for putting this opportunity over the work of the team, of which he was an important member. Others chimed in with examples of how he routinely did things "his way" without regard for other people's ideas or feelings, leading them to feel disempowered and less motivated. Josh sat brooding silently as people spoke, his face turning increasingly red and flushed. Finally, he erupted: "So it's all my fault, is it? Do you know how hard I have worked for this company? We would have been out of business years ago if it weren't for me! You guys are the ones who don't know how to lead, not me. If you don't appreciate what I've done for all of you, then maybe I should just quit and then you'll realize how bad off you are without me!" And he stormed out, slamming the conference room door.

Where did Josh go wrong? How did his strengths and drawbacks as a leader affect the outcomes on his team? Do you have a colleague, business partner, teammate, or company executive like Josh? Have there been times in your life when you wanted to point out that another person had let you down and sought the most constructive, compassionate way to provide this feedback, only to have that person close down or blow up defensively?

Like many business leaders, Josh lacked a certain type of accountability. Let's unpack this. First, Josh did not have a clear understanding of what others wanted or needed from him. Second, he did not appreciate the many ways his behaviors affected others around him, or the ripple effects those actions had throughout the organization. This constricted view made it challenging for Josh to keep in mind others' perspectives and to hear their feedback.

Josh's style as a manager also created certain accountability challenges. At times, he displayed a critical, harsh, top-down way of managing his team. This style inadvertently created an environment of risk aversion, stymied decision making, and inspired a fear of giving or receiving feedback—all of which lowered employee engagement. Alongside this, Josh's reluctance to admit mistakes or claim responsibility for his actions left him and the organization unable to move forward.

ISI's culture change initiative would not be successful unless Josh could display a more nuanced type of accountability and regard for himself, his team, and the organization as a whole.

## Why Accountability Matters

Accountability is the focus of this book. So, what is the new, more nuanced definition of accountability that we have been building toward? What do we actually mean when we say "accountability"? And why does accountability matter? Isn't it just another word for being answerable to someone? As long as we keep our heads down and get our work done on time, that means we're accountable, right?

Not quite. Accountability is at the heart of our work and our relationships. Think of accountability as the "secret sauce" that, when present and used well, leads to better results across many different spheres in life. And when it is used poorly or lacking entirely, it can have disastrous consequences.

We will talk more about what conscious accountability means in chapters 2 and 3. But at its core, we think of accountability as meaning *being responsible for your impact*—both the impact that you would like to have and the impact that you actually have. Being responsible for the impact that you would like to have (that is, for your intentions) means making sure you lay the groundwork for success. That includes being clear about the outcome you want to happen and exactly what is needed from you and others to realize it. It also means creating the conditions for you and others to be and do your best. Being accountable for your impact involves being willing to receive feedback about how you affect others and taking responsibility for the results you create through your actions or inactions.

Ultimately, accountability matters for a number of reasons, including the fact that accountability is present all around us, it greatly helps us get things done, and it strengthens trust.

## Accountability Is Everywhere

Humans are social creatures. We live in communities and depend on one another for survival. That means the social contracts we make with ourselves and others are essential for our sense of order, safety, and well-being. This interdependence not only keeps us alive, but it also helps us thrive.

In every relationship we have with an individual, group, or organization, there is an accountability equation at play. We need and expect things from others, and they need and expect things from us, even if these mutual expectations are implicit and unspoken. Parents and children expect and need things from one another, but there is usually no formal agreement or contract that they enter into. Whether we acknowledge it or not, relationships are the fabric of the human condition, and therefore accountability is always present and inescapable.

So if accountability is baked into us, it is clear that it is present in how we accomplish any task.

## Getting Things Done

Have you ever heard the expression, "If it weren't for the last minute, nothing would get done"? This saying speaks to the importance of deadlines to mobilize people toward completion. Even more motivating, though, can be answering to someone else or having others count on you.

In writing this book, for example, we had to be accountable to each other, to our editors, and to our publisher. And we have used family, friends, and colleagues as accountability partners to help us stay focused and meet our deadlines. Think about the things you are trying to accomplish—how does accountability to other people factor into it? What do others need and expect from you, and vice versa? How might you use the power of those connections to strengthen your own sense of accountability?

The enhanced accountability that human relationships provide is one of the reasons why coaching works. A coach, or someone in the role of a coach, serves as an accountability partner to help us stay true to and follow through with our own agendas. Indeed, there is empirical evidence that coaching helps people attain their goals while simultaneously increasing their resilience and well-being (Grant, Curtayne, and Burton 2009).

That is the power of accountability . . . and it also goes a long way toward building what every good relationship needs: trust.

## Building Trust

Trust is arguably the foundation of relationships for individuals, teams, and organizations. Without trust, relationships are at best distant and not especially effective, and at worst they're chaotic, dysfunctional, toxic, or dangerous. Accountability is the active ingredient for making or breaking trust. The relationship between accountability and trust is actually reciprocal: accountability builds trust, while trust allows people to be more accountable. Let's dig deeper into how that works.

We all have different baseline levels of trust, with different people being more or less trusting of others at the outset. Regardless of these baseline levels, trust can be strengthened or weakened by accountability. As future behavior is best predicted by past behavior, people assume (often rightfully) someone's level of trustworthiness based on how they have behaved previously (Ouellette and Wood 1998, Fishbein and Ajzen 1975). So when you do what you say you will do and act responsibly, it strengthens the perception that you're trustworthy. Conversely, if you do not do what you say you will do, it lowers trust. The bottom line is that if you want to build trusting relationships, it behooves you to be accountable.

The presence of trust can also help people engage in some of the behaviors that promote greater accountability. The more we trust other people, the easier it is to communicate more freely and fully—for example, to ask questions, raise concerns, admit mistakes, and give or receive feedback. These behaviors in turn promote a higher degree of accountability.

How does this work in your life? Think of someone in whom you have a high degree of trust. What makes them so trustworthy, reliable, and believable? In what ways have they been accountable in your relationship? How well do they communicate with you? How easy would it be for you to admit your mistakes or wrongdoings to them, or vice versa?

Now, in contrast, reflect on a relationship you have with someone whom you do not particularly trust. Why don't you trust that person? How does their level of accountability in their past behaviors factor into your feelings about them and your assessment of their trustworthiness? And how does this lack of trust affect how fully and freely you are able to communicate with them?

Interestingly, accountability and increased trust translate into better efficiency and cost savings at work. In *The Speed of Trust*, Stephen Covey (2008) argues that there is a direct relationship between trust on the one hand and speed and cost on the other. When trust increases, speed increases and costs go down. In other words, when trust decreases, speed decreases and costs go up, whereas when there is higher trust (for example, you trust that the information you are receiving is accurate), there is less need to double check or seek additional sources of information, which speeds up the process and ultimately saves money. So accountability breeds trust, and trust leads to efficiency and cost savings.

Being trustworthy can be a huge asset; it makes people more interested in engaging with you, seeing you as good and of value, and wanting to promote you or work or do business with you. Conversely, a bad reputation hinders success on all levels and can be difficult to shift or overcome. Behaving in ways that create accountability and build trust can make a substantial difference in how you are perceived in the world.

## The Time Is Now: Accountability Needs an Upgrade

In a traditional sense, we think of accountability as having to answer to, or justify behaviors and actions to, someone else. Governments need to be accountable to their citizens; politicians and lawmakers to their constituents; doctors and teachers to their patients and students; companies to their shareholders and customers; and teams to their leaders or managers.

This conceptualization of accountability places an undue emphasis on the underlying assumption that we answer only to those who have some power to influence or affect our capacity to continue doing our jobs. Citizens in a democracy can reelect or vote out an incumbent leader or party. Boards can remove CEOs or raise their compensation. Patients can file malpractice lawsuits. Customers can stop buying (or buy more) products and services. Team members can be fired or promoted by their managers. In all of these examples, accountability is defined by the potential to lose something should our behavior not measure up.

We refer to this traditional notion of accountability as "accountability 1.0," and it has serious flaws in how we interact with people on a personal and professional level.

### Limitations of Accountability 1.0

An obvious limitation to this style of accountability is that it is inherently transactional: If I do what I am supposed to do, I get something I want; if I do not do it, I receive some negative consequence. It relies on extrinsic motivation, rewards and punishments. This represents a problem because extrinsic motivation is not as powerful and sustainable a form of motivation as intrinsic motivation, which is driven by our deeper needs and values. And all this has crept into the meaning of the word *accountability* itself.

What comes immediately to mind when you think about accountability? In common parlance, we often mean, "Who is to blame? Who should be held responsible?" Holding others accountable, even yourself, can feel like assuming the role of a watchdog or an enforcer who gets people to do things by doling out threats. In this framing, accountability can feel sterile, individualistic, and even punitive. As a result, people being held accountable for something may expect punishment, retribution, or loss of credibility or status if they do not follow through and deliver; the motivation for action is therefore often fear, discomfort, or concern, rather than something more.

Accountability 1.0 can also lead us to ignore or discount stakeholders who may matter greatly but have less immediate power to reward or punish us. We prioritize, or outright ignore, some relationships at the expense of others. For example, more progressive organizations appreciate that employees—not just shareholders and customers—are critical stakeholders to whom employers are accountable. Similarly, healthcare professionals aiming to provide optimal patient care recognize the importance of building partnerships with and seeking input from not only patients but also the other important people in their lives. When our conception of those we are accountable to only extends up the power chain, such as to our boss, we can neglect those we rely on and those who rely on us, such as our teammates and others in the more outer reaches of impact.

In addition, in accountability 1.0 how well we get along and our commitment to the relationship is secondary, perhaps not even considered consciously, in our effort to get the stated job done. If the people we work with do not adequately follow through with a request, they may become defensive or reactive. Similarly, when making the request, we may become entitled or adversarial if the request is not fulfilled. At worst, accountability can become competitive, resulting in finger pointing and score keeping that drives people apart. In the opening example, Josh immediately heard his employees' complaints as a form of criticism, against which he defended himself strongly.

It is clear that accountability 1.0 fails to inspire our inner motivation, causes us to discount relationships outside a transaction, and de-emphasizes the quality of our relationships. Does relying on threats and depersonalizing our connections with our colleagues sound like the solution? In our opinion, the answer is a resounding, "No!" So what's the alternative to this way of exercising accountability? And what in our current world makes it crucially important that we adopt a more holistic view of accountability?

## The Way We Work Is Changing

Consider the following trends in the nature of work, which were present before the COVID-19 pandemic, but have been exacerbated by it:

- **Technology.** Changes in technology continue to revolutionize the way people live and work, such as increased use of artificial intelligence (AI), the proliferation of various digital communication platforms, the use of big data to drive decision making, and increasing reliance on software to conduct our business and run our lives from our phones. On the one hand, these changes can mean greater efficiency and flexibility to run our businesses and our lives. But to the extent that greater use of technology can separate us or reduce humanity in our decision making, how does that affect our sense of accountability? We have observed people expressing themselves on social media in ways that—we suspect— they would never do standing in front of another person. With greater disconnection comes a diminished sense of awareness of others or obligation to them, leading to a lowered sense of accountability.
- **Globalization.** Accompanying these changes in technology is the ability to more easily communicate and share information with

people all over the world. Globalization is reflected in the increase in organizations conducting business on a multinational scale, which includes having customers and employees around the world. To be successful in a global economy, it is important for people to be able to relate to, understand, and engage effectively with people who are culturally different. This poses challenges for accountability, both in terms of managing differences in work styles and managing differences in what it means to be accountable. In fact, the exact meaning of the word *accountability* varies across languages and cultures, ranging from responsibility to promises and vows to control to financial accounts (GEM Report 2017). In one ethnographic study of accountability, participants found it hard to describe what accountability meant, and "the more intent they became on pinning it down the more its meaning seemed to elude them" (Savage and Moore 2004).

- **Remote work.** Another important change is the growth in remote and hybrid workforces. As more business is done around the world, more work is being done from home or at other remote locations. And the outbreak of a pandemic in 2020 dramatically accelerated this trend even among companies and industries that were not previously in favor of it. In 2021, 58.6 percent of US workers were remote, which represented a 159 percent increase since 2009 (Steward 2021). Although working remotely has some compelling benefits for workers (for example, increased productivity, flexibility, and work-life integration), it also has some drawbacks (such as loneliness, challenges in communication and collaboration, and feeling less included in decisions). All these issues make accountability more difficult in remote and hybrid work environments.

- **Diversity, equity, and inclusion.** As movements for racial justice have come to the forefront, gained momentum, and led to improvements in broader participation, there has been a growing awareness on the part of organizations and employers that they can and should be active in creating change. For example, leaders who promote anti-racist policies recognize the systemic nature of racism and take active steps to dismantle systems of oppression and inequity within their organizations (Liu 2020). The focus on equity in the workplace has become amplified as companies are being called to demonstrate greater transparency around board and executive representation, compensation, hiring, advancement, and other aspects of talent management and organizational life. Accordingly, there will be increasing attention to accountability around implementing and sustaining these changes.

- **Teaming.** Working on a *team* (noun) continues to be important, but in many work contexts, there has been a rise in the need for *teaming* (verb). On a typical team, the membership is relatively stable, such that team members know who is on the team and who is not. In other cases, groups of people come together and work on temporary or short-term projects. In these conditions, having teaming skills— the ability to create strong relationships quickly and coordinate and collaborate with a potentially diverse group of stakeholders—will help build organizations that are able to respond and adapt faster to issues and challenges (Edmondson 2012). While teaming has many benefits, it may also complicate accountability. Within more traditional "vertical" organizations, accountability tends to be simpler, focused primarily between employees and their supervisors. In flat, team-based organizations, accountability occurs both within teams (members being accountable to each other) and across different teams and others laterally. An example of the differences in complexity, with more intersecting lines of accountability in team-based organizations, is shown in Figure 1-1.

**Figure 1-1.** Lines of Accountability

Lines of accountability in traditional vertical organizations

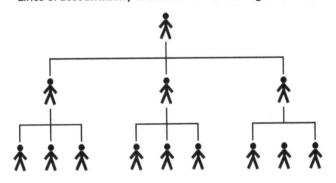

Lines of accountability in team-based organizations

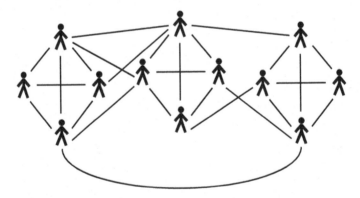

## Humans Are Struggling to Connect

While humans are inherently social in nature, the downside is that our natural ways of building connections at work may feel out of step with the trends in how we work (for example, less in-person and face-to-face interactions, and more communication through email, text, and other media). As a result, job turnover, loneliness, anxiety, depression, burnout, and suicide are on the rise. Growing evidence across disciplines including neuroscience, sociology, social psychology, psychiatry, and mental health suggests the importance of connection and the dangers of loneliness and isolation.

In studying social support and morbidity, Julianne Holt-Lunstad, professor of psychology and neuroscience at Brigham Young University, found that being socially connected significantly reduced the risk for premature mortality and that lacking social connectedness significantly increased the risk. Moreover, these risks exceed those associated with many other factors that receive substantial public health resources, including obesity, air pollution, smoking, and physical inactivity (Holt-Lunstad, Smith, and Layton 2010).

Data also links a lack of social connectedness to physical and mental health outcomes and limitations in a person's ability to function at work and in relationships. In particular, Generation Z reports higher levels of loneliness and worse mental health overall than other generations (AECF 2021; Bethune 2019). In contrast, people who feel more socially connected to others have lower rates of anxiety and depression, higher self-esteem, increased empathy, and are more trusting and cooperative with others; as a result, others are more trusting and cooperative with them (Seppälä 2014).

Taken together, these findings underscore the importance of creating ways of working together that are not only effective from a task performance, bottom-line perspective, but are also sustainable—in that they also help nurture, support, and foster the growth of the people involved.

## We Need Conscious Accountability

It is easy to see how accountability 1.0 is shortsighted, too narrow in its focus, less sustainable and profitable, and adversely affects our well-being. But the concept of accountability itself is not completely to blame. Accountability holds promise as a much more positive, powerful, and universal idea, one that can change us, our relationships, our workplaces, our communities, and indeed our world. We refer to this next evolution of accountability as conscious accountability.

*Conscious accountability* is a practice of working together in ways that catalyze interpersonal connections and produce excellent task outcomes. In this model, people who are consciously accountable to one another are deeply motivated not just by their shared goals but also by the quality of their relationships with one another. Accountability stems not from fear of reprisal or retribution but from wanting to do right by oneself and others. Awareness of one's own strengths, weaknesses, intentions, and emotions—and being aware of or curious about those of others—figures prominently in how we practice conscious accountability. Failing to produce is not a black-and-white invitation for reprisal but a learning moment, supported by the relationship that has experienced the lapse in accountability.

Take a moment and imagine working alongside people who you feel strongly connected to and aligned within your common purpose. A group that makes you feel free to be your most authentic self and still fully belong. How wonderful would it be to see yourself achieving remarkable results and fulfilling your mission in a way that allows everyone involved to learn and grow as individuals? Further, wouldn't your experience generate learning and improvement at the group level to bolster your collective capacity to do more and be even more effective together over time? This state of affairs defines what it means to be an effective team and represents the potential that conscious accountability holds (see, for example, Wageman et al. 2014).

In the next chapter, we'll share our understanding of consciousness, why this notion is of vital importance for accountability, and what it means to expand your consciousness.

# CHAPTER 2

# Becoming More Aware

*Awareness is like the sun. When it shines*
*on things, they are transformed.*

THICH NHAT HANH

Aaron is a data management specialist working in a small hospital in the Southwest. A hard worker and a dedicated, well-intentioned teammate, Aaron is always quick to lend his support when colleagues need help on a project. Recently, however, he's fallen behind in some of his responsibilities. This was the case when Aaron agreed to help Elizabeth research potential vendors to upgrade their hospital's electronic health records system. Working under a tight timeframe, Elizabeth had only a month to pick vendors and complete the request for proposals (RFP) process. After the first week, Elizabeth checked in, and Aaron, while a little vague, said he was on track to share a list the following week. But Aaron never did end up delivering his research. The second week passed and Elizabeth, frustrated, moved on to doing the research and reminded herself not to ask for Aaron's help again.

Little did Elizabeth know of Aaron's struggles to feel close to people, which cause him anxiety in his relationships. He values connection and yearns to feel secure in his personal and professional relationships, yet this has proven challenging for him in the past. This tension results in his behaving in ways that are overly accommodating. He tends to immediately agree to requests because he fears if he says no, the relationships will be harmed or even broken. As a result, he ends up taking on tasks and responsibilities that are more than he can handle, causing him to feel overwhelmed, despondent, and resentful. More often than not, he cannot complete all that he takes on. This has gained him the reputation of overpromising and underdelivering. Ironically, his attempts to forge stronger relationships end up putting significant strain on them.

Do you relate to any part of Aaron and Elizabeth's story? Many people have a reflexive inclination to want to please others, and, like Aaron, say yes when they should say no. Or perhaps you've been in Elizabeth's position, frustrated by people around you who drop the ball. What do you think could help prevent these demoralizing, everyday failures in accountability from happening?

The answer is conscious awareness. Had Aaron been more aware of his relationship anxiety and how that leads him to overcommit, he might have handled Elizabeth's request differently. Likewise, had Elizabeth been more aware of Aaron's current workload or his tendency toward people pleasing, she might have had a different kind of conversation with him about the work upfront.

Conscious awareness is the key differentiator between accountability 1.0, which is more transactional, and conscious accountability, which is more transformational. By holding our own needs, proclivities, and capacities in mind, and considering the perspectives and needs of others, we can simultaneously improve the quality of our relationships and the quality of results. With greater awareness, we can better hold ourselves and others accountable. Conscious awareness is what allows for a more holistic and humanistic understanding of the big picture as we pursue our goals. Therefore, one of the ways we can improve our practice of conscious accountability is to work actively and deliberately to expand our conscious awareness.

## What Do We Mean by "Conscious"?

Consciousness is something that has been pondered and scrutinized by philosophers and scientists for centuries, yet there is no consensus on what consciousness is or how to define it precisely (Koch 2018). For our purposes, we define *consciousness* as "awareness of experience." That means being aware of our own experiences, as well as being aware of the experiences of others.

Conscious accountability focuses on bringing experiences that are out of awareness into the light, allowing us to become more conscious of the influences on us and on others. Each time we become aware of an influence of which we were previously unaware, a connection is made. In this way, we see consciousness as a growing network of connections (Figure 2-1).

**Figure 2-1.** Consciousness as a Network of Connections

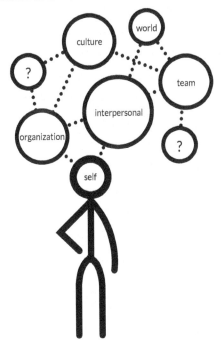

Once we make those connections, we can use this awareness to make better choices—choices that are more in alignment with our intentions. Let's share a personal example.

In a graduate-level leadership class that David teaches, students complete a weekly reflection journal assignment. Designed to help them reflect more deeply on themselves and their experiences in the course, the journal becomes an important source of learning. One student's submission described his negative reaction to an article David had assigned in class: *"Such articles do little to advance discourse and reflect poor judgment and scientific illiteracy by the authors and professors who post them."*

David felt that the student missed the point of the assignment and responded with the following comment: *"Sorry you did not find much value in the article, which was intended to spark debate and critical thinking, albeit in a somewhat provocative manner."* But later that night David was unable to sleep, as he reflected more deeply about how he felt about the student's comments.

The next day David wrote in his journal about it and spoke about the interchange with a trusted colleague. Through his own process of reflecting alone and with others, David became more aware that he was actually feeling angry and hurt by the student's statements. And further, he was concerned that if this was how the student went about giving feedback to others, it could have a detrimental impact on his future as a leader (not to mention on the people he will lead). David also became aware that his commitment to the student as his instructor was to help him increase his capacity to be more interpersonally effective.

After a few days, David realized that withholding more detailed feedback was counter to his intentions for the student's learning, so he logged into the online grading system and sent the student this message:

In the spirit of conscious accountability, I have some feedback for you, given with the hope that this allows you to continue to improve as a leader over time. When I reflected on your comments, I experienced them as unnecessarily harsh and condescending.

The part of the feedback I reacted to was your assertion that assigning the article demonstrated my "poor judgment and scientific illiteracy."

Please know that I completely support (and applaud!) your capacity to think critically and to voice those criticisms. This kind of behavior helps teams avoid groupthink and allows for constructive debate that ultimately leads to the best thinking and outputs. Here are some suggestions for how you could improve your delivery of feedback in the future: (1) separate your criticism of ideas from criticism of people; (2) when you need to criticize or critique people, (a) focus on behavior not character or things more intrinsic to personhood, and (b) frame your feedback with empathy and with some intention to help them improve.

The student replied:

Hi Professor, thank you for taking the time to provide detailed feedback and making this a teaching moment. Your point about separating the idea from the person was powerful and something I took to heart. In the future, I will reflect on my writing to make sure I'm being fair to the people I'm writing about and not make unwarranted personal judgments.

Ultimately, David's ability to become aware of his own feelings and what he was really committed to sparked the action that created some potentially important awareness for the student. By giving him this feedback, David shared the impact the student had on him, which allowed the student to self-reflect and learn from the experience.

## Two Kinds of Consciousness

For the purposes of this book, it's helpful to think of consciousness as falling into two domains: self-awareness and social awareness. Both kinds of consciousness are crucial for the practice of conscious accountability.

## Self-Awareness

Earlier we noted that our definition of *consciousness* was "awareness of experience." Our experience is inclusive of many things: thoughts, perceptions, beliefs, physical sensations, feelings and emotions, actions, behaviors, motives, values, preferences, interpretations, stories, and memories—to name more than a few. Self-awareness includes the ability to observe all of these different aspects of our own experience.

Self-awareness as a concept dates back to ancient times. Plato is credited with saying, "Know thyself." But what does it really mean to know thyself? A formal theory of self-awareness emerged in 1972 when social psychologists Shelley Duval and Robert Wicklund proposed that self-awareness occurs when we consciously focus on the self as an object. There is the part of ourselves that thinks, feels, and behaves, and there is a part of ourselves that is aware of our thoughts, feelings, and behaviors. For example, your mind can be busy with worried thoughts about a deadline, and then there is a part of your mind that notices you are having worried thoughts. This is the phenomenon of self-awareness: the ability to think about our thinking, as well as about our feelings and our behaviors. In other words, we are not our experiences. We are the observers of our experiences.

Take a moment now and try practicing self-awareness by observing your experience in this moment:

- **Bring attention to your mind.** What are you thinking right now? Notice that there is a part of you that is thinking and there is another part of you that is observing what you are thinking.
- **Bring your attention to your body.** What physical sensations are you noticing? To assist, try this five senses exercise. Name five things you can see, four things you can feel, three things you can hear, two things you can smell, and one thing you can taste.
- **Bring your attention to your emotions.** What emotions are you experiencing right now? Are some stronger than others? Where are they present in your body? Can you label them with feeling words?

It is quite a lot to notice and be aware of within ourselves! The good news is that we can improve our awareness of all these rich experiences with practice.

Let's try another exercise in self-awareness. Take a moment to think about your day and reflect on these questions:

- What were the important things that happened?
- What meaning did you make of what happened?
- What was the story you told yourself about what happened?
- What were some of the thoughts that occupied your mind?
- What emotions did you experience?
- What did you choose to do (or not do) today?
- Why did you make those choices?
- How are your values reflected in these stories, thoughts, emotions, and choices?

What was that like to answer some of these questions? Many of us go through our days without giving much thought to what we are thinking and feeling. But by contemplating such questions, we can reveal hidden clues in the habits of both our thoughts and actions that point to what really matters to us. When we bring our attention to ourselves, we can engage in self-evaluation and assess how we are measuring up to our personal standards and values. Some days this leads to satisfaction and pride, and other days it may lead to dissatisfaction or regret. In either case, this kind of reflection promotes a deeper understanding of our emotions and of the impact of our actions on ourselves and others, which in turn opens the door to changing our behavior.

While we have our own sense of awareness and knowledge of ourselves, other people also can have knowledge and awareness about us. So how do we understand the similarities and differences between our self-perceptions and other people's perceptions of us? In 1955, psychologists Joseph Luft and Harrington Ingham created a schema depicting the things we know about ourselves compared with others' knowledge of us, called the Johari window (Figure 2-2). The window has four panes: Open, Blind, Hidden, and Unknown. Here is how we would explain their meanings: Some knowledge of yourself, like your name, may be open and known to others (quadrant 1); while other things, like the private thoughts you have about others, are known only to you (quadrant 3). There are also things about you that you can be blind to, but that others see (quadrant 2). An example of this is what the back of your head looks like, or the exact thoughts and feelings that someone else is having in response to how you are interacting with them. And, finally, there are things about you that are unknown to you and to others. This can include what you dream about but do not recall, or some of the unconscious motivations that are driving your behavior outside your awareness (quadrant 4).

**Figure 2-2.** Johari Window

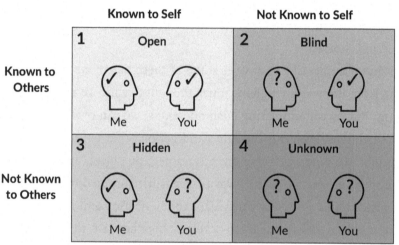

The Johari window is useful in a number of ways. First, it helps us appreciate that everyone has blind spots and that there are things about us that we have yet to discover; we need other people in order to understand ourselves more fully. Second, it also points us toward a good way to grow our self-awareness: by asking others for feedback. Third, it shows that for others to become more aware of us, we need to share the things about us that they cannot necessarily see or know. Finally, this schema also bridges the ideas of self-awareness and awareness of others. Greater mutual knowledge and awareness expands the pool of information that everyone has about each other. By striving to make the Open pane larger, we learn more about ourselves and others, which helps build trust and improve communication.

Consider what things about yourself you might you not be able to see well. How would knowledge of those things make you better? Who might be able to help you see some of the things you do not see as clearly?

## Social Awareness

Social awareness relates to being able to accurately discern what others are feeling, thinking, or experiencing. It is closely related to empathy or the ability to take on the perspectives of others and find validity in them (or at least appreciation of why—given their life experience—they hold those perspectives). Social awareness applies our understanding of other individuals, groups of people, or social situations.

Think about someone in your life who really gets you. How does that person know you so well? Maybe this person has been in your life for years and has taken the time to get to know you. Or perhaps this person has become exceptionally attuned to you by listening carefully to what you say and the emotional tone in your voice, by reading your facial expressions and body language, and by asking questions that help them know more about you. Social awareness goes a long way in helping us feel connected and close to each other.

In our own work, we have had the privilege of engaging with many leaders who go the extra mile in understanding and connecting with their team members. One example is the chief medical officer of a local healthcare consortium. Prior to rounding each morning, the CMO personally visits one floor of the hospital, both to find out how the night shift went and also to convey to staff that she is available to answer their questions at any point. If she sees that one of her staff members looks upset or concerned, she pulls them aside and encourages them to describe what they may be feeling or the challenge they may be facing. Over the course of the week, the CMO is careful to rotate these visits between the different floors of the hospital. The CMO also makes a point of visiting patients on the floor, asking them how they are doing and if they need anything. There is no job that this CMO will not do, should she be called upon to assist. By tapping into her awareness of others and her ability to connect, the CMO is able to establish this spirit of engagement and involvement and send the message that everyone's work has value and that she stands behind her team and employees.

Social awareness also applies to being aware of the experiences of groups of people and even larger communities. People who are socially aware in this way can read the mood of a group, understand why others think or feel what they do, and make good judgments about what to say (or what not to say) in a given moment.

As consultants, one of the things we like to do is check in at the start of a meeting to take the group's temperature. On one occasion, Daryn and David were working with a family business. They had mapped out a series of meetings designed to produce their five-year strategic plan. Not long into one of those meetings, however, they noticed that people seemed quieter than usual and there was some friction in the room.

Reflecting this back to the group, Daryn observed, "I sense a little tension in the room, and I'd like to invite us to discuss it. I'd welcome anyone's perspective on what may be going on." That led to one family member disclosing that there had been a hotly contentious political argument over the weekend at a family event, and people were still upset about it. In response, Daryn and David put aside their agenda for the day and helped everyone process their feelings about it with each other to get to a better place. Had Daryn and David noticed but not invited conversation on this issue early on, the quality of their work with this family would have been greatly diminished.

Let's try an exercise around social awareness. Think about your day again. This time, think about any people you spent time with or encountered.

- What do you think they were thinking about?
- What do you think they were feeling?
- What kind of mood do you think they were in?
- What do you think they needed or wanted from their interaction with you?

- How do you think they perceived you or your behavior toward them?
- What mattered to them? What was important for them?
- What specifically led you to those conclusions? What about the other people did you notice?

We may not always deliberately examine our interactions with others, yet by asking these and other questions, we can understand the people around us, which is pivotal for our ability to work well with them. Ultimately, expanding our social awareness starts with the acknowledgment that we often do not really know how other individuals or groups experience things, but that being curious, open minded, and interested in understanding others is key to helping us connect more fully with them. It is through deeper listening and asking questions that we can open our eyes to see things from different vantage points.

This sounds easy enough, but listening deeply, keeping an open mind, and expanding our curiosity involves inhibiting some of our self-focused thoughts. It requires shifting our focus to the person we are with and away from our inner chatter about how what they are saying relates to us, or what we want to say next. This inhibition takes emotional and mental energy. As an experiment, try for one day to really tune in to the people you care about. Express your curiosity, ask them to tell you more, and refrain from adding your two cents. See what it is like—how did it feel for you? What was the impact? As you engage in this more and more, it gets easier and easier.

## Why Be More Conscious?

Like space or time, consciousness is infinite and limitless. Freud's 1915 iceberg theory of consciousness posited that what we are aware of is just "the tip of the iceberg" and that a much bigger portion of ourselves lies below the surface, outside our awareness. Although we can never "arrive at the destination" of being fully conscious or fully aware about everything, we can make efforts to grow in awareness. In doing so, we expand our knowledge and elevate our perspective. There are considerable benefits in doing so.

## Unlock Personal Growth

Self-awareness helps us comprehend who we are; why we think, feel, and behave the way we do; and what we need to thrive in our personal relationships and work lives, while social awareness helps us comprehend this about others. As psychologists, we have spent a great deal of time helping people raise their self- and social awareness and also working on our own. For example, over time David has learned that when he deprives himself of sleep, it takes a huge toll on his physical energy, mental well-being, and productivity.

Although it may be challenging or scary to face our own lack of awareness, it is the first step in personal and professional growth. We cannot improve what we are not aware of. Whenever we are coaching someone, one of the early steps in the process is helping the client get a clear understanding of who they are today and how they are perceived by others. Once the client becomes more aware of what is working (and not working) about how they think and behave, they can take the necessary steps to align who they are with who they want to be.

## Elevate Results

Self-awareness matters because in every situation and interaction, we can never remove the unique lens through which we see the world—the lens of ourselves. The following quote (most frequently attributed to Anaïs Nin 1961) captures this truth that removing the lens of ourselves is beyond our capabilities: "We do not see things as they are, we see things as we are." This is the ever-present reality of being human. We can never be truly, fully objective. In every interaction, we bring an entire menu of personal perspectives and viewpoints that we develop across our lifespan, due to influences of both nature and nurture. By focusing on improving our self- and social awareness, we can acknowledge the influence of our own subjective outlook, and get outside ourselves a bit more.

This greater consciousness allows us to make more clear, intentional, and informed decisions. These are decisions that can be in better alignment with our own values and those of our teammates and our organizations—decisions that will result in better outcomes and better relationships. The benefit of greater consciousness is that you will have a broader and deeper understanding of what really matters to you, as well as the other people and forces involved. This allows for necessary shifts and adjustments, and it helps anticipate problems and enables individuals and teams to plan accordingly. The result is more informed decisions, which in turn increases the likelihood of greater success and satisfaction.

## Deepen Relationships

The more that we are clear about what we want, what matters to us, and why, the more that we can make our wants, needs, expectations, and motives known to others. That allows other people to know us and, as a result, do a better job of being responsive to us. Sometimes we want the people around us to be mind readers. We think they should be able to intuit our needs and to meet them, without our having to say anything. Who wouldn't want that? But the reality is that our needs are rarely met unless we ask for what we need. And that is predicated on being *aware* of what we need.

Knowing ourselves and then sharing that knowledge with others builds and strengthens human bonds. To quote the wisdom of Fred Rogers, "Anything that's human is mentionable, and anything that is mentionable can be more manageable." While we may feel unique and alone in our struggles, to be human means that we will all struggle. When we share our struggles, we are better able to gather our resources and chart a course of action. Simultaneously, sharing our struggles helps others feel less alone in their experience while forging meaningful bonds that can sustain us.

## Becoming More Conscious

Expanding our consciousness means learning to become aware of things that generally exist beyond the scope of our awareness. It means learning to see what we now do not see, to hear what we now do not hear, to feel what we now do not feel, and to understand what we now do not understand. It involves the humility to recognize that our perspective on everything, including ourselves, is limited. It means being curious about many questions, like "What don't I know?" or "What am I not seeing here?" And it involves taking actions like deeper reflection or asking others for their perspectives to broaden our own.

We have discussed consciousness as a network of connections. In becoming more conscious, we can actually forge new neural connections and modify certain aspects of our neuroanatomy. For example, studies of consciousness-enhancing activities such as meditation have shown consistent differences in eight brain regions of meditators compared with the brain regions of non-meditators (Fox et al. 2014). In particular, some studies have concluded that meditation can change your neural circuitry in ways that make you more compassionate and empathetic (Klimecki et al. 2013).

Let's return to the example of Aaron from earlier in the chapter. Realizing he needed to build his self-awareness, Aaron took some free online assessments to help him clarify his strengths, preferences, and values. Then he asked several significant people in his life what impact his behavior has had on them. He specifically asked questions related to how his behavior affected how close they felt to him, as his goal was to forge closer relationships. Then he spent time reflecting on the feedback and journaling about it.

Subsequently, when Sean approached Aaron for help reviewing new platforms for fostering physician continuing education, Aaron did not respond with an immediate "yes." Instead, he replied that the work sounded interesting and that he would like to support Sean to the best of his ability, but he needed to look at his other obligations before committing. This type of response allowed Aaron to take some time to think, so that he could respond from a place of greater self-awareness.

After assessing what he was capable of, and what he was willing and wanting to take on, Aaron returned to Sean with an honest answer—he could take on part of the task but would not be able to complete the entire task by the deadline. Sean appreciated Aaron's honesty and integrity. Aaron and Sean's relationship deepened as they pursued this project together.

## Summary: Elevating Our Perspective

The conscious accountability model specifies consciousness as the key differentiator between transactional accountability and transformational accountability. Awareness makes us better equipped to be more accountable to ourselves and others. By holding ourselves and the perspectives of others in mind, we argue that we can create a more collaborative, interdependent kind of accountability that strives to improve the quality of relationships and the quality of results. Conscious awareness is what allows for a more holistic and humanistic understanding of the big picture as we pursue our goals. Therefore, one of the ways we can improve our practice of conscious accountability is to work actively and deliberately to expand our conscious awareness itself.

Think about the benefit of becoming more conscious this way: If you are standing in the bottom of a valley, you have one perspective of your surroundings. As you climb up to the top of the mountain next to the valley, you can see not only the valley below but also how it is connected to the greater landscape that surrounds it and of which it is a part. This capacity for an elevated perspective provides more information and therefore greater power to operate.

To promote more consciousness of ourselves and others, we need to engage in specific mindsets and behaviors that help raise awareness and promote continuous learning. In the next chapter we further describe conscious accountability, including the practices that bring it to life.

# CHAPTER 3

# The Power of Conscious Accountability

> *With awareness comes responsibility and choice.*
> AMANDA LINDHOUT

Conscious accountability can be the thing that differentiates the good from the truly exceptional, something Kevin Jackson, a managing partner at Gridiron Capital, knows well. Gridiron Capital is a private equity firm with an intentional focus on building strong partnerships based on trust and shared values to help all stakeholders (including customers, employees, managers, and investors) win together.

For Kevin and for Gridiron Capital, a culture of accountability is a game changer for teams and organizations. It represents three things. The first is an *ownership mindset*, where everyone thinks and acts as owners, everyone takes responsibility, and no one wants to let anyone else down. The second is an *action focus*, where people move quickly and may fail fast but don't stay down. They get up, learn, and keep moving forward together. And the third is alignment through *clarity on strategy*.

"When everyone agrees on where they are going and how they'll get there," Kevin says, "they can focus on the limited number of key things they will do, and align on the things they will not do, in order to build lasting value."

Gridiron Capital also looks for strong cultures of accountability in their partnership companies. According to Kevin, these companies often succeed because their cultures of accountability are palpable. It starts at the top—not just in one individual but from a whole team that leads by example. In many cases, they have been able to boil down their culture of accountability to a mantra that is well known and understood throughout the organization. For example, one company's mantra is "expect to win."

"For them, this meant refusing to lose but also not over-celebrating the wins," Kevin says. "There is a level of excellence that is always there in everything that they do. If you walk into their warehouses, people on the ground floor know what that mantra means, and it helps build a tremendous sense of pride and camaraderie."

Communication is also key, Kevin observes. This company puts a great deal of effort and thought into communication, making sure to communicate clearly with customers and everyone else involved. Part of this communication is aligning incentives with the team winning, which helps create an atmosphere of freely sharing best practices. That allows everyone to continually learn and get better. "The culture flows through everything they do, and it's quite unstoppable," Kevin adds.

To build a culture of accountability, there needs to be a relationship of trust. "We are very much in the people business," Kevin explains. So Gridiron Capital strives to make its performance metrics and KPIs straightforward and easy to understand. That way, people don't have to guess at how they are performing—they know what winning looks like. "And when people experience winning together," Kevin concludes, "it is a relationship builder, a trust builder, and a retention builder."

The power of conscious accountability lies in its potential to change leaders and teams from good—getting things done, getting pretty good results—to fantastic. That means getting things done with excellence, greater consistency, and doing it in a way that drives learning and connection. This leads to greater joy, passion, and satisfaction in the work itself. Imagine getting up every day and feeling like this and working with others who feel similarly. When we bring conscious awareness together with accountability, we take accountability to an entirely new level.

## How Is Conscious Accountability Different?

We define *conscious accountability* as expanding awareness to create deliberate intentions, take informed actions, and be responsible for our impact. Let's break that down a bit further. By *awareness*, we mean awareness of ourselves, awareness of other people, and awareness of the interdependence between self and others. *Deliberate intentions* refers to having preconceived ideas about what we want to do and about the desired effects we want to have on others. *Informed actions* are actions that are both informed by our awareness and consistent with our intentions. Finally, being *responsible for our impact* means acknowledging that our actions (and inactions) affect other people, and that we are willing to own the results that follow from our choices.

There are a few key ways that conscious accountability differs from traditional notions of accountability:

- It focuses on two outcomes: relationship and results.
- It moves beyond transactional ways of engaging to a more transformational way of working.
- It is a more forward-thinking approach to accountability, as opposed to a "rearview mirror" approach.

Let's unpack these differences a bit further.

### One Outcome Versus Two

Joe was a financial executive who developed a strong reputation for being able to turn around start-up organizations that were performing poorly and in financial trouble. He was able to go into organizations, quickly identify the opportunities for change, and then drive those changes in a way that produced remarkable fiscal improvements within six months. He attributed his success, in part, to his ability to hold people accountable to do what they were hired to do.

However, Joe had difficulty dealing with his fellow leaders, who were focused on the toll that his changes took on people. His relationships with these leaders were often strained, and therefore he typically did not stay in organizations after he made change happen. Joe believed it was an either-or proposition: either you can have happy people and good relationships, or you can have positive results, but not both. His perspective invites the question, "Can you have it all?"

Our answer to that question is a resounding "Yes, you can!"

Amy Edmondson (2014), professor of management and leadership at Harvard Business School, highlighted the importance of psychological safety and accountability for getting into the "learning zone" of optimal teamwork and learning. Inspired by her rubric, we have developed a similar matrix to capture how conscious accountability can both result from and foster high-quality relationships and task performance.

To be a person who operates with conscious accountability, you need to hold these two things in your mind at once, and you have to behave in ways that consider both of these dimensions. Let's look at what happens when you put performance or relationships before the other, or in the worst case, prioritize neither (Table 3-1).

**Table 3-1.** The Two Dimensions That Drive Conscious Accountability

| | | Task Performance | |
| --- | --- | --- | --- |
| | | Low | High |
| Relationship Quality | High | The Harmonizer | The Conscious Performer |
| | Low | The Neutralist | The Hard Driver |

People who have a high focus on relationship quality but low focus on task performance are *Harmonizers*. They feel best when working in a group where everyone gets along well. Conflict is hard for them, and they prefer for people to be agreeable. If their team succeeds at a task but there are hard feelings, they believe they've failed. People and relationships come before performance and profits. In this situation, their team's productivity may suffer and dissatisfaction may ensue from a lack of challenge or from a collective sense of underperforming.

When people weigh task performance over relationship quality, they may create a climate where productivity and efficient output are maximized at all costs. They are known as *Hard Drivers*. They consistently strive to do their best, and they expect everyone around them to do the same. They like bottom-line outcomes: They either hit their mark or they don't. They consider explanations excuses. They believe people need to take responsibility for their work and if they can't perform, they need to move on. Under these conditions, people might feel undervalued, underappreciated, and unseen, as well as anxious about their performance. They may also be afraid to admit mistakes, ask for help, or show other signs of vulnerability or weakness.

If people do not take task performance or relationship quality into consideration, they are called *Neutralizers*. They may pride themselves on being easygoing and adaptable. When decisions need to be made, they are comfortable deferring to the expert in the room, voting neutrally, or abstaining altogether. It feels good when their team gets along and performs well, but they are not going to lose any sleep over any challenges they face. Work may not be where they get significant meaning in life, so they are not going to knock themselves out over any of it. In this kind of environment, people can easily slide into disengagement from one another, and from the work at hand.

As you think about these descriptions, can you think of a time when you were in a situation in which either task performance or relationship quality was emphasized at the cost of the other? What did that feel like? How would it have been different if both were emphasized equally?

*Conscious performers* are the people who can balance and include a focus on both task performance and relationship quality. They tend to be observant and are sure to notice a team's energy. They like to dig deep to uncover the root causes of challenges. For them, when people understand and appreciate each other, they can drive better results. They think divergent opinions and approaches are essential for optimizing outcomes, and that everyone's voice should be heard. They cannot optimize results without optimizing their team dynamics. To them, the two go hand in hand.

People who approach accountability in this way become increasingly aware of themselves and each other's influences, more deeply connected to each other, and more efficient and able to work consistently at high levels of performance. They do not see their work interactions as a series of transactions to be met.

## Transactional Versus Transformational

*Transformational leadership* was originally defined as a process in which "leaders and followers help each other to advance to a higher level of morale and motivation" by leadership authority James MacGregor Burns (1978). It is distinct from *transactional leadership*, which is based on a series of exchanges or transactions between leaders and followers, each giving something to get something they need. But exactly how do transformational leaders boost morale? Fellow leadership expert Bernard Bass (1985) described four elements that explain how transformational leaders motivate their followers to work harder and achieve more:

- **Individual consideration.** Attending to each follower's needs, acting as a mentor or coach to the follower, and listening to the follower's concerns
- **Intellectual stimulation**. Encouraging the follower's creativity, challenging followers to think and learn, and soliciting the follower's ideas
- **Inspirational motivation**. Articulating a compelling vision, communicating optimism about future goals, and challenging followers to achieve high standards
- **Idealized influence.** Being a charismatic role model for ethical behavior, and instilling pride, respect, and trust

The result of these behaviors is that followers become intrinsically motivated because their sense of self-actualization and self-esteem resonate with the mission and collective identity of the team. They are also inspired to perform based on their trust in and appreciation for the leader.

So how does this relate to accountability? Traditional accountability has been more transactional in scope, with an emphasis on making sure things get done as they should, with each person involved responsible for their own piece of the activity. While there is nothing wrong with this, transactional accountability does leave much untapped potential and could be a setup for problems down the line.

If everyone is charged with getting their own piece done, their attention is mostly on themselves and what they independently need to do. They can say, "I've done my part. I can check that off the list. I'm all set." But here's the twist: That approach runs the risk of losing sight of the larger goals and the other people involved. We see this frequently in organizations where different teams, departments, or locations have to collaborate with one another. More often than not, there is a lack of awareness, friction, competition, or—at worst—animosity between these different people or groups. Customer service is frustrated with sales for overpromising, sales blames operations for underperforming, operations blames engineering for design flaws, and so on.

Conscious accountability is more transformational, because it recognizes the value of attending to people and relationships as crucial for achieving success. Grounded in awareness of ourselves and others, conscious accountability embodies important elements of transformational leadership: considering individuals' needs, engaging them intellectually, motivating them personally, and building relationships of trust and respect. If everyone is more aware of one another and working together toward a higher goal, then each person is responsible for their own piece and has a greater sense of ownership for the shared outcomes. Another aspect of untapped potential is the satisfaction that comes from having accomplished something together and being part of something larger than yourself. Therein lies the difference between "good" and "exceptional."

## Backward Looking Versus Forward Looking

If you look up the word *accountable* in *Merriam-Webster's* dictionary, one of the first definitions you will see is "subject to giving an account, answerable." Traditional ideas of accountability may conform to this understanding of what it means to be accountable and therefore focus on the question "Who needs to explain the reasons for their actions or decisions?" This leads to a reactive, backward looking approach to accountability. When something bad happens, people often say "Who needs to be held accountable for this?"

This is what people were saying in February 2021, when a terrible winter storm in Texas led to widespread power failures, which resulted in food scarcity, contaminated water, freezing cold temperatures, and at least 57 deaths across the state, mostly from hypothermia (Sparber 2021). In the wake of this crisis, the outcry for accountability led to the firing or resignation of executives and board members both in the Electric Reliability Council of Texas (which managed the power grid) and the Public Utility Commission (which oversaw the grid's operator).

Conscious accountability is a bit different in its emphasis. It is not solely focused on who is to blame for the problem but instead looks at who is responsible for the solution. It is not about justice—it is about creating the capacity for learning and improvement over time. It is not a reactive approach to accountability, but a proactive approach that understands that many things in life—including complex teamwork—are quite difficult to do perfectly every time. There will be challenges and failures along the way, but these can and should be viewed as opportunities to learn, grow, and improve.

An example of this more proactive, forward-looking approach to accountability is captured in the RACI matrix, also known as the responsibility assignment matrix. You can use the matrix to clarify and define key roles and responsibilities in cross-functional or multi-departmental collaborations. Each of the four letters in RACI describes a different role:

- **R = Responsible:** person responsible for doing the work to complete the task

- **A = Accountable:** person who is answerable for the correct and timely completion of the deliverable and the ultimate approving authority with regard to the task
- **C = Consulted:** people who are consulted as subject matter experts with regard to the task
- **I = Informed:** people who are informed and kept up to date about the status of the project, but their input is not sought

Although one person is designated as "accountable," others are also asked to think about and contribute to the final product. When a group of people assign responsibilities in this way, it allows for creating clear expectations up front, as well as discussion of what is important to people in how they work together from the outset of the collaboration.

Conscious accountability has the power to change the way you think about relationships and results. Table 3-2 presents a summary of the key differences between accountability 1.0 and conscious accountability.

**Table 3-2.** Accountability 1.0 Versus Conscious Accountability

| Accountability 1.0 | Conscious Accountability |
|---|---|
| Single outcome: results | Two outcomes: results and relationships |
| Transactional | Transformational |
| On your own | Shared with others |
| Backward looking | Forward looking |
| Reactive | Proactive |
| Blame | Learning |
| Punishment | Try again |

## What Does Conscious Accountability Look Like?

To help illustrate what it means to operate with conscious accountability, let's look at three examples from our experience: a leader, a team, and an organization.

## Leader Profile: Sanjay, the Velvet Hammer

Sanjay was a nonprofit leader who spent his entire career in the service of people with developmental disabilities. He'd grown up with a younger brother with Down's syndrome, so he was passionate about the cause. While in college, he began working at a nonprofit focused on empowering young adults with developmental disabilities. He started as a recreational therapist, taking on increasing responsibility until he eventually became the executive director.

Sanjay set a high bar for himself and everyone else. When managing others, he delivered direct, clear feedback about what needed to change, but also expressed care, encouragement, and specific ideas about how to be more successful. This earned him the nickname "the Velvet Hammer." And, within five years, he was able to more than double the size of the organization (as measured by annual budget, number of staff employed, and clients served).

One of the biggest tests of Sanjay's leadership came when it was discovered that a major gifts officer was embezzling portions of several sizable charitable contributions. Sanjay was devastated by the news. After dismissing the employee and involving legal authorities, he came into the office on a Saturday to support the finance and development teams as they pieced together how it had happened. He knew he had an uphill climb to restore trust in the organization, the donor base, and other important stakeholders. But he went right to it, having countless conversations with his board, the staff, major supporters, media, clients, and families. In each conversation, he shared information, listened deeply, and took responsibility for not having better systems in place to prevent fraudulent behavior. He commissioned an independent audit of their processes and took a pay reduction to offset losses that were unrecoverable. Ultimately, his transparency and integrity preserved the goodwill of the organization's major funders, and they were able to weather the crisis successfully.

A number of Sanjay's qualities allowed him to live the practices of conscious accountability. In particular, he showed a steadfast commitment to results and relationships with his team and other stakeholders. But he did not look backward to assign blame and then wash his hands of the problem. He was willing to take ownership of problems and be responsible for them.

## Team Profile: Super Nurses

When Daryn and David started working with the nursing management team at a regional hospital, we knew there was something special about this group. The members had a camaraderie that was palpable. They were quite diverse with respect to race, gender, sexual orientation, and personality styles. Notably, they believed that the richness of their team members' backgrounds helped them think about clinical needs more holistically and thus serve staff and patients even better.

Although they had never discussed it in great detail, each member of the team described feeling aligned in their common goals and the values that motivated them. They all wanted to support their staff in providing exceptional care for their patients and the community at large. And they all "walked the talk" on being supportive to one another. There were countless stories and examples of how they could call on one another, whatever time of day or night, and get advice and support on how to handle difficult situations. When one member went out on a leave to care for her husband after he had a stroke, the other team members covered her responsibilities until she came back, without a second thought.

Not that it was always rosy. Each team member managed a different nursing function or treatment unit within the hospital and their outpatient clinics. There were different needs and challenges, and they had to come together as a group to solve system-wide issues. Sometimes that meant having to make hard decisions about which functions or units received resources. Initially they locked horns a lot, and it took a while for the team to learn how to have those conversations productively without taking things personally or seeing it as a win-lose situation. Members learned to advocate for their own teams, as well as align behind final decisions so they could represent them to their respective staffs with clarity and confidence. A key behavior that helped preserve the psychological safety and trust they had established was to explain their thinking, motives, and behaviors with transparency.

After learning how to really listen with deeper empathy for one another and how to have robust but respectful disagreements and debates, they were able to cultivate a system-wide mindset. This change in thinking allowed them to simultaneously hold the needs of their own teams and see and understand the needs of the system. When that began to happen, it was a game changer for their functioning and performance, as measured by increases in scores on staff engagement and patient safety.

This team demonstrates conscious accountability in three important ways. First, they created and maintained a high level of engagement, commitment, and psychological safety within the nursing department. Second, they were committed both to providing excellent services and to each other. And third, team members learned to be aware of the ways they were interdependent and could then see beyond their own agendas in the service of something larger than any of them.

## Company Profile: Sibling Act, Fifth Generation

During Daryn and David's first meeting with the Hutchinson family, they saw hints of the many strengths that had kept this family in business for more than 100 years. The original business involved manufacturing theater curtains, but over time it grew to be the leading supplier of specialty lighting and sound systems for entertainment venues worldwide. Three siblings in the fifth generation led the company: Diane was CEO, Audrey was CFO, and Jerome was chief product officer. Their father had recently retired, at which time each of the siblings transitioned into their current roles. The siblings were getting along and doing well, but they chose to engage us proactively, to make sure that their familial and professional relationships stayed strong and in balance as they grew into their new roles.

We quickly learned about the strong set of values that was guiding family interactions and business decisions. Fairness and meritocracy existed at the center, with family members having to earn each job they assumed. With the requisite education and outside experience, each sibling had successfully competed against other candidates for their respective positions. The siblings also paid themselves and other staff members fair salaries, which met or mildly exceeded industry averages.

The emphasis on employee engagement and inclusion was also apparent. Every quarter the siblings sought to include employees in decision making using anonymous surveys to gather feedback. After reviewing the results, the siblings conducted town hall meetings to share what they learned and their plans to address any concerns raised. This approach seemed to reap rewards, with employees reporting that they felt like valued members of the Hutchinson family and expressing pride in being the market leader in their industry. Employee engagement scores were consistently well above national averages.

Leadership's commitment to transparent communication also informed the financial information they shared. During quarterly town halls, leaders openly discussed how well the company was tracking toward top-line and bottom-line revenue goals. They also created and deployed metrics to gauge the productivity of each department. This information was updated weekly (and in some cases, daily), allowing employees to assess their own progress and how their work influenced the company's bigger picture.

Relationships across the organization were enhanced through effective dialogue. When disagreements arose, leaders would engage in a constructive conflict protocol, which was developed by a committee that took inputs from across the organization. They also conducted after-action reviews when new policies and procedures were put in place, allowing everyone to capture what they learned—both in terms of what went well and should be repeated—and what should be amended in the future.

The organization consistently received awards and recognition for being a great place to work. When attending these ceremonies, they would invite team members to accept the awards, which were often dedicated to front-line staff.

In reflecting on their success, the siblings saw they drew strength from their support of one another and the model their forebears had set, which elevated working hard and building trusting professional relationships. The company exemplifies several key tenets of conscious accountability. Leaders and managers were transparent about goals, expectations, and markers of progress. Strong metrics helped everyone see how they were performing. There was a commitment to learning through feedback, both at the individual and team level, and trying again. Employee empowerment and sense of belonging also deepened relationships and commitment to the organization as a whole.

## The Seven Practices of Conscious Accountability

We consider conscious accountability to be a state that emerges as a result of engaging in a number of practices. This book describes seven practices, which we call the CONNECT framework (Figure 3-1), with each letter representing a different set of actions and mindsets meant to enhance conscious accountability.

**Figure 3-1.** The CONNECT Framework

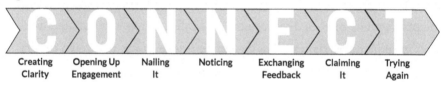

| Creating Clarity | Opening Up Engagement | Nailing It | Noticing | Exchanging Feedback | Claiming It | Trying Again |

Here is a quick summary of the practices, and a bit about what you will learn in each of the coming chapters.

- **Creating clarity.** This practice establishes a clear vision and shared goals and expectations. It requires strong, crisp communication in which people can negotiate the terms of interacting together, so that they can identify and iron out any areas of potential disagreement or misalignment.

- **Opening up engagement.** This practice creates the conditions in which people feel safe and free to express themselves and are motivated to work together to complete the tasks at hand.

- **Nailing it.** This practice means doing what you say you will do and ensuring that others are doing the same. It often involves managing competing priorities so balls do not get dropped and helping others organize toward task completion.

- **Noticing.** In this practice, people pay attention to what they are seeing outwardly and experiencing internally, actively checking in with others to share observations, and ensure that others are OK and things are on track.

- **Exchanging feedback.** This involves soliciting, receiving, and giving feedback to help oneself and others expand awareness, learn what is or is not working, and make any necessary course corrections.
- **Claiming it.** This practice is all about taking ownership and responsibility for the results—both the successes and the failures—and consolidating the learning.
- **Trying again.** This practice allows us to take what we have learned from our experience and apply it in the next situation. It requires that people get re-energized and recommitted to their plans and is crucial for creating a cycle of continuous improvement.

## Guiding Assumptions

Throughout this book, we will highlight the key mindsets that help someone engage most fully in each of the seven CONNECT practices of conscious accountability. Here we highlight four overarching assumptions that can help you stay centered as you bring the tenets of conscious accountability to life:

- **Accountability is a skill that can be developed.** Although we all come into this world with our natural strengths and weaknesses, we believe that people can increase their proficiency in accountability. We do not subscribe to the opinion that being accountable is a personality or character trait. Instead, we believe that anyone's accountability can be improved by holding a growth mindset—one that underscores our ability to continuously grow and learn. We propose that by understanding how accountability is best actualized through strong relationships and task performance, everyone—with practice—will be able to improve their adeptness.
- **Growth is a vulnerable process.** It can feel vulnerable and uncomfortable to develop your capacity to be more conscious and accountable. It is not unusual for us to be afraid to take a closer look at what is operating below the surface. You may find yourself saying,

"I don't want to go there. Who wants to open that can of worms?" People may also have the fear that if they open that door, even just a crack, there will be a flood of information they are not prepared to handle. This is natural and normal. All beings instinctively move away from pain, whether the pain is real, anticipated, or imagined. The fact is that, yes, there might be some discomfort in uncovering influences that are not readily in your consciousness. But in many cases, growth requires taking risks that move us outside our comfort zone. We invite you to build muscle around accepting vulnerability and tolerating discomfort in the service of your growth.

- **We learn best when we feel supported.** Support can help manage discomfort along a journey. When we are in an environment where we feel safe and cared for, our parasympathetic nervous system activates. Conversely, our sympathetic nervous system activates when we perceive a threat, triggering a flight or fight response. Our brains are most able to acquire, assimilate, consolidate, and apply information when our parasympathetic nervous system is activated. Because caring relationships help activate our parasympathetic nervous system they put us in the best position for growth and performance. That also includes having self-compassion by being gentle and forgiving with ourselves for mistakes, shortcomings, or failures—real or perceived.

- **Just like me.** Human beings share several basic needs. According to self-determination theory, the three most universal psychological needs (beyond the most basic needs of food, clothing, and shelter) are autonomy, mastery, and relatedness (Ryan and Deci 2000). We all want to have a sense of freedom and independence (autonomy) while also feeling connected and part of a group (relatedness). Experiencing a sense of competence—that we are able to engage in a task in a full, masterful way—is also a critical driver. Within the conscious accountability framework, we encourage you to keep these needs in mind—both for yourself and for others. In embracing the Dalai Lama's "just like me" ethos of compassion, we acknowledge and honor that others have the same needs as us (Lama and Stril-Rever 2010). Even in times of conflict, we can bridge a connection by recalling that this person wants to be competent, just like me; this person wants to have freedom of choice, just like me; and this person wants to feel connected to others, just like me.

## Summary: Beginning Your Practice of Conscious Accountability

As you will see in the chapters that follow, each of the seven CONNECT practices can stand on its own as an important piece in enhancing relationships and results. And, as you will also learn, each of these practices may be important to different stages of a group project or endeavor. For example, creating clarity is an important practice at many points, but it's especially crucial at the outset of a project, so that the terms of engagement and expectations are clear. The same is true with opening up engagement—promoting commitment and psychological safety from the outset sets the tone for the entire project going forward. In contrast, claiming it and trying again typically come later, after a project has been completed and your team would like to reflect on how it has gone.

In the coming chapters, we will describe what each practice entails in terms of the mindsets you need to practice, as well as the behaviors required. We will also illustrate the practice with examples, and each chapter will encourage you to reflect on your own experience with this practice, suggesting strategies for developing it further.

Remember that these are skills you can practice and continue to hone over your lifetime. You do not have to do it all at once. You may wish to identify which you are proficient at, and which are the most challenging for you. Or maybe most rewarding would be identifying and working on the practices you believe will have the biggest influence on your success. Figure 3-2 reviews the mindsets and behaviors of the seven practices, which we'll elaborate on in Part 2. Feel free to skip around and focus on what catches your attention and what your needs are currently. Let's get started!

**Figure 3-2.** Summary of the CONNECT Model of Conscious Accountability

| Practice | Mindsets | Strategies |
|---|---|---|
| Creating Clarity | Humility and Patience | • Clarify your intention.<br>• Consider your audience.<br>• Communicate the message.<br>• Check for understanding. |
| Opening Up Engagement | All In | • Align values.<br>• Honor individual needs.<br>• Model vulnerable learning.<br>• Be inclusive. |
| Nailing It | Grit and Grace | • Activate knowledge of self and others.<br>• Organize for task completion.<br>• Stay together. |
| Noticing | Compassionate Curiosity | • Prepare.<br>• Be aware.<br>• Share. |
| Exchanging Feedback | Courage | • Connect to your intentions.<br>• Make it safer.<br>• Prepare.<br>• Listen actively and seek information.<br>• Manage emotions and resistance.<br>• Express gratitude.<br>• Make a follow-up plan. |
| Claiming It | Objectivity and Acceptance | • Identify what the actual results were. (versus the expected results).<br>• Determine the root cause of the results.<br>• Respond to the results and what was learned from them.<br>• Consider how to apply this learning next time. |
| Trying Again | Growth | • Refuel.<br>• Recommit.<br>• Rerun the experiment. |

# PART 2
## CONNECT:
## The Seven Practices

# CHAPTER 4

# Creating Clarity

*The single biggest problem in communication
is the illusion that it has taken place.*
GEORGE BERNARD SHAW

Think of a time when you needed someone to do something, but along the way you discovered a disconnect. You might have fired off an email to a colleague. Or you might have brought up a deliverable during a meeting. Or at home you might have just asked your partner or family member to take out the trash or pick up something from the grocery store. Did you ensure that your request was heard and understood? Or did you just assume it was, only to later find out that the other person heard you in an entirely different way than you intended? Let's look at an example text exchange between David and Marianne, as they were working to finalize the launch of a client project.

**David, Sunday, 12:49 p.m.:** Hi! Checking in. I'm gonna be working for the next couple of hours and wanted to see what support you needed from me to complete the draft of the survey and make final decisions about the assessment. My goal is to have the platform ready with all the team members added before I record the video, which I will send out tomorrow.

**Marianne, Sunday, 12:55 p.m.:** Hey! I'm working on it now. For the survey, I need clarity on what to include. So a cleaned-up version of the doc you created would be great. I left a bunch of comments. For the assessment, I got some feedback and decided which one to include. However, we can change it if you have different thoughts. How does all this sound?

**David, Sunday, 1:00 p.m.:** Sounds good. I will make a clean version of the survey questions and will give you some feedback about the assessment.

**Marianne, Sunday, 3:08 p.m.:** Hey there. Friendly check-in. Hope things are progressing. Thinking I should have said earlier that I am hoping to be done by 4 p.m. to have a free evening. The only piece I have left is the survey. I started it, but I don't want to go any further until I get your input. When can I expect the clean version?

**David, Sunday, 3:26 p.m.:** Oh gosh, sorry. . . . I did not realize you had some time constraints. I just finished grading some papers and was going to turn my attention to the survey, but I need to take my son to the park now.

**Marianne, Sunday, 3:29 p.m.:** Yeah, I realized I made an assumption when you texted you'd be working for the next couple of hours. I assumed you were working only on the survey. Oh the joys of communication! I am exhausted and need some downtime to refuel before Monday hits.

**David, Sunday, 3:38 p.m.:** Thanks for letting me know. I can understand why you made the assumptions you did—not unreasonable given my text. Let's regroup when I get back from the park and figure out a plan.

This exchange between Marianne and David illustrates the ease of miscommunications and how those moments can affect how (or whether) things get done properly. And these miscommunications also can affect how people feel about each other, even momentarily. For example, Marianne felt increasingly irritated because she did not get the work back from David when she expected, and then was frustrated at the idea of having to work later than she had planned. After learning about Marianne's timeframe, David felt slightly saddened yet frustrated, as he thought to himself, "Well, that would have been nice to know a little earlier!" and "Duh, why didn't I just clarify our timeframe up front?"

In this chapter, we will first show you why clarity matters so much in how we communicate and set goals and expectations. Next, we will discuss two key mindsets for the practice of creating clarity. Then we will describe a number of important action steps that will help you increase the odds that your practice of communication will result in crystal clarity, mutual understanding, and better connections with the people involved. Finally, we share some examples, tips, and an exercise to help you get going.

## Why Does Clarity Matter?

Both in life and at work, having a clear understanding about the overarching goals and what is expected at the outset of any task or endeavor is vital. The hundreds of people we have talked to during workshops in both academic and business spaces can attest to its importance. And the opposite is also true: Having poor workplace communication is associated with some pretty steep costs. Poor communication leads to failed project delivery, workplace injuries, and increased employee absenteeism and turnover—with associated annual costs of $62.4 million in large companies (100,000+ employees) and $420,000 in smaller organizations (100 employees or fewer; Grossman 2016; Hamilton 2009). In the most extreme cases, the costs of poor communication can be counted in lives lost. The worst aviation accident in history—the 1977 Tenerife disaster, in which 583 people died—occurred because the pilot took off prematurely after a series of miscommunications between the cockpit, the tower, and another aircraft that was still on the runway.

How does this relate to conscious accountability? Recall that conscious accountability's goal is twofold: to get things done and to build relationships in the process. Poor communication is often cited as one of the top problems in relationships. While communication is important for relationships in general, *clarity around goals and expectations* is especially crucial for accountability—and that is the focus of this chapter. It is impossible to be accountable if we do not know to what or whom we are accountable. We cannot keep an agreement or meet others' expectations if we are not clear about what we agreed to or what was expected in the first place. When goals and expectations aren't clear, not only are the outcomes generally worse, but it can often lead to frustrations and hurt feelings that strain relationships. And given that, there is more complexity in how clarity gets negotiated and communicated.

Accordingly, the first practice of conscious accountability is to create clarity, such that goals and expectations for tasks and relationships are fully understood by everyone involved. When this happens up front, the process that follows is easier and more efficient. When it does not happen initially, circling back at some point to deal with the disconnects becomes inevitable. Creating clarity sounds simple enough: "If I am just really crisp, direct, and straightforward with what I am asking for, people will get it and we will have a mutual understanding." Not so fast.

In reality, we have only communicated clearly when all relevant people involved have a shared understanding of ideas, goals, expectations, or circumstances. For many reasons, this is often difficult to realize in one-on-one relationships, let alone in larger groups of people, like families, teams, classrooms, or organizations. So how do you communicate clearly around a task while keeping the relationships in mind at the same time?

## Key Mindsets: Humility and Patience

The practice of creating clarity involves a number of steps and behaviors, which we will explore shortly. But even prior to those actions, we think it is helpful to introduce the idea of mindset. *Mindset* has been described as the attitudes, assumptions, and notions that people hold about something, either at a particular point in time or more globally. Being in the right frame of mind can help you engage in behaviors more fully, meaningfully, and effectively. In this case, the question is, "What mental framing or attitude can I bring to creating clarity in tasks and relationships?"

## Humility

In the opening of the chapter, we shared a text exchange during which David and Marianne were not quite in sync in their expectations—in this case, for the timing of their work together. There comes the inevitable moment when you discover that—*once again*—communication has failed or gone wrong. For a moment, it can feel frustrating and demoralizing. Even when you thought it out in advance, even when you chose your words carefully and tried hard to be clear, miscommunications happen.

The overarching challenge with clear communication is how we construct meaning through the communication process, both verbal and nonverbal. Unfortunately, language is not nearly as precise as we often hope it to be, because it is symbolic. We use words to represent ideas, but variations in meaning can create confusion and misunderstanding. Then add to the mix that much of what we convey to other people comes through nonverbal communication, like our posture, gestures, or body language; the physical distance between us and another person; our clothing and appearance; our rate of speech, pitch, or loudness; and our speaking style. Given that much of what gets communicated actually happens through nonverbal channels, and that all information involved in communication is subject to interpretation anyway, it is no wonder so many communication problems emerge.

Miscommunications happen to everyone. So the mindset of humility—or freedom from pride or arrogance—is useful here. It helps because it sets up the understanding that no one is above communication mishaps. Most of the time it is not fun, but these mishaps are common and very human. Go easy on yourself, and everyone else.

## Patience

Another mindset, which in some ways relates to the idea of humility, is patience. Think about a time when you were trying to communicate with someone and the two of you did not understand one another readily. Perhaps you were traveling in another country, or maybe you encountered someone who was not able to speak your language fluently. Or maybe you were trying to communicate with someone who had difficulty speaking or hearing what you were saying. What was that like? It probably wasn't easy and took a lot more effort than most conversations. Perhaps it felt awkward or uncomfortable or frustrating. Now imagine that same conversation, but this time, picture taking a breath and inviting yourself to slow down and take your time. Set aside having to get it exactly right and stay in the moment with the person. What happens when you bring in a mindset of patience?

Communicating to create mutually understood goals and expectations is usually not a single transaction but a process. The process entails multiple rounds of clarifying not just what people said, but what others heard, and what was actually meant. And to get to the point where there is buy-in from everyone also requires some discussion to arrive at the place of mutual understanding. All of that takes time as well as perseverance to stay with the process. That means being patient with other people and being patient with yourself too.

## Four Strategies for Implementing the Practice of Clarity

As a reminder, conscious accountability means expanding your awareness to create deliberate intentions, take informed actions, and be responsible for your impact. That pertains to impact both on task results and the relationships involved. These ideas are embedded within the four strategies we suggest for improving your capacity to create clarity:

- Clarify the intention.
- Consider who is involved.
- Communicate or receive the message.
- Check for understanding.

Although much of what we will discuss relates to how you should send a message, the most powerful communication skills we can develop are our listening skills. After all, conscious accountability is an interpersonal endeavor—not practiced in isolation but with others. In the same vein, clear communication around goals and expectations is a two-way street, a dynamic process with two (or more) individuals. One of the best things we can do to achieve clarity is to refine our listening skills, so we can hear beyond what others say to what they really mean. In each of the four strategies, we have a shared responsibility to clarify intent, consider who you are communicating with, communicate or receive the message optimally, and check for understanding.

## Clarify the Intention

Effective communication starts when we get clear on three things: *Why* the communication is happening, *who* is involved in the communication, and *what* is being communicated.

- The question of *why* is about determining the communication's broader purpose. Connecting to one's purpose is a powerful way to initiate any communication. It helps us better appreciate our own needs, wishes, and motives, and it can help us figure out what needs to be said to whom. Knowing the why is especially important for conscious accountability because it helps others better understand where we are coming from and what we are hoping to achieve. This leads to a deeper level of understanding, greater connection, and shared commitment.

- Determining *who* should get the message is also important to consider, including who absolutely needs to know (and who does not), who wants to know, and who may be in some way affected by what is being communicated. Many people generally appreciate the risks of not involving enough people (for example, a key player does not receive critical information, which prevents them from taking an important action). However, there are also problems associated with being overly inclusive in communication (such as excessive emails or meetings that can take a toll on speed, productivity, and morale).

- Deciding *what* to communicate entails considering all of the possible information, context, and details, and narrowing them down to what's most critical and relevant to convey. Another key consideration is not just what you want, but what you want them to know about you. How might sharing this information help deepen the relationship? And finally, what do you want the audience to feel? This is especially important for conscious accountability, as it has lasting effects on motivation for the task at hand and on how others connect with you. As Maya Angelou noted: "People will forget what you said, people will forget what you did, but people will never forget how you made them feel."

### Consider Who Is Involved

Think about someone you know very well and find easy to talk to. You probably know how they are feeling based on their facial expressions, tone of voice, or the words they are using. You might already know what matters to them, what excites them or sets them off. Given everything you know, it is probably easier to connect with that person and be on the same page than it is with a stranger or someone you know less well. It is also easier to frame your communication in a way that it is better understood.

Understanding who you are communicating with is important for conscious accountability for two reasons. First, knowledge of others helps you tailor your messaging so it lands and is understood, which helps with the task dimension of conscious accountability. Second, this knowledge can help you communicate with greater empathy, allowing you to convey the sense that you understand who your recipients are and what they need. This supports the relationship dimension of conscious accountability.

It is helpful to consider how other people may be different from us, how those differences may affect the way our communication is received, and what similarities exist that can help build connection.

## Facets of Human Diversity

The ways in which people vary with regard to styles, perspectives, and experiences are considerable. Before you initiate communication, it is helpful to step back and consider: what will this person (or group of people) need to fully understand what I am communicating? And what are the points of similarity that could help me connect to them more effectively? Here is a brief list of things to keep in mind, as you think more deeply about your audience:

- **Language and culture.** One of the most obvious barriers to communication is a language difference, where words can be mistranslated, misheard, or misunderstood. Similarly, people from different cultural backgrounds communicate differently (for example, some cultures are more direct and concrete in communication, whereas others are more indirect and nuanced). If others involved are linguistically or culturally dissimilar from you, how might that affect clarity and mutual understanding?

- **Personality and thinking style.** Personality and stylistic differences affect how people prefer to take in and process information. For example, some people prefer to have a big picture understanding, while others think immediately in specific details. Some people prefer a logical, factual, or unemotional approach, while others would rather have an emotional or person-centered approach. How might you craft your message so that it aligns with different styles?

- **Lived experience and social identity.** People have many different kinds of life experiences, which are often influenced by their social identities, including gender identity, race, ethnicity, age, sexual orientation, ability status, mental or physical illness, military service, history with the legal system, religious affiliation, and body type. When people have experienced themselves as different from the majority, they can feel like they are excluded—frequently based on personal experiences with bias or discrimination. So how can you check your own biases and communicate in a way that builds connection and trust?

- **Location.** Sometimes people have different perspectives based on their location. This could mean a physical location (for example, the London office versus the Dubai office), or it could mean your place within the organizational hierarchy and power structure (for example, frontline staff, middle management, or the C-suite). Consider who is involved and what their experience might be like based on their location.

### Human Differences Affect Clarity in Communication

Our ability to process what someone else says is influenced by our own individual filters, such as our beliefs, biases, interpretations, and assumptions. This is a kind of "psychological noise" that can prevent us from hearing messages as intended (Rothwell 2004). These filters affect both the data we pay attention to and how we make meaning of that data.

The bottom line is that our personal backgrounds very much affect how we experience our world in general and how we receive information from others. Therefore, the meaning of communication can become distorted based on the filters that we and others bring to it.

It is difficult (if not impossible) to predict exactly how people will perceive what we say. Building awareness about other people is a never-ending endeavor that requires curiosity, inquiry, deep reflection, active listening, and the persistent effort to uncover and hear additional perspectives. To the extent you know about the other people you are engaged with—who they are, what is important to them, and what they need from you—the better able you are to articulate and deliver your message in a way that can be more readily understood and better received.

## Communicate or Receive the Message

Once the "who, what, and why" have been established, executing clear communication of the message is the next step. You probably know at least one person who you think of as a very strong or compelling communicator. What is it about their communication that makes it impactful? Or how about people whose communication style you find challenging, difficult to follow, or frustrating? What are the qualities that distinguish one from the other? Some of the things that we think make a difference include selecting the right communication channels, having good timing, sharing your intentions, and delivering a clear, specific message that is consistent with emotions.

## Choose the Best Channels and Timing

When and how you communicate are important to consider. What is the best way to communicate to get the desired outcome? Now more than ever, there are many different options and possibilities for communicating (such as in-person, phone, e-mail, text message, voice message, video message, or social media), each of which may have advantages or disadvantages based on the context or circumstances. In addition to selecting the appropriate channel, the timing is important. Again, knowledge of the receiver's context and preferences is of central importance to time messages appropriately. When is your audience likely to be in the best mental or emotional place to receive a message? Likely not when they are highly emotional or overwhelmed or distracted by something else. Whether you want receivers to think about the information or act on it immediately may dictate whether you deliver the communication on Friday afternoon or Monday morning. A good way to determine the best option is by asking others directly to share their preferences about channels and timing.

## Share the Purpose

When initiating the message it is useful to begin by sharing your purpose for communicating. Ideally, this purpose is one that others involved also care about. It frames the message in a larger context that can include both the task ("I want to share with you some important information about our work . . .") and the relationship (". . . so we can feel more aligned and better supported by one another").

## Keep It Concise, Specific, and Simple

Sometimes people think that communicating clearly means explaining every detail. But often, too much explanation can be more confusing and may make others work harder to figure out what they should be paying attention to. When it comes to conversations involving accountability, try bottom-lining it; for example, "Here are the three things you need to know" or "Please be sure that you do these two things." Then state them as concisely as possible.

When we're unsure about whether we'll be able to meet a deadline or reach our goal, it feels easier or safer to communicate in generalities. "I'll get that report to you next week" helps us, as the speaker, assert some degree of control by being vague and noncommittal regarding our intention. While this may have short-term benefits, the lack of specificity can result in confusion and uncertainty for others. This confusion can then affect how fully we practice conscious accountability. Unless we push ourselves to articulate (or make sure we understand) the specifics, we are increasing the likelihood that miscommunication will occur.

Another communication pitfall is the use of overly technical language or jargon. This kind of language may make other people feel confused or excluded, and places the burden on them to ask for clarification. This may be more challenging, especially if there are power differentials between the message sender and the audience.

## Align the Message With How You Deliver It

There is one additional factor that will enhance the effectiveness of your message, and that is alignment—or congruence—between what you are saying (the content) and how you are saying it (the nonverbal and emotional aspects). When there is consistency between verbal and emotional or nonverbal dimensions, the message is both clearer and often experienced as more authentic, believable, and powerful. To a large extent, this is an exercise in using emotional intelligence skills, such as the capacity to understand what emotions are called for (in you and in others) and the ability to embody and to elicit those emotions in the process of communication.

## Check for Understanding

Once the message has been delivered or received, a critical step, which often gets left out, is checking in for understanding. In the military, use of backbriefs—summaries of information repeated back by personnel to commanding officers—helps ensure that instructions are fully understood. As US Army Col. Pilar Ryan (ret.) puts it: "I don't know what I've said until you tell me what you heard." This acknowledges that what you say and what people hear or what gets communicated are not always the same thing. To understand the impact of our delivery, we must first check in and use listening skills to elicit information about what the audience heard, how they reacted to it, and anything that might need to be clarified further.

### Check In

The purpose of check-ins is to make sure the full, intended meaning of the message is clear and understandable. This typically involves some back-and-forth dialogue between the message sender and receiver to increase clarity and understanding. Examples of check-in questions could include: "What stood out to you as the important points of what I shared?" or "What was the feeling you got in receiving this message?" or "What part of this deserves further clarification?"

### Listen Carefully

As we negotiate expectations with others, it is our capacity to listen and observe carefully that can help us identify gaps between what we intended to communicate and what was heard, and whether others truly understand or are simply going through the motions of agreement. Here are some strategies for increasing the quality of your listening:

- **Be fully present.** This means being free from distraction and really taking the other person in. Pay attention to verbal and nonverbal cues (like tone, facial expressions, and pauses) and read the emotions that the person is sharing in their communication. We can also demonstrate our presence by making eye contact or avoiding distracting behaviors like checking our email or phone.

- **State what you hear.** When we reflect, paraphrase, and summarize what we are hearing through the conversation, it helps the speaker hear themselves and offers the opportunity for adding anything that was missing or clarifying anything that was not fully understood.

- **Inquire with curiosity and interest.** We can engage others through our listening by taking on a stance of active curiosity and interest. This is a powerful way to build connection while eliciting further information. By asking open-ended, clarifying questions, we invite responders to share more information.

- **Show empathy.** Finally, listening in a way that demonstrates empathy can make the difference between something transactional (only focusing on the deliverable) versus something more transformational (holding the relationship and the task in mind simultaneously). We can show empathy by attuning to emotions and feelings, by acknowledging and validating the speaker's perspectives, and by suspending judgment, criticism, or advice giving.

### Close the Loop

Now that the message has been sufficiently clarified in terms of the sender's intended meaning, there is the opportunity to finalize specific details of the message and more fully align expectations of the sender with those of the receiver. This kind of conversation will help establish mutual expectations, which is an important step in increasing buy-in and commitment (both of which will be more fully discussed in chapter 5). People are more likely to feel invested when they have had the opportunity to contribute to the process.

The things that may need exploration include the receiver's sense of self-efficacy—or the extent to which the receivers believe they are capable of doing whatever might be required by the sender's request. Studies have documented that when people have greater levels of self-efficacy, they are more likely to complete the action successfully (Bouffard-Bouchard 1990).

It is also important to discuss both how success will be measured and over what timeframe. Clear metrics that leave no room for interpretation are essential for tracking progress, verifying whether goals were achieved, and keeping everyone accountable.

Finally, confirm the agreement by restating it and making sure that all parties are, in fact, agreeing to the same thing. This should be followed up by putting the agreement into writing or in a form that allows people to revisit and refresh their understanding if needed. Doing this prevents confusion or potential disagreements about the expectations in the future. There are many other ways to create visual representations of commitments that can help keep them top of mind as well (such as team charters, value statements, dashboards, or project management software applications).

## Revisiting the Text Exchange

Let's revisit the texting example from the beginning of this chapter. Keeping in mind the strategies just discussed, take a moment to go back and reread that exchange. Ask yourself, which strategies were done well? What went wrong? What could have been done better?

As you can see, we took a shot at improving the communication ourselves. The changes we made are in italics.

**David, Sunday, 12:49 p.m.:** Hi! Checking in. I'm gonna be working *until about 3:30 p.m.* and wanted to see what support you needed from me to complete the draft of the survey and to make final decisions about the assessment. My goal is to have the platform ready with all the team members added before I record the video, which I will send out tomorrow.

**Marianne, Sunday, 12:55 p.m.:** Hey! *Thanks for checking in.* I'm working on it now. For the survey, I need clarity on what to include. So a cleaned-up version of the doc you created would be great. I left a bunch of comments. For the assessment, I got some feedback and decided which one to include. However, we can change it if you have different thoughts. How does all this sound?

**David, Sunday, 1:00 p.m.:** Sounds good. I will make a clean version of the survey questions and will give you some feedback about the assessment.

**Marianne, Sunday 1:01 p.m.:** *Great! I'm hoping to finish up working today by 4 p.m. to have some free time before Monday hits. When do you think you will get the clean version and your feedback to me?*

**David, Sunday 1:02 p.m.:** *Oh, good to know. I have some other work to do as well. So, I'll prioritize this and get it to you by 2 p.m. Will that work?*

**Marianne, Sunday 1:03 p.m.:** Yep, that will work. Thanks!

Here, increasing the specificity of times improved the clarity of the text exchange.

Although "a couple" can mean two hours, it is not always used that way in practice and leaves some room for interpretation. This also happens with similar words like *few* and *several*. When possible, being as specific as possible helps reduce the likelihood of miscommunication.

Also, Marianne's disclosing that she would like to finish work by 4 p.m. sheds light on what is important to her. This is an example of how one can be intentional about increasing the "known" window of the Johari window, discussed in chapter 2. Deliberately telling others relevant personal information allows them to more fully understand us and better communicate with us. With this information, David was able to better consider his audience and honor Marianne's needs.

Lastly, by adding, "Thanks for checking in," Marianne is able to quickly acknowledge David's actions and express her gratitude for his offer of support and information. These simple exchanges may seem superfluous upon first glance. However, the additive impact of these small gestures can be powerful. Each one is like a penny in the bank of your social capital account. Over time, this capital builds and when things go wrong, as they inevitably will, there is enough goodwill to draw from without incurring a significant deficit in the relationship.

Let's take a look at the practice of creating clarity in action.

## Leadership by Example: Shalini, Seeking to Clearly Share Information With Her Team

Shalini Desai is a top leader at a multinational venture capital firm. From her office in Boston, she manages a global team of investors who are looking to invest in startups that are innovating climate-change solutions. Half of her team is in the US, with the other half in India. During a recent session with her executive coach, in which they reviewed the results from her latest 360, Shalini was proud to learn that she is seen as personable, caring, and an able communicator by team members in both countries. She has been with the firm for almost a decade and is well liked by most of her colleagues.

However, a few of her direct reports in the US noted that they sometimes hold back on telling Shalini about emerging problems because she can be quick to react and make decisions without asking them for their full input and knowledge about the issue. This has resulted in frustration that team members' expertise is being overlooked and sidelined in favor of Shalini's quick and sometimes uninformed responses.

As a result, these direct reports will occasionally withhold their concerns and try to solve problems on their own, even in situations where they know that Shalini's input, early in the process, could prove very valuable. Her US-based direct reports would love for Shalini to be able to listen more calmly and fully to their concerns during moments of stress, so that they could directly collaborate with her to resolve crucial issues.

Always open to growing as a leader, Shalini appreciated this feedback from all members of her team and began thinking about ways to communicate to her staff—particularly in the US—her openness to hearing their perspectives on critical business issues. Shalini also took note of the fact that she did not receive the same feedback from members of her India-based team, but that she should consider clueing them in so that everyone on the team understood and agreed to any changes in their workplace norms and ways of solving problems together. She started planning for a meeting in which she would discuss these issues with her team.

Two days later, Shalini learned from the board that because of a recent market depression, the company was not able to raise the capital needed for its latest investment fund. Top leadership, with Shalini included, held an emergency meeting and came to the difficult decision that a 10 percent staff reduction across the organization was now required. Shalini was sobered to realize that she would need to cut staff across the two locations of her team.

While she wished circumstances were different, Shalini knew that the best thing to do was communicate this difficult news to her staff in a clear, direct, and empathetic manner. But she was also aware of how disempowering this information might feel, especially given some of the concerns that Shalini sometimes made rash decisions without consulting them or having all the information available to her.

How could Shalini most effectively let her team know what she needs and expects from them at this difficult time, while doing so in a way that acknowledges how painful the layoffs might be for them? How could she address the concerns raised about her openness to feedback and collaboration with team members, if this decision about layoffs might come across as unexpected and unilateral? And how could she communicate that they were all members of the same team, even if there were different workplace issues under consideration at the two offices?

## Exercise: How Would You Handle Shalini's Situation?

To prepare for these complex conversations, Shalini circled back with her leadership coach. Together, they developed and worked through a set of questions that were focused on helping Shalini (and all of us!) communicate as openly, clearly, and respectfully as possible. As a thought exercise, you (the reader) can work through these questions too. If you were in Shalini's situation, what would you do?

- **Clarity of intentions:**
  - What does she want her team to understand about how and why she and the rest of the leadership team came to the decision about the layoffs?
  - What is the most important information she wants to get across about this news and its potential impact on her team?
  - How will she address the fact that she received different feedback from both of her teams and is working to address this while still encouraging the full cohesion of the group?
  - How could she most effectively communicate not just the decision, but also her feelings about it? What—on an emotional level—does she most want to convey to the recipients of this news?

- **Consider who is involved:**
  - How might her team members receive the news about the layoffs?
  - What considerations of cultural differences across her teams should Shalini make when delivering the news of the layoffs?
  - How will Shalini communicate her openness to addressing the unique needs of the staff members slated to be laid off?
  - How can Shalini both deliver the hard news about layoffs while also reassuring her team of her desire to be more open to their input and feedback going forward?

- **Communicate her message:**
  - How will Shalini alert her staff about this meeting?
  - How could Shalini frame her message so that it is concise, caring, easily understandable, and culturally sensitive?
  - How will Shalini handle her body language, tone of voice, and other elements of nonverbal communication to ensure that her feelings about the decision are in sync with the information she is sharing?

- **Check for understanding:**
  - How will Shalini create space for her team to ask any questions they may have?
  - What sorts of questions will Shalini ask them, to gauge whether they have fully understood her message about the layoffs and her desire to collaborate going forward?
  - What resources will team members have access to following the meeting, so they can retain what was said and continue learning about the terms of the layoffs?

## Leadership by Example, Shalini's Response

In the end, Shalini chose a hybrid approach to address her two main concerns: the impending layoffs and the impression by her US staff members that she was not as open to collaboration as they would like. Given her prior knowledge that many of the people across her team have a more independent style of working, Shalini decided it would be best to first communicate news of the layoffs in one-to-one meetings with those affected. But, while she felt well versed in communicating difficult news to her staff in the US, Shalini was less certain of appropriate moves for such a conversation in India. She therefore reached out to her company's HR department in India to learn about important cultural codes to follow when delivering difficult news in this different cultural context.

To lessen the likelihood of the rumor mill churning, Shalini first sent a memo letting all team members know that layoffs were coming and that she would be in touch with people individually over the next three days. She then held meetings and remained receptive to each person's concerns; she came equipped with information about severance pay and the other supports that HR could provide. And Shalini made sure to keep open office hours over the course of that week, so that anyone on her team could reach out to her for more information or support.

Following these one-on-ones and office hours, Shalini held a larger team meeting, billed as an opportunity to discuss team dynamics and well-being, with all members of her team. She did her best to schedule this meeting around time-zone differences. Shalini started by addressing the issue of layoffs more broadly. She transparently shared all of the relevant information about why the layoffs were occurring, and also described the support the company would offer those affected. She also video recorded the meeting for those who were unable to attend in person.

Shalini next highlighted her second concern, focusing on the feedback she received about her decision-making style. She explained that she understood the feedback and asked questions to more specifically understand how different colleagues (in different cultural contexts) felt about her openness to collaboration with them. As issues of cultural differences in opinion around leadership came up, Shalini encouraged dialogue by asking candid questions about her team members' perspectives. Shalini repeatedly voiced that she remained very open to learning more from staff members (either directly or through an anonymous chat board she had created). She also laid out a few ideas she had for enhancing collaboration across all levels of the team, and again encouraged feedback on the cultural sensitivity of her suggestions.

The upshot? The team members who were laid off were understandably upset but also felt buoyed by the support that Shalini provided. The team members who were worried about Shalini's openness to hearing their perspectives felt heard and were excited by the prospect of working in greater understanding with her. And all team members felt that the door had been opened, widely, to more honest exchange about the cultural richness of their group.

## Summary: Managing the Challenges of Practicing Clarity

Creating clarity is an important practice for promoting conscious accountability. In fact, it is so central that we position it as the first of the seven practices. Clarity in goals and expectations increases the likelihood that tasks will be completed and supports stronger relationships. It also helps support the implementation of the other practices.

Despite our best efforts, clarity is often not easy to achieve, and practicing it requires the mindsets of humility and patience. The challenges of communication become even more complex when the number of people involved increases or when human diversity increases. Diversity of experiences opens up the likelihood that people will perceive communication differently. Fortunately, there are four strategies for increasing clarity and reducing or preventing the occurrence of communication problems:

- Clarify the intention.
- Consider who is involved.
- Communicate or receive the message.
- Check for understanding.

Normally, we might communicate with far less forethought and intentionality. Conscious accountability calls us to bring more awareness to what we say, how we think and plan, and how we listen and respond. In the next chapter, we will discuss another practice that also lays the groundwork for subsequent practices: opening up engagement.

# Opening Up Engagement

Fred Rogers, the beloved children's television personality, is an example of someone who deeply engaged not only his viewers but also the people with whom he worked and collaborated. His continuous message that he liked you "just the way you are," and his reiteration of how important and special each and every person is in their own unique way created the sense that everyone could fully be themselves without fear of embarrassment.

Behind the scenes, Rogers's leadership allowed for extraordinary creativity and innovation. He created a unique kind of programming that was very accessible to children yet tackled difficult personal and social issues ranging from death to racism.

Jeanne Marie Laskas, a longtime friend of Rogers, penned an article about him in the *New York Times* in 2019. She wrote the following about a discussion she had with him on the nature of his program: "'An atmosphere,' he said. What he was trying to create with *Mister Rogers' Neighborhood* was 'an atmosphere that allows people to be comfortable enough to be who they are.' He continued: 'I really don't want to superimpose anything on anybody. If people are comfortable in that atmosphere, they can grow from there, in their own way.'

"That was the vibe in Studio A," continued Laskas, explaining what it was like to spend time on the set of the TV program. "Fred was intentional about the atmosphere he created on the program as well as on the set. If you could provide an environment that allowed people to be comfortable enough to be, simply, who they are, what would happen? Who would they become?"

She was not the only one who felt this vibe. In Laskas' *New York Times* article, Johnny Costa, a musician from the show, expressed a similar sentiment about Rogers and what it felt like to work for him: "Fred knows that I have something to give that's important. And he lets me give it, and I give it freely, and then I'm part of it, a part of his creation" (Laskas 2019). Costa said pretty much everyone felt that way. "That's what makes us so tight. It's because Fred lets us give. And what a thing that is, huh?"

Becoming "tight," being free to give, and feeling like a contributing and important part of the work—these are all desired outcomes of conscious accountability. Like Fred Rogers, conscious accountability encourages people to be authentic and bring their whole selves to work and life more generally. It lets people give all they have to offer. If we could create the conditions where this could happen, what an accomplishment that would be.

## What Is Engagement and Why Does It Matter?

Engagement in the workplace means being passionate about what you do, being committed to your team and organization, and being willing to exert effort above and beyond what is required. When we are deeply engaged, we experience a powerful connection to what we are doing, who we are doing it with, or—in the best of circumstances—both.

Can you think of a time when this was true for you? How did you feel about the tasks? And how did you feel about who you were doing them with? It was probably a high point kind of experience.

David has been involved in musical theater productions off and on since high school. Some of his best memories were from shows when the cast members were fully engaged and formed a tight bond that allowed everyone to take more risks and have greater freedom to play together. This collective enthusiasm and comfort resulted in stellar, memorable performances.

Meanwhile, Marianne has had the pleasure of working on a multi-disciplinary startup team to develop technology to assist folks with opioid use disorder. This work was filled with repeated moments of deep engagement; it was contentious at times, but continuously full of meaning and devotion to their shared purpose. This fueled them when they had to meet the demanding deadlines set by a technology boot camp that required extended work hours and the temporary sacrifice of other areas of their lives. The result has been a fuller appreciation of their perspectives, and a product that none of them could have conceived or built on their own.

And, when Daryn works with her coaching clients, she opens herself to the emotions they're expressing and the energy in the room. Sometimes, through honest, caring conversation, Daryn and her clients will click, allowing each of them to become more deeply engaged and immersed in the discussion. When such moments of connection blossom, Daryn feels more strongly drawn to her clients and increasingly invested in helping them actualize their hopes for personal growth and professional development.

In your own work and relationships, you too may have felt connected to someone in this deeper, more engaged way. Engagement makes a big difference with regard to improving relationships and results. Higher employee engagement is linked to greater productivity, higher morale, and better profits. And disengaged employees cost US companies between $450 and $500 billion per year (Smarp 2021). Given the stakes at play, we believe that the practices of conscious accountability and opening up engagement are important.

Our treatment of the concept of engagement focuses on two different dimensions that open up engagement: commitment and psychological safety.

## Commitment

Commitment is such a complex notion that it has been studied across disciplines for decades. Despite this impressive volume and scope, there is no consensus on how to define it. Given this ambiguity, we turned to the most in-depth review of scholarship on commitment for the basis of our definition. Organization and leadership development expert Zachary A. Mercurio (2015) conducted an extensive review, analysis, and synthesis of the scholarly writings on commitment over the prior 50 years. He concluded the core essence of commitment was affective (or emotional) commitment.

Our interest is in improving not only outcomes for performance but also interpersonal relationships. Thus, we too put affective commitment, or emotional attachment, at the core of our definition and describe *commitment* as a psychological state reflecting how strongly one is emotionally attached to the targeted result and relationship.

In essence, commitment is a promise to complete a task and to do so in a way that deepens our connection to the people involved. Each commitment is an opportunity to develop both our behavioral performance and interpersonal effectiveness. It requires specificity in both the task and strategy, as well as transparency around people's intentions, motives, and behaviors. We propose that focusing on building commitment will lead to both improved performance and interpersonal effectiveness, which are the goals of conscious accountability. In fact, research shows that commitment is linked to positive outcomes and the absence of it is linked to negative outcomes. Let's look closer at both aspects:

- **Performance outcomes.** Commitment is strongly linked to turnover, absenteeism, and organizational citizenship behaviors. If employees feel a strong emotional attachment to the organization, they are more likely to stay, show up regularly, and go above and beyond expectations (Mercucio 2015). Extrapolating to accountability among teams, it seems fair to assert that if individuals are emotionally attached to their team, they are more likely to remain a member of that team, follow through on team commitments, and go out of their way to meet or exceed expectations.

- **Relationship outcomes.** The need for attachment is an intrinsic part of being human. Studies on attachment in romantic relationships shed light on the importance of commitment in how we experience and behave in relationships. Commitment has been linked to higher relationship satisfaction as well as greater persistence and longer-term stability (Ho et al. 2012; Bui, Peplau, and Hill 1999; Etcheverry and Le 2005). It also helps create a buffer against feelings of rejection, while enhancing feelings of acceptance (Tran and Simpson 2009). People who are more committed will also enact more constructive behaviors and fewer destructive behaviors (Wieselquist et al. 1999). If we extrapolate these findings to relationships at work, when people feel emotionally committed, they are more likely to persevere when things get rocky and interact in ways that support relationships over time. We have survived and thrived because of our ability to cooperate and exist in groups. Our social and emotional connections allow us to communicate complex ideas and coordinate behaviors across time and space (Harari 2018). If affiliation is a kind of human superpower, emotional commitment leverages that power to ensure things get done.

Commitment can be a double-edged sword. On the one hand, it can help us feel motivated and inspire us to action; however, it may also weigh us down with feelings of pressure, obligation, and fear of failure. This is referred to as the paradox of commitment, which requires us to find the sweet spot that works for us.

Commitment on the surface may seem like it is task focused and action oriented. In reality, commitment is centered deep in our hearts. And when one's heart is on the line, it is crucial to make sure it is in a safe place. Making sure psychological safety is fostered while building commitment may help us feel more fully involved in our tasks. Therefore, we advocate for creating both of these constructs concurrently because they are interdependent and each builds upon the other, brick by brick.

## Psychological Safety

Nobody wants to look bad. Most people do not want to appear like they do not know what they are doing, that they are complainers or that they are disagreeable. When we informally asked our peers, "What makes accountability hard for you?" people shared comments such as:

- Fear of failing
- I will lose social capital and be on the receiving end of backlash
- Accountability takes away from the facade of appearing like you have it together

Humans are continuously evaluating the cost-benefit of putting themselves out there. This dilemma can lead to a tendency to avoid asking questions, sharing our thoughts and feelings, offering honest feedback, trying something new, or attempting to work collaboratively together.

Psychological safety is what allows us to put ourselves out there. The term *psychological safety* was first studied in the 1960s and then became a topic of renewed interest when Amy Edmondson, an organizational behavioral scientist at Harvard Business School, rediscovered it in her attempts to understand the conditions under which serious medication errors occurred in hospitals. She found that, among healthcare teams with greater levels of psychological safety, there was an increased willingness to report and discuss errors. Edmondson defined psychological safety as "a general belief that one is comfortable being oneself—being open, authentic, and direct—in a particular setting or role" (Nembhard and Edmondson 2011).

Psychological safety has a big impact on how teams behave around emotional or controversial topics. When we feel psychologically safe, we feel we can show up fully, share ideas freely, and take risks without the worrying we will be embarrassed or ostracized. The potential benefit of saying something outweighs the risk of looking bad or losing social standing. It does not mean that the atmosphere is devoid of pressure, worries, and problems. Rather, it is an environment where discourse and dialogue around these difficult situations occurs.

Shining a light on challenges may even give the appearance that there is dysfunction in the team because issues that may typically go underground are brought to the surface. However, this type of discourse is key to addressing team disharmony and improving outcomes, because having the brave conversation conveys trust between individuals and allows for problems to actually get fixed.

For example, in a meeting of partners of a startup communication consulting firm who were discussing some changes in their operating agreement, individuals were able to share their personal concerns, objections, and candid feelings about proposed changes. Other partners were able to hear and appreciate these contributions—even though it was uncomfortable and meant that there was not going to be a quick solution.

By contrast, another group of partners in a law firm with long-standing relationships were so worried about discussions becoming heated or individuals getting hurt that they held back and did not bring their authentic perspectives to light. They avoided tough topics and more substantive collaborations. Over time, this led to many side conversations instead of direct conversations and bred serious mistrust because of what was seen as a lack of transparency and hidden agendas.

Having a sense of psychological safety makes it much easier for people to engage in conscious accountability. Let's revisit our definition of conscious accountability: *expanding awareness to create deliberate intentions, to take informed actions, and to be responsible for our impact.* Here are some examples of how psychological safety promotes various aspects of conscious accountability:

- **Expanded awareness.** When we are less concerned about self-protection and the need to avoid looking bad, it frees us up to think more about others and what they think, feel, experience, and need. We can also more readily delve inside ourselves to come in contact with deeper intrinsic motivations, beyond impression management.

- **Taking informed actions.** Being able to take informed actions requires having access to a deeper pool of information on which to base those actions. When people feel psychologically safe, they can provide and receive better quality information by sharing ideas more fully, asking tough questions, and exchanging honest feedback.
- **Being responsible for impact.** Admitting mistakes, errors, and problems requires a great deal of courage and humility. When people feel certain that they will not be judged harshly for these mistakes, they become more open and willing to not only acknowledge them, but to discuss and learn from them (Edmondson 2012).

## Key Mindset: "All In"

The key mindset for the practice of opening up engagement is the state of being "all in." When someone says, "I'm all in," what does that convey to you? If you are playing poker, "all in" means putting all your chips—everything that you have—into the pot. In other areas of life, it is often shorthand for "I am 100 percent committed." If some friends asked you to go on vacation with them, "I'm all in" conveys that nothing could stop you from joining them; here's my credit card—book the tickets now!

Being all in relates to other people as well. In relationships, the idea of being all in means being highly committed to the person and the relationship. How does it make you feel when you know someone is committed to you? That they will be there and still connect with you, even when you disagree or get mad or forget something important or screw up? If we are lucky, we have at least one person in our lives like that: a parent, a partner, or a best friend. Relationships like that make us feel safe and relieved—like we can be more fully ourselves and accepted for who we are, even if we are having a bad day or a bad moment.

At work, all in means you are fully engaged and committed to doing your best for yourself, for the results you are trying to achieve, and for the people you are working with. Consider this example. Nikita and Michael were software engineers working on a program with important strategic significance for their company. The two of them were tasked with bringing this initiative to life and had been working together closely, developing the product for 18 months. The day before the program was scheduled to go live, and in the midst of a whirlwind of last-minute bug fixes, a storm knocked out power to Michael's location. Nikita, who lived 45 minutes away, was able to send her sister to pick up Michael and together they completed the fixes, resulting in a successful rollout the next day. Nikita and Michael were all in, both with regard to their work commitment and to their relationship as colleagues.

In this way, embracing an all-in mindset means committing to both the endeavor and the people involved. When we do that, it conveys commitment, promotes safety, and opens ourselves and others to robust, honest, and fuller engagement both in the work and in relationships. But also note that being all in does not preclude you from having healthy boundaries. Good boundaries help people understand what is expected, what is appropriate, and what the limits are—all of which can contribute to building a sense of psychological safety. And when people feel safe, it is even easier for them to be all in.

## 4 Strategies for Opening Up Engagement

Opening up engagement through building safety and commitment may sound straightforward, but it is actually a process that can be complex and requires both time and effort. We offer four strategies for driving engagement, which contribute to commitment, psychological safety, or both:

- Align values.
- Honor individual needs.
- Model vulnerable learning.
- Be inclusive.

Opening up engagement happens throughout the team's work together. It's not something you check off before work starts and then do not revisit. With these four strategies, the first one is the most important to reach agreement beforehand, while the others (plus the first) are advanced in every interaction.

## Align Values

Values refer to the guiding principles that influence how we behave and react. Conscious accountability looks at values as what is important to individuals deep down in their hearts. Values tend to be stable and serve as the driving force behind our decisions. They determine our priorities and serve as the metric to gauge how we are living. When we are living according to our values, life feels good. When we are not, we typically feel an internal dissonance and life feels like a struggle. Every individual has a set of values, whether they are aware of it or not. Within organizations, values determine decisions, such as strategic direction, customer strategy, and responses to fluctuations in the market. An organization's values are also operating whether or not people are aware of them. Getting clear on and communicating the organization's values is an imperative of leaders.

The aim with regard to values in conscious accountability is to find alignment or congruence among team members' values, or between individual and organizational values. Values congruence is linked to numerous outcomes, including greater organizational commitment and engagement (Harris and Mossholder 1996). Think about it: When the work you are doing or the way you are working lines up with what is important to you, it is incredibly energizing and increases the sense of connection, passion, and meaning you experience.

So how can you create that alignment? Various strategies exist to strengthen values congruence. First, it is essential to be clear on what your values (or your team's or organization's values) actually are. And not just values you *aspire to*, but the ones you really live and use to guide everyday decisions. As US president Joe Biden (2008) once said: "Don't tell me what you value. Show me your budget, and I'll tell you what you value."

Once you are clear on your own values, it is important to talk about them with others and learn more about what they value. From there you can explore areas of overlap and issues of fit. The process involves taking time to understand what really matters and resonates with people. Here are some of the questions we have used to help people talk about values:

- What personal motivation do you have in being involved with this project, team, and company? What matters most to you?
- What qualities would you look for most when hiring team members and why?
- What kind of team or company culture are you looking to build and why? Be as specific as possible (for example, work-life balance, freedom to work from home, and so forth).
- If you could name three to five values that define this team or company, what would they be?

Note that these conversations are not always easy, especially when there isn't immediate agreement on what values are most important. The critical question is whether there is sufficient commonality to remain engaged together, and how to make the most of shared values to advance the endeavor or team.

One of our clients who runs a manufacturing company does this routinely when hiring new executives. Prior to joining the team, the executive completes a series of assessments, one of which examines the person's values. The assessment results explain not only what people value but also the implications for the environments where they work best. This has served as a great springboard to get to know people more quickly to gauge the extent to which their values match those within the team. As the CEO explained, "We've seen this practice speed up onboarding, because we have real dialogue that builds mutual understanding and trust, right out of the gate."

## Honor Individual Needs

People are more engaged not only when they are connected to their values but also when their primary needs are being met. According to self-determination theory—which was popularized by Dan Pink in *Drive* and his 2009 TED talk—all humans are driven by three basic universal needs: autonomy, mastery, and relatedness (Deci and Ryan 1985). *Autonomy* refers to an individual's freedom of choice around performing an activity. *Mastery* is a sense of growing competence in a given activity. And, *relatedness* is a feeling of connection to others involved in the same activity.

Each of these factors influences engagement. The greater the sense of autonomy around choosing an activity, the more likely the person will carry it out. Similarly, if task difficulty is high enough to engage interest but low enough that steady improvement is possible, it will lead to a sense of mastery. This is positively correlated with commitment and performance. Finally, the more connected or related an individual feels to others engaged in the activity, the more persistently they will pursue it. Thus, designing tasks and interactions with people's needs in mind will increase commitment to both the task and the team. This can be done by keeping the following guiding principles in mind:

- **Always autonomous.** Specify the desired end state ("where we're going"), not the means ("how we're getting there"). Give as much freedom of choice as possible when deciding on task and team assignments. When autonomy is not possible, state that you wish you could have given them the choice and that you will offer a choice in some other way.

- **Gradual mastery.** Break down larger initiatives into smaller steps that can create an incremental sense of accomplishment. The steps should be "just hard enough," meaning they offer a stretch but are not impossible. Be sure to break down steps so they're small enough to allow learning while maximizing the likelihood of success. Do this by repeatedly asking, "What would be the step before that?" until a plan to mastery unfolds.

- **Keep relating.** Share team members' progress and reactions to the work and allow for ongoing discussion. On one team David led, their use of a group text conversation was instrumental for sharing just-in-time information, while building a sense of camaraderie, appreciation, and belonging among the team members.

When we are aware of others' individual needs and are able to acknowledge or meet them, it helps others to feel seen, understood, and cared for. This can strengthen relationships, drive reciprocity, and increase willingness to be mutually accountable.

## Model Vulnerable Learning

Psychological safety sounds comforting and inviting and, well . . . safe. Ironically, creating it often feels nothing like that, as this example from our work with learning teams at Yale School of Management demonstrates. The learning team (also known as the "Lab Group," because it is an interpersonal learning laboratory) was made up of a collection of students of varying races, ethnicities, nationalities, religious backgrounds, and sexual orientations. For the first two sessions, they were very cautious and tentative, sticking to innocuous topics and not inquiring about or disclosing anything that was too personal or revealing. It was awkward and strained with long uncomfortable silences.

In the third session, Carla had been quiet for the first hour; when one of the facilitators noticed this, they asked her if she was OK. Carla responded with a statement that changed everything.

"When I was a child, my father was an alcoholic," she said. "When he would come home drunk, he often became loud, argumentative, and menacing. Me and my siblings had to walk on eggshells all the time and had to hold everything in, so we didn't set him off. Being in this group reminds me of having to walk on eggshells, and I am sick and tired of feeling that way. Can we please stop censoring ourselves here? What are we all so afraid of?"

That led to a cascade of more authentic sharing of reactions and feelings from the other group members, as well as discussions of the things people were afraid of. It was a major turning point for the group, which started connecting and becoming a safe place to learn.

Time and time again, we have observed that one person's vulnerability usually leads to others being vulnerable too. But here is the rub: Someone has to be willing to go first. And this responsibility for deliberately creating psychological safety falls squarely on the shoulders of leaders. Inspired by Amy

Edmondson, Charles Duhigg, Brené Brown, Dan Coyle, and others, here are some ideas for how a leader can help create safety:

- Talk about the importance of learning in the relationship or within the team. Learning often requires making mistakes and missteps, which are normal and expected, and talking about errors is not only acceptable but also necessary for getting better.
- Demonstrate fallibility by being open about your own mistakes, past and present. Don't be afraid to say, "I made a mistake," or "I'm sorry."
- Admit that you do not know the answer. Be willing to say, "I don't know" or "I need your help." This paves the way for others to be similarly open, to rely on others, and to promote team problem solving.
- When others admit mistakes or ask for help, be supportive and encouraging. Positively reinforce their willingness to talk about it and help extract the learning.
- Model curiosity and interest by asking lots of questions. This conveys that it is OK to dig deeper and inquire to find the solutions. Equally important is to respond to questions with openness and appreciation. No topic should be off limits.
- Ask supportive questions like, "What are you dealing with right now?" "What's holding you back?" and "How can I help you?"
- Ensure that everyone gets equal time to speak and offer individual team members the opportunity to contribute if they have not done so.

If you recall in the introduction, we learned about Kendra's leadership practices. She went beyond making it acceptable to be vulnerable, take risks, and fail. She made it a required rite of passage to becoming a full-fledged member of her team, and she celebrated the occurrence of a team member's first mess up. Kendra also modeled vulnerability by sharing stories of her past mistakes, continuously owning up to not knowing the answer, and apologizing when she falls short.

In sum, it is up to the leader to set the tone, go first, and model behaviors that promote safety and greater engagement. Moreover, the leader needs to do this repeatedly and frequently. But not just C-suite leaders. The onus of creating and maintaining psychological safety falls on leaders and managers at all levels of the workplace.

## Be Inclusive

Researchers at Google studied 180 teams over five years and found themselves stumped as to what made some teams more successful than others. Every variable they hypothesized—including demographics such as educational background, gender, personalities, and socialization—would explain what made some teams more successful than others fell short. Eventually, they stumbled upon the concept of psychological safety in academic papers and suddenly it all made sense. The researchers realized it was not *who* was on the team that was critical; rather, it was *how* the team worked together. Other dynamics were important too, but none as important as psychological safety. It was the necessary foundation. And in their study, two variables were critical for creating psychological safety: "equality in conversational turn-taking" and "social sensitivity." Equality in conversational turn-taking meant that every team member had roughly equal airtime in meetings, while social sensitivity meant that team members were skilled at intuiting how others felt based on their tone of voice, their expressions, and other nonverbal cues (Duhigg 2016).

Inclusive leaders use "a specific strategy of openness and accessibility to create a dynamic that promotes a diversity of opinions" when working to forward shared team goals (Mitchell et al. 2015). Making people feel seen, heard, and included means actively seeking out their opinions and input. It means engaging others with openness and curiosity and listening to their perspectives and feelings with total receptivity. This is especially crucial in the case of underrepresented minorities that have historically been excluded, overlooked, and unheard, and whose own past experiences of exclusion or nonbelonging may understandably result in a reluctance to speak up.

Fostering inclusivity may look like a leader saying to the group, "We've been hearing a lot of great things from Tom and Kevin. I would like to get some other voices in the room. Sharon, you've been looking pensive. I am interested in what you are thinking if you don't mind sharing. Your viewpoint and insights are important and valued here." Alternatively, if a leader does not want to single out a person, another possibility is to invite someone to play the role of the skeptic. This might sound something like, "We've been hearing a lot of great things from Tom and Kevin. Let's make sure we are discussing this from all angles. Who would like to be the skeptic and poke some holes in what has been said?" In this way, an individual who has some alternative thoughts about what is being discussed but is reluctant to be the outlier is now invited to share contradictory opinions in a safe way.

## Leadership by Example:
## Erik, Creating a Community of Engagement

Erik Schreter, founder of Venwise, is an outstanding example of a leader who has been able to create deep levels of engagement, commitment, and psychological safety among a population where opening up is typically seen as a huge risk. Venwise is a community of high-growth tech startups head-quartered in New York City. The tech startup world is highly competitive, constantly changing, and full of risk. The viability statistics are daunting. The vast majority of startups fail, about 90 percent (Ward 2021). Founders face a plethora of challenges, most of which are similar across the board. It boils down to the fact that they are all trying to build the business and team, and secure funding, at the same time. On top of this, finding a safe space for founders to get high-quality support and advice for their most vulnerable questions is nearly impossible. Exposing challenges to other founders, board members, partners, and employees would leave founders even more vulnerable in an environment where impressions can make or break a company.

Erik saw this situation and was driven to create a safe space where startup executives could get answers to their most pressing concerns. He envisioned groups of startup professionals meeting regularly to share challenges, wisdom, support, resources, and advice. The creation of these groups, called "pods," involved three critical steps:

- Getting buy-in
- Committing to a structure
- Visualizing what good looks like

Erik knew the first step, to get people to buy into the concept, would require their emotional attachment to what he was creating. In his words, "People become accountable to things they care for. Whether it is a person you are working for, the community you are joining, or the relationship you are in, you are not going to be accountable unless you care and actually have an emotional attachment." He continues, "In this way, emotional attachment became a business resource for Venwise."

Erik is deeply committed to creating a culture of care and mutual benefit. When people join the community, he communicates, "I care about you, you care about me. Let's make this valuable for both of us." He makes sure to find out what is important to each person. The first questions he asks every new member are, "Why are you here?" and "What are you looking for?" He goes further by inquiring, "If we were to measure success in 12 months from now, what would that look like?"

He then shifts his focus to the second critical step, structure. This is about how the group behaves to achieve what each of them wants. He invites members to co-author this step, relating, "Let's build an infrastructure for this meeting that makes this a valuable asset for all of us." This infrastructure includes strict ground rules that all community members must adhere to, such as being present, open, and respectful. "These ground rules are the commitments to me," he explains. "This is where they become attached. This is where they help to co-author relationships together." In this way, they are embracing a mindset of being all in.

Third, he helps pod members visualize what a good group looks like using the Johari window (introduced in chapter 2). Using this tool helps them see that by being vulnerable, by sharing, and by being curious about others, the Open window becomes larger, communication is improved, self-awareness grows, and relationships deepen.

Membership has grown steadily, and Venwise members continue to gain tremendous value from the community. If you visit their website, you can view glowing testimonials, such as this one from the CTO of Peloton: "Last year our engineering team experienced 100 percent growth and needed to be restructured. My Venwise Pod helped me adjust my strategy to better align with our annual goals and has had a direct impact on the organizational structure of Peloton." And this one from the CEO of Betterment, "The immediate usefulness surprised me. I came in skeptical and walked away with a handful of learnings while thinking, wow, that was a great three hours; let's do that again. Four years later, I continue to feel that way."

## Exercise: Assess Engagement, Commitment, and Safety

Because high levels of engagement, commitment, and safety are so crucial to ensuring optimal teamwork, it is important to touch base frequently with team members about how safe, committed, and engaged they actually are feeling about the tasks at hand. The questions in this exercise—inspired by more formal assessments, including those from Edmondson (2019) and Monday, Steers, and Porter (1979)—can serve as a guide to priming team members to necessary conversations about commitment, safety, and overall engagement. Feel free to adapt them as you learn more about your team and what they need to work together most effectively.

**Figure 5-1.** Engagement, Safety, Commitment Check-In

**Quick ESC (Engagement, Safety, Commitment) Check-In**
*Please rate your response to the following statements on a scale from 1 to 5.*
*(1 = not at all; 5 = completely)*

|  | 1 | 2 | 3 | 4 | 5 |
|---|---|---|---|---|---|
| How committed are you to completing the task that we are working on? |  |  |  |  |  |
| How psychologically safe do you feel on this team? |  |  |  |  |  |
| What is your overall level of engagement with the task at hand? |  |  |  |  |  |

**Slightly Longer ESC Check-In**

*Please rate your response to the following statements on a scale from 1 to 7.*
*(1 = completely disagree; 7 = completely agree)*

| | 1 | 2 | 3 | 4 | 5 | 6 | 7 |
|---|---|---|---|---|---|---|---|
| **Commitment** | | | | | | | |
| I believe in the values and goals associated with this task. | | | | | | | |
| I am willing to exert considerable effort on behalf of this team. | | | | | | | |
| I have a strong desire to maintain membership in this team. | | | | | | | |
| **Safety** | | | | | | | |
| I feel comfortable speaking up. | | | | | | | |
| I feel comfortable experimenting. | | | | | | | |
| I feel comfortable collaborating. | | | | | | | |
| **Engagement** | | | | | | | |
| I feel completely engaged with the task at hand. | | | | | | | |
| I feel completely engaged working with my team members. | | | | | | | |
| If you are in need of a boost on either of the last two questions, please name one thing that could create a shift on our team to increase your levels of engagement. | | | | | | | |

Here are some additional tips for increasing engagement:

- Introduce and normalize frequent conversations about safety and commitment. Explain these concepts and invite your team members to also share their perspectives on how safety and commitment could increase engagement and overall team performance.
- Set a strong tone of psychological safety in these conversations by creating space for everyone to share their perspectives and potential concerns, and by making clear that all viewpoints will be welcomed and considered.
- If you sense that there are deeper-seated concerns with safety and commitment on your team, engage a coach to help the team navigate and discuss these issues constructively.

- Keep your approach to these topics flexible, light, and accepting. If team members seem hesitant to answer questions about commitment and safety directly, you could create an anonymous survey that you ask everyone to complete in advance of your meeting.
- After you have assessed commitment and safety and have a better understanding of where your team stands, you will want to move toward building upon their current levels of emotional buy-in and strengthening the climate of safety. The strategies for opening up engagement (discussed earlier) can help guide you to do so. Awareness about typical challenges to commitment and safety will help you strategize about how to proceed.

## Summary: Two Critical Factors for Opening Up Engagement

In this chapter we focused on the practice of opening up engagement as foundational for promoting conscious accountability. And we explored two related and at times intersecting paths that strengthen engagement: commitment and psychological safety. Awareness of these factors allows you to gauge how committed others are to both the task and the team and if they feel safe moving forward. It also helps determine who may need support increasing their engagement. And, it opens up an opportunity to check in on assumptions and sets the stage for the exchange of feedback.

In the absence of information, leaders may be under the assumption that the team is strongly committed and psychologically safe because they have not been informed otherwise. However, because voicing dissent is challenging, inviting other perspectives as a matter of course will help break this barrier to disclosure. These two factors are critical because they serve as the fuel for your goal. When challenges arise, as they do, if you are committed and feel safe, you will be more likely to find solutions and persevere. When the initial sparks of inspiration and excitement dissipate, it is your commitment to the task that will sustain you and your sense of safety that will allow you to keep trying.

# CHAPTER 6

# Nailing It

> *Accountability means to say what you do, do what you say.*
> PEARL ZHU

## David's Journal Entry, May 14, 2021

*As I am sitting down to revise this chapter on nailing it, I am aware that this whole book project has been an exercise in nailing it. It's ironic to me, because on the one hand this practice is so essential to conscious accountability—yet it is something that I have really struggled with at different points in my life. I remember friends in college joking that my name should have been "David Late" because I could never quite manage to show up at the agreed upon time—and I did not like the idea that people saw me as not fully reliable or responsible. And then there was that fundraising initiative at a nonprofit that I led, which flopped. We had a lofty but seemingly attainable goal, but in the end, we could not summon the necessary collective energy and action required to pull it off. Subsequently, our morale and sense of collective connection seemed to diminish.*

*Accountability failures like these still make me cringe a little when I think about them. But they have afforded me the opportunity to think about what I have learned, and who I aspire to be.*

*I just read this great quote from Charles Duhigg: "The difference between who you are and who you want to be is what you do." And I do want to be someone who others experience as reliable, dependable, and trustworthy. So that means if I said I'll do something, I damn well better do it. (And it also means being very careful about what I say yes to!)*

*One of the reasons why I wanted to write this book with co-authors is because I have learned that it's easier for me to nail it when I have made clear commitments to other people and when we have a common goal that motivates us.*

## What Is Nailing It and Why Does It Matter?

If you had to get something done and could pick anyone you know to ensure that would happen, who would you choose? How would you describe this person? Do you like them? Do you trust them? What about them made you want to select them? Most likely, this person has proved to be good on their word because they do what they say they will do.

In essence, the practice of nailing it means *doing what you say you will do, at the same time that you deepen the relationships that are essential to getting it done.* It invites you to consider two questions: "How can I rely on and leverage my relationships to level up outcomes?" and "How can I use this task or project as a vehicle to build better relationships with others?" There is a dynamic flow here, and this practice allows for the deepening of engagement, psychological safety, and commitment, as well as actualizing your goals.

As we will see, it is not always possible to do these things in equal measure. That is OK. And, it is not always possible to get things done perfectly or completely the first time around. That is also OK. What matters is that you feel comfortable relying on relationships when completing tasks and you work on tasks with goodwill, effort, and determination so your relationships continue to grow and flourish. As long as the communication is open and authentic, and people share their intentions and capacity to complete the tasks, the process of getting things done can move forward, even if metrics and milestones have to be altered or shifted due to changing realities and shifting priorities.

Recall the dual outcomes of conscious accountability (Table 6-1). If we only focus on building relationships but do not deliver on what we had intended to do (the harmonizer), we may feel good, but the lack of productivity can hurt the team's reputation and lower morale. Likewise, if we get the work done at the expense of our relationships (the hard driver), then we may have a good short-term outcome but may negatively affect our ability to work together with others in the long run.

**Table 6-1.** Dual Outcomes of Conscious Accountability

| | | Task Performance | |
| --- | --- | --- | --- |
| | | Low | High |
| **Relationship Quality** | High | The Harmonizer | The Conscious Performer |
| | Low | The Neutralist | The Hard Driver |

This is why it is crucial, when we nail it, to both attend to our relationships and the outcomes that our collaborations produce. And this also gets to the heart of the importance of this practice: When we nail it with attention to results and relationships, we build sustainability in our leadership effectiveness. In other words, we lower the chances that people will become disengaged or burn out from either lack of appreciation or lack of performance.

## What Gets in the Way?

Getting things done can be a big challenge for people individually and collectively. Most people who set individual goals, such as New Year's resolutions, do not reach them. And two-thirds of well-formulated business strategies fail because of poor execution (Carucci 2017). In our executive education seminars, which have included hundreds of leaders and managers across various sectors, we routinely ask the question, "What are the most common barriers to nailing it?" Here are the five most-cited:

- **Problems with motivation.** This includes a lack of commitment, inadequate buy-in, or low sense of ownership in the endeavor, as well as procrastinating or not moving to action.

- **Problems with priorities.** When people prioritize inappropriately (or focus on the wrong things), when priorities change frequently, or when priorities compete or conflict with one another, it can be more challenging to get things done and fulfill commitments.
- **Insufficient resources.** If the resources needed to complete the job are not sufficiently present (such as knowledge, skills, time, money, or people), this increases the likelihood of problems in execution.
- **Unforeseen obstacles.** It is difficult to plan for everything that might come up, and unexpected disruptions, bottlenecks, mistakes, and other unwelcome surprises raise the risk of failure to deliver.
- **Problems with communication.** This category includes a number of common challenges like misinterpretations, misunderstandings, breakdowns, and coordination failures.

The conscious accountability approach to nailing it emphasizes the idea of not just taking action but taking *informed* action. That is, actions that are informed by awareness of ourselves, others, and the interdependencies between us and others. This additional bit of intelligence can serve as a key advantage to surmount the aforementioned list of barriers to nailing it. Heightened awareness of ourselves and others helps us have greater knowledge about different people's motives, priorities, styles, and challenges, which can lead to a more proactive approach to communicating about how to integrate and account for these differences. Plus, this approach underscores the idea that no one has to go it alone. Instead, we can rely on and be connected with others as we get things done. In the rest of this chapter, you will find ideas to help you navigate the barriers and realize success in getting things done.

## Key Mindsets: Grit and Grace

We recommend holding two distinct frames of mind when you are in the practice of nailing it: grit and grace. *Grit* is the spirit of fierce tenacity and persistence, even in the face of the slings and arrows of all sorts of challenges that arise during the process. It is a kind of resilience that allows you to get up after being knocked down by setbacks and disappointments. When the chips are down, when you are exhausted, or when it feels overwhelming or impossible, grit is the thing that allows you and your teammates to dig deep within yourselves to find the strength you need to keep moving forward.

*Grace* is the spirit of responding to what happens with openness, equanimity, and acceptance. This entails having compassion for yourself when you are not at your best and having compassion for others as well. When things go wrong, most of us can experience frustration, anger, and demoralization. Grace allows us to not stay stuck in these feelings, enabling us to hold a wiser, more soothing presence for ourselves and others.

For example, Daryn and David were facilitating a leadership retreat for the Yale Greenberg World Fellows program, an annual fellowship that brings together 16 highly accomplished, mid-career professionals from around the globe to study at Yale for a semester. The day before the retreat was supposed to kick off, Daryn's husband had to leave town unexpectedly, so she had to stay home to take care of her family. This required David to pivot and handle a number of logistical and programmatic details that Daryn was not able to cover. He took on the extra work and responsibility with resilience, while giving himself the latitude to not have everything be perfect. The retreat went on as planned and was a successful experience for all. While Daryn's reasons for missing the retreat were entirely understandable, she felt bad that she'd left David with an additional burden. But after many years as colleagues, Daryn trusted that David would step up and handle their shared work with competence and professionalism.

## 3 Strategies for Nailing It

Dialing up awareness of yourself and others, prioritizing and planning, and maintaining effective communication and teamwork will put you in a strong position to succeed and readily navigate the bumps in the road. There are also a number of strategies you can use to ensure that communication and positive regard remain central as you collaborate with others effectively. It is this focus on both the task and the people that we believe creates the secret sauce to taking your work to the next level.

Outlined in the next sections are three strategies you can use to organize yourself and others throughout the process of conscious accountability:

- Activate knowledge about self and others.
- Organize for task completion.
- Stay together.

## Activate Knowledge of Self and Others

Conscious accountability asks us to get work done while we make use of our knowledge of ourselves and others, and to also remain receptive to being guided by the knowledge that others have about us. With this awareness, we can tailor the process of getting things done in a way that maximizes the likelihood of success and allows the people involved to come away having experienced some type of interpersonal growth. This might include feeling fulfilled or more connected, or it might be growth in understanding others. While there are potentially many different facets to be aware of with regard to ourselves and others, three keys for nailing it in a consciously accountable way include knowledge of motivation, capacity, and stylistic preferences.

### Motivation

Motivation is the sometimes-elusive drive we draw on to inspire us to action and fill us with sustaining energy. The wise and well-known motivational author and speaker Zig Ziglar is credited with asserting that "people often say that motivation doesn't last. Well, neither does bathing—that's why we recommend it daily." We understand that motivation can wax and wane due to any number of circumstances and that it needs to be refreshed repeatedly. Motivation, like the ability to make good on stated intentions, requires us to harbor a realistic perspective of what we truly want to do in a given situation. It also requires us to take a good, hard look at our motives for doing a given task.

There are two primary types of motivation: intrinsic and extrinsic (Deci and Ryan 1985). When our motivation on a task is intrinsic, the reward—in the form of joy, happiness, productivity, and sense of completion—is born from the actual engagement in the task itself. When the motivation is extrinsic, the reward is external to us and is usually a secondary derivative of the task, such as the money we will earn, the praise we might receive, or the criticism we hope to avoid. While both intrinsic and extrinsic motivation are drivers for action, we may feel differently depending on which one is activated for us around a given task. Although extrinsic motivation can be helpful (such as for tasks that are not inherently rewarding), intrinsic motivation is more powerful (Cho and Perry 2011). For example, a number of studies suggest that intrinsic motivation is more effective for improving long-term performance and retaining employees (Kuvaas et al. 2017; Dysvik and Kuvaas 2008).

To assess the degree and type of motivation you are experiencing, slow down and think about the details of a task you need to accomplish. Without judgment, see how you feel, on a visceral level, when you imagine doing the various steps of the task:

- If, when you think about the task, you feel energized and excited, and the ideas start flowing, then it is likely that you have intrinsic motivation to do it. The nature of the task itself is somehow pleasant and makes you want to get involved. This intrinsic motivation will serve you well as you engage in the task.

- If, when you think about the task, you are less interested in the details and instead focus on the external rewards (money, improved status, or relief about not being criticized or scolded), it is likely that you have extrinsic motivation for it. These reinforcers will help you to stay focused when you engage in the task, but they may not be sufficient in helping you to complete a task that you might otherwise find boring, tedious, or unenjoyable.

- If, however, you feel sluggish, resistant, or find yourself making up excuses when you think about doing the task, then it is likely that you are not intrinsically motivated to do it. If the thought of external reinforcements (money, recognition, or avoiding some kind of anticipated punishment) do not overcome this internal ambivalence, then you probably are not extrinsically motivated either. In this case, it makes sense to rethink the wisdom of engaging with the task at all, although you may not have that choice, in which case you'll have to find a way to push past your own inertia.

So what happens if you or someone else you are relying on is showing signs of insufficient motivation? Here are some ideas for how to boost motivation borrowed from the science of motivational interviewing—a person-centered approach to eliciting behavior change by helping people explore and resolve their ambivalence about taking action. This process unfolds by asking yourself (or someone else) a series of questions (Pantalon 2011):

- On a scale of 1–10, how motivated are you to bring about a given change or do a given task?
- Considering the number you just chose, why didn't you choose a lower number? (In answering this question, people will identify the reasons why a given change or activity makes sense for them, which will help them feel more motivated).
- Imagine you changed or did the task. What would the positive outcomes be?
- Why are those outcomes important to you?

These questions begin to help you connect to the more intrinsic aspects of your motivation to do something because they support your basic need for autonomy—to have the sense that you are making your own choices about things. Appealing to other human needs, like mastery and relatedness, helps us derive greater meaning and motivation:

- How might this task help me become more competent or masterful?
- How might this task support others or relationships that matter to me?

When we align with our own needs, interests, strengths, or values, we are more likely to find intrinsic motivation and reward in the work, which in turn makes it more likely for us to follow through to the end of a task.

Reminding ourselves of these intrinsic motivators over the arc of the overall process to get things done helps refresh our motivation and keeps us engaged in a more natural state of flow.

## Capacity

Each of us must work within the constraints of the 24 hours we get in a day. Some of those hours must be filled with activities that keep us alive and healthy (eating, drinking, sleeping, health maintenance, and personal hygiene, for example) and that involve caring for others. The time needed for these activities will ebb and flow throughout our lives and will affect the types of work that we take on in different stages of our careers. Sometimes we may need more time to focus on younger children, ailing parents, or ourselves during moments of illness or stress. Within the workday itself, we also have limits to our time and capacity, which are affected by dynamic forces. Meetings come up out of nowhere, long-term projects get put on the back burner when more immediate and pressing demands arise, and our levels of energy will naturally fluctuate.

When you think about taking on a given activity, it is important to ask yourself whether you have the bandwidth for it, given the other demands on your schedule and in your life. This can be difficult for people to do accurately because of the planning fallacy. The planning fallacy is an optimism bias that people have when predicting how much time will be needed to complete a future task, in which they underestimate the time needed (Kahneman and Tversky 1977). Here are some questions you can ask yourself to help offset this bias:

- How long, realistically, will this task take? If you are unsure (or if you notoriously under- or overestimate the amount of time required to get something done), you can ask others for input.
- Is this a novel type of activity that will require you to devote additional time and energy to learning new skills or working with a new team? Or is this something you have done many times before or with known

team members, such that your relative expertise and knowledge about others' work habits will expedite your efforts?

- What is the deadline for this task? Do you have the actual number of hours required before the deadline to get this job done? How much wiggle room is there, in case stumbling blocks emerge?

- How much energy will this task take? Do you have other things going on in your life that may increase or decrease the amount of expendable energy that you have for this task?

- And if your capacity is stretched, but you say "yes" to the task, what will you need to say "no" to doing to create the needed space to complete the task successfully?

For many people, it is not easy to say "no" or "not right now." They may worry about disappointing others or appearing selfish, unhelpful, or not a team player. So it is useful to think of this kind of focused time appraisal as an act of caretaking for yourself and others, because it facilitates a more successful output while minimizing feeling unduly burdened or burned out. The more realistic and aware you are about your own or others' capacity, the more likely you will be able to do what you say you will do, and avoid the disappointments that come with minimal follow through or task incompletion.

## Stylistic Preferences

Which hand do you prefer writing with? If you are not ambidextrous, observe that you can write with your nondominant hand, but the process—at least initially—is likely to be slower, less comfortable, and the results are probably not as good. Stylistic preferences capture our preferred way of thinking, decision making, communicating, working through tasks, and dealing with stress, to name a few. When we are able to work in alignment with our preferences, it feels easier, requires less effort, demands less energy, and the results are often superior. It is a way of playing to your strengths.

For example, David prefers big-picture thinking and brainstorming ideas and possibilities. He is an extrovert who likes feeling connected to others while getting work done. And he also tends to be prompted by pressure and needs hard deadlines to get things done. Daryn loves to engage with others in strategic, systems-level program development and related projects. Introverted and self-directed, Daryn then prefers to tackle her work independently before seeking feedback from close collaborators and colleagues. She has found that she works best on projects marked by defined expectations and set deadlines. As an ambivert, Marianne thrives with a combination of solo and group work. Highly people-oriented, Marianne prefers a caring, connected environment and becomes inspired and motivated when work is transparent and collaborative. She enjoys sharing ideas and seeks different perspectives. Setting clear goals is important to her; however, she then likes to hold them lightly to allow for a flexible, process-based approach.

Accurately appraising your relative strengths and your work-style preferences and those of your team members can allow for the delegation of tasks in line with these strengths, which can increase efficiency and output overall. Here are a few ways to evaluate these relative strengths:

- Ask team members what they most enjoy doing and why. Take this into consideration when assigning tasks.
- Use empirically validated tools to assess team members' strengths and preferences for things like problem solving and decision making.
- Find out which members of the team are eager to learn new skills. Delegate in accordance with existing skills and potential learning opportunities. And then commit to supporting those to whom you delegate by providing continued instruction, guidance, and opportunities for ongoing skills development (Nawaz 2016).

For example, one of our clients is a consulting firm that has used assessments of strengths and thinking style preferences in the onboarding process, so management can have a better sense of what kind of working conditions will allow each employee to thrive. When the employee is placed on a team, team members share their preferences with one another. This allows everyone to know who among them are the big-picture thinkers, analysts, relationship tenders, and implementers. From there, they can assign tasks accordingly in a way that leverages the unique preferences of each person. They also know who else on the team they can call on if they need to deal with issues that require someone else's areas of strength. And finally, in learning more about one another's preferences, team members develop a better understanding about how best to communicate and work together.

Kate, the CEO, described the impact of this practice for the team's effectiveness: "We learned that, as a firm, we had a lot of strengths in certain areas. We had a lot of right-brain thinkers—ideators, learners, and strategists. But for certain projects and teams, it was important that we had a balance of strengths and styles in the room, so we made sure to get some left-brain thinkers in there too, who were more detail- and execution-focused."

## Organize for Task Completion

Getting things done, both in results and the process of execution, does not just happen by itself. It requires a certain amount of forethought. In the workplace, when we know in detail what we are getting into—what the final deliverable is, by what date, and how we are going to team with others—we can feel relatively confident that we will get the job done. At the same time, we may find that unexpected obstacles come up as we embark on a given task, requiring a reevaluation of priorities and plans midstream. This is OK and to be expected. From a conscious accountability perspective, the trick is handling the process of reprioritization in such a way that the work can still be completed and that our essential relationships are nurtured and supported. Here we will describe three things people can do to organize for task completion: prioritize, make a plan, and take action.

### Prioritize

In getting ready to execute, one of the biggest questions to answer is how to prioritize your activities wisely, so that you make the best use of your time and energy. With conscious accountability, we also consider the question of how to prioritize not only to be most efficient but also to improve interpersonal effectiveness.

In her leadership development work with clinician-scientists in university settings, Daryn often partners with her coachees to address their concerns about how best to identify and then work in line with their priorities. Many of her clients have so many priorities—some of which seem to conflict with one another—that it can be difficult to know when to engage in which task. What are the best ways to manage dueling clinical and research responsibilities? How much time should they spend overseeing the workflow of lab members who are cooperating on a research project? How can they fulfill their intentions to support their trainees' development? And how can they find time to enjoy other parts of their life and navigate other responsibilities, such as caring for family members, while working a job that occasionally demands immediate responsiveness?

A first-line prioritization tool we offer our clients is the Eisenhower matrix. Later popularized in Stephen Covey's 1989 book, *The Seven Habits of Highly Effective People*, the Eisenhower matrix (yes, created by US president Dwight Eisenhower) invites users to sort tasks based on their urgency and importance. The following example of a busy physician-scientist highlights how using this urgency-importance framework can help professionals prioritize certain activities and responsibilities over others. This matrix, specified for this example, is shown in Figure 6-1.

Dr. Joanna Smith is an oncologist who maintains a busy clinical practice. She is also a research associate in her university's oncology department, where she oversees grants for several active clinical trials. On Tuesday morning, she arrives at her clinic ready to roll. In the 15 minutes before she is to see her first patient, she opens her email and remembers that she needs to email her son's teacher about setting up an additional parent-teacher conference to discuss his academic progress over the last few months. This is an important task but not urgent; Dr. Smith knows that if she sends the email by the end of the week, she and her son will be OK. The same is true for several other emails she needs to send to schedule some other appointments, which she decides she'll work on during her lunch break. As she continues to scan her inbox, Dr. Smith sees three emails from the chair of her department asking her to attend a number of upcoming departmental and university meetings. Responding to these timely emails is urgent, but it is not important for Dr. Smith to answer them personally. So, she delegates this to her assistant, asking him to look at her calendar and send emails responding to the various requests.

Dr. Smith closes her email and sees three patients in a row. She finishes up and leaves the clinic for her 30-minute lunch break. As she sits down in the hospital cafeteria and starts eating her sandwich, she listens to a new voicemail from a representative at a lab supply company, highlighting deals on lab equipment that members of her team might use in their research studies next year. Responding directly to this request is neither urgent nor important, so she deletes the voicemail, knowing that she can reach out to the company at any later point. As she takes the first bite of her apple, Dr. Smith suddenly gets a text from her lab manager, alerting her to a mishap in her research laboratory that requires her immediate attention. Very concerned about this urgent matter, Dr. Smith packs up her lunch and runs over to her lab. In transit, she calls her colleague to reschedule a clinical case consultation meeting they were supposed to have in 30 minutes.

Now, let's use the Eisenhower Matrix to plot each of Dr. Smith's priorities (Figure 6-1).

**Figure 6-1.** Dr. Smith's Use of the Eisenhower Matrix

|  | Urgent | Not Urgent |
|---|---|---|
| **Important** | Do it now!<br>Deal with lab mishap | Decide when to do it<br>Call school to schedule conference |
| **Not Important** | Delegate<br>Respond to chair's email | Delete<br>Calling the lab equipment company |

As Figure 6-1 shows, the matrix can help you figure out what to do *now*, what to schedule time for in your calendar, what to delegate, and what to drop entirely. This will help you stay focused on the things that matter most, and to re-evaluate priorities as things shift.

Managing time and prioritizing tasks in the team environment can be more nuanced. When teamwork and interdependence are required for getting things done, it is necessary to have consistent open communication around each team member's needs, capacity, and time constraints. It is also necessary to make sure that everyone's estimates about workload and expectations are clearly aligned.

In her book *Dare to Lead*, Brené Brown (2018) highlights one approach to team-based time management: the "turn and learn" technique, in which everyone on her team is invited to write down how much time they think each project needs and how to prioritize competing demands. Shielded from the potential pressure of agreeing with the opinions of the team leader or the majority, team members each make their own appraisal and then reveal their time estimates to one another. They can then discuss everyone's perspectives on the task at hand and how to best align with one another.

Teams can also use the Eisenhower Matrix to establish and reshuffle collective priorities. In highly collaborative work, vibrant and dynamic discussion is needed, especially when changes arise (such as in available resources) that affect expectations, goals, and corresponding priorities. Inherent in prioritization of tasks on teams is an understanding that the team, as a whole, needs to get the task done and that the team is adaptable, with different individuals capable of stepping in and out of tasks as needed so that everyone performs within their capacity at a given time. Prioritizing on teams requires enhanced interpersonal flexibility, compassion, and understanding.

When David was coaching Tyler, a director in a healthcare system, they developed an innovative approach to prioritization and time management. Rather than organize his to-do list by tasks, they organized it by the people Tyler was supporting or working with in some way. This helped keep Tyler's awareness on the people first—what they were responsible for accomplishing and how he could help develop their leadership capacity—which, over time, allowed him to maintain a higher strategic focus.

Once your priorities have been reasonably well established, the next critical step in organizing for task completion is planning. The advantage of prioritizing first is that it allows the plan to be aligned with those top priorities.

## Make a Plan

Think of a time when you were in a meeting where the agenda was completely overstacked. Perhaps the pressure to get through everything meant that you took fewer or no breaks. And the urgency to plow through it all meant that there was insufficient time for deeper dialogue and exchange of perspectives. How did you feel at the end of that meeting? Exhausted? Disappointed? Frustrated? Unheard? In this example, not only are human needs at risk for neglect, but the ideas that come out of such a process may not be fully thought through. The way to avoid snags like these is to conduct more conscious planning.

A solid plan reinforces and promotes the clarity we discussed in chapter 4 by providing the answers to a number of key questions:

- Where are we going? (Or what is our goal?)
- How will we get there? (What specific actions or steps do we need to take)?
- Who needs to do each of those actions? By when?
- What supports and resources do we need to get the job done?
- How will we know how we are doing and when we have arrived? (What are the metrics for measuring progress and success?)
- What could come up that could take us off course, and how will we deal with those things?

From a conscious accountability perspective, planning means making use of a heightened sense of awareness of yourself and others throughout the planning process. Sometimes, we can be so focused on the results that we neglect human needs (our own and other people's) in the process. To avoid this, ask yourself a few additional questions:

- What is important to me in this plan?
- What will it take to get the job done and make me and my teammates feel great about how our work together went?

- What will help me build stronger relationships with the other people I will engage with in executing this plan?

Then, it is important to bring other people into your planning process. Their perspectives can help you see what you do not see, as well as consider angles and needs that you had not imagined. Consider reviewing the plan with others and asking some questions of team members or other people involved in the work (or even a family member, friend, or partner):

- What do you want me to keep in mind as we do this together?
- How realistic do these timeframes seem to you?
- How else might we measure progress?
- How well do the metrics capture our key actions and desired outcomes?
- What do you need in this process to do your part (either in support or resources)?
- What else could go wrong? How might we deal with that?
- What else should be on my to-do list that I have not considered?

You can also plan for additional aspects of the process (which we will explore more thoroughly in chapters 7 and 8):

- How do we want to communicate and keep each other apprised of progress?
- What happens if we see someone going off track or underperforming? How do we want to handle that?
- How will we give and receive feedback along the way?

By engaging others in this additional level of planning, you can better anticipate their needs, have greater buy-in to the plan, and also get out in front of any potentially sensitive conversations that may emerge along the way.

In a class David teaches that emphasizes teamwork, each team is required to put together a project plan that allows the team to look at the outcomes they seek and the actions needed to support those outcomes. The actions are both task focused (for example, action steps needed to be taken each week) and process focused (such as behavioral norms that the team strives to uphold). Having a plan at the outset not only creates a clear road map for the team, but it also serves as a great accountability tool. Toward the end of the project, teams go back to the plan and reflect on the extent to which they upheld it, in action and interpersonally, both as individuals and collectively.

## Take Action

All of the best prioritizing and planning in the world will remain incomplete in the absence of action. Actually doing the things that make progress happen is essential to the practice of nailing it. People who are really skilled in taking action have a number of things in common. They do not get bogged down in the planning, such that they need not have every detail and contingency covered before they take action. So they plan just enough, but they do not overplan. They are also able to jump on opportunities that come up unexpectedly. This means they can make relatively quick decisions that allow them to respond to their environment and not get stuck in paralysis by analysis (Barnfield and Lombardo 2014). Action-oriented people can also summon a great deal of focus when completing tasks. They bring a single-minded, eyes-on-the-prize approach to pursuing their goals.

When Marianne began working with Peter, a senior manager at a tech startup, he had a lot of trouble taking action. This came back as a major finding in his 360-degree feedback report, in which a number of his peers and direct reports acknowledged feeling frustrated with Peter because they were often waiting on him to make decisions. He was starting to get a reputation for being a bottleneck. As Marianne and Peter unpacked the reasons for this pattern, they observed a number of worries or anxieties underneath.

In Peter, this often showed up as a fear of making the wrong move. He was preoccupied with the risks of taking certain actions, often worrying that the results of his actions would be less than ideal. For example, he stalled when trying to decide whether to purchase a more expensive software package that was better than what they were currently using, but only solved 75 percent of their current problems. If he could not arrive at what seemed like a completely winning solution, he would either spend more time puzzling about it or shift his focus to other tasks. Further, he felt like he had to make decisions alone, because he thought asking for help was a weakness.

When he was able to bring more awareness to these fears and to challenge them, he began to take more decisive action and relied more on others to help him do so. He had to remind himself that "the perfect solution is the enemy of the good-enough solution." And if he still had doubts, he could ask others for help in giving their opinions and feedback about whether action was warranted. This further reduced his anxiety and built his confidence.

The need for clarity of expectations in a project—through a written plan, concrete deadlines, and metrics for gauging progress—is important for self-accountability and when working with others on a shared task. Table 6-2 provides a list of guidelines to follow when working solo or in a group or team.

**Table 6-2.** Guidelines for Nailing It: Working Individually and in Teams

| For Yourself | In Your Work With Others |
|---|---|
| Create a written plan of action, including overall goals, desired outcomes, metrics, and realistic targets. | Re-address expectations and goals to ensure a shared understanding and clarity regarding the scope of the project and each person's role. |
| Set deadlines, a game plan, or schedule various steps in the actualization process. | Assign actions and tasks in line with people's stated affinities and strengths. |
| Be realistic about the amount of time a given task will take. Amend the schedule as needed, if you learn that something is taking longer than you expected. | Note what each person needs to do their part as well as boundaries to their efforts (when applicable). Set realistic timeframes for interdependent efforts. |
| Ensure that the resources you need to complete the task are available. | Continually ensure that you and others have the resources you need to get the job done. |
| Keep a record of the steps you accomplished. | Use a shared dashboard or joint project management tools. |
| Be flexible and kind to yourself as irregularities of the process unfold. Use an accountability partner to share your plans, and check in throughout the process. | Communicate frequently and honestly to ensure that everyone understands the task, emerging timelines, and changing details of project. Set and host regular check-in meetings. |

## Stay Together

Peter's case leads us to another important strategy for nailing it the conscious accountability way: staying together with others through the process. This third strategy underscores the importance of maintaining awareness of and connection with other people as you are prioritizing, planning, and taking action. This might take some extra time and effort, but the improvements to the outcomes in results and relationships will be worth it. Three ways to ensure that you stay together are to overcommunicate, ask for and offer help, and use accountability partners.

### Overcommunicate

Overcommunicating means keeping people in the loop on things as they are happening, and being fully transparent about your thoughts, needs, and motives. Daryn and David worked with a religious organization that was responsible for orchestrating large events around certain holidays. They noticed that in the days before the events, sometimes the group would stumble on execution because needs would come up suddenly, but others who could potentially help were unaware of those needs. The team came to embrace the idea of overcommunication as a way to ensure that everyone was aware of the latest plan and changes afoot. Now, during more hectic periods, team members are extra-inclusive of those in their email correspondence and text messaging groups, which allows others to step in and support one another as needed.

### Ask for and Offer Help

Peter's case shows the value of asking for help when you need it. That help could take the form of needed resources, ideas that help you get unstuck, moral support, or practical, hands-on support to get something done. Asking for help can also be an act of vulnerability, which—if responded to well—can contribute to greater psychological safety and trust among team members. Offering help is another way to stay together through working to execute on a project successfully.

On most mornings, media executive Tanya, who is a proponent of management by walking around, visits all her team members and asks them if they need any help from her. She does this especially during crunch times, for example when they are getting an issue ready to go to print.

## Use Accountability Partners

Sometimes it is very helpful to have at least one person you can rely on to provide support and accountability. Having an appointment with someone else to talk about your goal dramatically increases the likelihood that you will reach your goal. Accountability partners can help not just with task completion but also with relationship and interpersonal behaviors. When David was working with Rene, the CFO and a member of the executive team at a successful manufacturing firm, Rene received feedback that he sometimes came across as unclear or confusing when presenting information. As he worked to correct this communication issue, he enlisted two other team members that he felt the closest to and trusted to help him see opportunities for improving his clarity. Over time, this kind of accountability helped Rene become more effective and strengthened his ties with the colleagues who supported him.

# Leadership by Example: Sonja, Laying the Groundwork for Her Team to Get Things Done

Gaylord HealthCare is a specialty healthcare system that provides inpatient and outpatient rehabilitative services for a range of neurological and orthopedic ailments and injuries. Since January 2019, Sonja LaBarbera has served as the first woman CEO and president in the history of this organization, which was founded in 1902.

When she assumed this post, Sonja had been working successfully at Gaylord for several years in a number of different roles. As a team member and team leader, she was known for her tremendous ability to unleash fellow employees' capacity, helping them complete assignments big and small in a way that made them feel seen in their successes and supported in their struggles. With her strong interpersonal warmth, optimism, and can-do attitude, Sonja is a model case study in creating the culture to nail it.

In working with others, Sonja knows the importance of activating her awareness of what motivates them and what their individual stylistic preferences are for getting things done. She fosters engagement with the task at hand by giving others whatever flexibility they need.

"Everybody has their own way of accomplishing something. Some people follow a straight path, some veer off, and some take a circuitous route," Sonja says. "It's short sighted to hold everyone to the same narrow path or same prescription for action." In fact, having people approach something in different ways gives her team a better holistic picture of the problem or goal to begin with.

Sonja taps into her employees' motivation by listening and asking for their opinions, having them be involved in decision making, and recognizing their efforts. "I've always found that the more you can build in flexibility, creativity, and individualism, the better the results, because it all comes back to people, not a set process," she shares. And Sonja engages them by setting the framework for helping people understand why they are doing a task, what the benefit of doing it is, and what everyone's role is. "People want to be engaged, understand the task, and feel like they are doing something for a purpose, not just because someone told them to do it," she adds.

Sonja understands accountability does not just mean that someone meets the goal and is all done. It is an ongoing process in which people stay together and communicate where they are in their progress toward the goal. "Accountability is doing what you say you'll do. It's being someone who can be counted on," she says. "But it is really an iterative process involving open discussion and then agreement about what will be done by everyone. You can't effectively hold someone accountable without having built rapport and a relationship with them first. It's really more about relationships than checking a box."

Sonja has nurtured a psychologically safe environment where people are willing to ask for help and can come to her when something stands in the way, so she can help them eliminate barriers or challenges, or help redefine when goals need to change. This starts with her ability to react with grace when others do not meet expectations.

"My first response is to meet with them and have a discussion regarding the barriers that got in the way," she says. Then she will ask, "What prevented this person from reaching the goal? Is it still a reasonable goal? How can I help them to reach this or a different goal?" After discussion, they then work to set a new path, together, that they agree is reasonable and doable.

And when people complete a given task, Sonja is quick to appreciate and celebrate it. "Don't take for granted that people will do a good job," she shares. "You should always take time to appreciate and celebrate their accomplishments. When you do, people will then continue to try harder for you."

## Exercise 1. Plot the Scenarios

Nailing it within the framework of conscious accountability means to deliver on results and relationships. When you are in the midst of doing the work, it is a good time to assess whether you are maintaining good task performance and relationship quality (Table 6-3).

**Table 6-3.** Dual Outcomes of Conscious Accountability

| | | Task Performance | |
| --- | --- | --- | --- |
| | | Low | High |
| Relationship Quality | High | The Harmonizer | The Conscious Performer |
| | Low | The Neutralist | The Hard Driver |

In the scenarios below, the people described are attempting to nail it. With this in mind, review each situation and indicate where you would plot the behavior of the person in terms of task performance and relationship quality as indicated in Table 6-3.

1. Gene arrives at the weekly team meeting having completed all of the items assigned to him. In fact, he got these done before the deadline and started pushing ahead on other work that's due next week.

However, he had not been checking the Slack channel and let several emails from his colleagues slide, so he missed updates that drastically changed the nature of his assignment.

2. Pat designed t-shirts for the team and had them delivered to each member with a note of encouragement. She hand wrote each note. This took more time than she anticipated, and therefore she did not complete the financial projections the team needed to make important decisions about the road map of their new product.

3. Nada attends a whiteboard session with her team to plan out their priorities for the next quarter. She listens to others as they share ideas and answers questions when asked. When it is time to prioritize tasks, Nada remarks that she is flexible and is fine with whatever the team decides.

4. Sunil checks his team's shared project-management tool every morning. He sees that his teammate, Alex, has not completed an assignment that he has been waiting on. Sunil emails Alex to check in, asking how it is going and if he has what he needs to complete the task.

**Answer Key:**

1. Gene is a hard driver. His completion of all items falls into the high category of task performance. However, his decision to not check in with his colleagues on Slack and to not attend closely to his emails falls into the low category for relationship quality, which adversely affected the relevance of his final product.

2. Pat is a harmonizer. Her personal attention to each team member falls into the high category for relationship quality. However, failing to complete the financial projections falls into the low category for task performance.

3. Nada is a neutralist. She attends, listens, and answers at the session, but does not initiate, ask questions, express curiosity, or invite others to share their thoughts. This type of participation falls in the low

relationship category. She also does not share any of her knowledge, experience, or expertise to help the team prioritize the tasks. This behavior falls in the low task performance category.

4. Sunil is a conscious performer. His daily tracking of work on the project management tool is a behavior that promotes high task performance, as well as his noticing of tasks that are not completed. Checking in with his teammate in a curious and supportive way is conduct that exemplifies high relationship quality.

## Exercise 2. Plot Yourself

Now think about a time when you had to work with a group of people. How did it go? How did you prefer to show up and behave? What was the typical way that you approached each task? How did you usually interact with others? After reflecting on this experience, where would you plot yourself in the table? How might you shift your mindset and behaviors to be more consciously accountable?

## Summary: The Nuances of Nailing It

Nailing it—*doing what you say you will do, at the same time that you deepen the relationships that are essential to getting it done*—is essential for conscious accountability. And while this seems straightforward, there are predictable obstacles that arise when trying to nail it, including problems with motivation, priorities, resources, unforeseen obstacles, and communication. Having the mindsets of grit (perseverance) and grace (compassion) will help you stay focused and manage the challenges that inevitably arise.

We have posed three strategies for nailing it:

- Activating knowledge of self and others (including motivation, capacity, and stylistic preferences)
- Organizing for task completion through prioritizing, planning, and taking action
- Remaining engaged with others by overcommunicating, asking for help, and using accountability partners

Next, in chapter 7, we will look at the practice of noticing as a way to turn our awareness into observations that can be used to check in with others, offer support, and invite course corrections wherever they might be needed.

# Noticing

> *Learn to be quiet enough to hear the genuine in*
> *yourself, so that you can hear it in others.*
> MARIAN WRIGHT EDELMAN

In 2007, Peter Boyd was hired as CEO of Virgin Mobile South Africa. Not too long after settling into the role, he received a number of reports from supervisors who were frustrated because workers were arriving late, sometimes multiple times a week. The behavior continued even after warnings were issued. Some supervisors advocated for taking a more punitive approach with these employees. However, Peter noticed that no one seemed to have a clear understanding of an important question: *Why were these employees frequently arriving late?*

So he began asking them directly about their experiences. The initial responses were a bit vague—"the commute is a bit tricky" or "well, it's hard to explain." Then, one employee invited Peter to come out and try the commute sometime. Much to everyone's surprise, Peter agreed to join them on a Friday evening commute home.

The public transportation system in that part of South Africa was not well developed, so employees had to rely on minibuses. Most people had to take a minimum of two buses to get home. Peter quickly came to understand that the commute was long, unpredictable, and stressful. At bus depots, it was not always clear where buses were going or what the fares were. People formed lines for different destinations, but many drivers would only stop at the longer lines to quickly fill their buses. It was not uncommon to wait for unknown amounts of time.

When Peter brought this experience back to the team, it changed everyone's thinking. What looked like a group of disengaged, underperforming employees was just the opposite: These workers were committed to getting to work despite facing numerous logistical challenges.

In so many cases in life, we behave more like the supervisors from this example than the CEO. When we observe something, we immediately judge what we see as good or bad, right or wrong, and then quickly jump to our own conclusions and actions. But Peter's approach reveals a different path: slowing down, becoming curious, and displaying willingness to learn more about someone else's perspective as you work together toward a common goal.

Once you have a plan for how you are going to nail your goals, it is helpful to develop a practice that allows you to gauge how that plan is turning out. The main purpose of noticing is to maintain momentum and keep the work going while addressing challenges or relationship dynamics that emerge, so the outcomes for both work and relationships are enhanced. Prioritizing time to observe the process of your efforts toward nailing it allows space for intentional reflection and learning, which are needed to make course corrections and propel progress. This is a continuous, fluid, dynamic process that involves checking in with yourself and others.

In this chapter, you will learn how to intentionally and comprehensively reflect on the process of nailing it through the practice of noticing. This will include not only noticing what is observable but also noticing internal processes within yourself with the intention of bringing unconscious influences to the surface. This will help you keep top of mind the goal of conscious accountability, which is to improve both performance and relationships. We will define what we mean by noticing, discuss why it is particularly important to conscious accountability, delineate typical barriers to noticing, and, finally, offer a framework for effective noticing. Let's start with diving into what we actually mean by *noticing*.

## What Do We Mean By Noticing?

So, what exactly are we noticing? Given that conscious accountability considers relationships and task outcomes of equal importance, we are noticing not just behaviors, but feelings and thoughts at a variety of different levels. In this way, we are striving to improve our awareness of influences and connections. In Figure 7-1 you can see the various levels or places we can direct our curiosity and attention when we notice.

**Figure 7-1.** Levels of Noticing

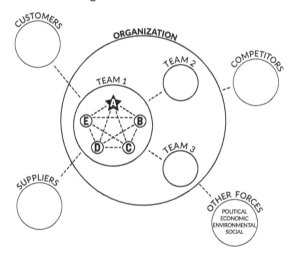

They include what's happening within yourself (Person A), what's happening for individuals (Persons B, C, D, E), what's occurring within individual relationships (dashed lines between people), and what's happening with the team or group as a whole (the circle that surrounds persons A–E). Beyond that, there is further room to consider other stakeholders and systems that the team is connected to, such as other teams, external stakeholders (like customers, suppliers, and competitors), the organization as a whole, and various influences outside the organization that affect it (for example, political, economic, social, and environmental forces). If considering all of these levels is overwhelming, start with the primary group or team and the individuals that comprise it.

As we proposed in chapter 2, becoming more conscious of influences affecting us on different levels (that is, individual, interpersonal, team, and so forth) improves our interpersonal effectiveness and task performance. The practice of noticing in this continuously consciousness-raising fashion will require us to use some strategic skills.

Noticing involves the act of seeing, hearing, becoming aware, and paying attention. However—and this is crucial—it doesn't include evaluating those observations. This is why we chose the word *noticing* for this important practice. By *noticing*, we mean observing without judgment. This process is closely related to the concept of *mindfulness*, which emphasizes present-moment awareness of experiences (such as, thoughts, feelings, bodily sensations, and surrounding environment) with acceptance and nonjudgment.

We emphasize observing *without judgment* for three important reasons:

- It allows you to gather a fuller range of data than if you were just seeking to evaluate, which essentially cuts short the data collection to either confirm your preconceptions or gather just enough information to communicate your perspective.
- Noticing without judgment also helps you separate the facts from your interpretation of those facts. Therefore, you may see "what is" more clearly, resulting in better data quality. It also allows you to remain open to others without being clouded by your judgments, reactions, assumptions, and biases.
- When people feel judged or evaluated, they are more likely to feel anxious or threatened, which engenders defensiveness and closing down to receiving new information. By contrast, a nonjudgmental approach allows for a more productive conversation as the observations are shared.

Evaluation of the outcomes and impact is an important piece of conscious accountability as well, which we will address in the next chapter on exchanging feedback. However, here we want to emphasize the importance of continuous, nonjudgmental observation for creating a fuller practice of conscious accountability.

## Why Does Noticing Matter?

Noticing is an essential practice for three specific reasons:

- It increases awareness and intentionality.
- It deepens relationships.
- It catalyzes growth, change, and therefore improvements in behavior and outcomes.

Let's address each in turn.

### Increasing Awareness and Intentionality

The practice of conscious accountability regards consciousness as a network of connections. Increased awareness is how connections are made. When we notice without judgment, we allow sufficient space to pause and reflect. This can result in increased awareness about how we think about, feel about, and typically might behave in a given situation. With this self-awareness, we can then inquire about our intention—what do we want to happen, and how do we need to proceed to realize that intention? Perhaps we may want to course correct, or maybe our current course of action was affirmed. Either way, noticing is what allows us to grow our awareness around our current process of nailing it.

Here is an example: Daryn and David were coaching a team and had asked them to complete a brief survey before the next session. David issued reminders to the team about the deadline, but less than half of the team completed the survey. As they prepared for their next coaching meeting with the team, David observed that he was feeling frustrated, and both Daryn and David noticed that they were beginning to feel skeptical about the team's capacity for progress. Just before the meeting, they learned that a crisis situation had occurred and demanded many long days and extra hours from most of the team. Given that Daryn and David's intention was to boost the team's commitment and ownership of the change process, they decided to share their concerns about the team's progress, but in a way that did not come across as critical or punitive. Rather, they normalized how difficult moments of crisis can be and then encouraged the team to look at what happened with curiosity and interest toward the questions of how to get things done even when unexpected things happen. And they helped the team consider how they could take ownership of their path forward, even when obstacles arise.

## Deepening Relationships

Noticing also helps us forge stronger and deeper relationships with others. To notice in the practice of conscious accountability is to see oneself and others with curiosity and compassion. It means to bear witness without judgment. This act, in and of itself, brings individuals closer. It is key to satisfying the universal human need of relatedness described in self-determination theory. If you are interested in creating more meaningful relationships, a simple yet powerful tool to use is noticing.

Tara supervises the customer service team at a shipping and logistics firm. Over the course of a couple days, she saw that Lisa, one of her representatives, was working an additional 30-60 minutes after the time her shift ended. Tara approached Lisa and said, "Hey, I've seen that you have been working late every evening over the past few days. Is there some way I can support you in getting out of here sooner? I really appreciate your conscientiousness and effort, but I also want to help you have more time for your life outside work if that is something you would like." Lisa was able to share what was slowing her down and receive some suggestions that helped her work more efficiently. Moreover, she experienced Tara's observation as supportive and ended up feeling like Tara had her back.

## Catalyzing Growth and Change

Noticing is also an effective way to catalyze growth and change. It is difficult to change or improve without awareness. There is an extensive body of research showing that self-monitoring or keeping track of a behavior will result in desired improvement in that behavior, because it promotes greater awareness and increased accountability (Bandura 1998).

For instance, when we work with people who are trying to get better at managing their emotions, we often ask them to start by recording their emotions periodically throughout the day in a notebook or a mood tracker app. We might invite them to set alarms to remind them to do so, or the app might prompt them to stop and notice their current mood. The act of pausing and tuning into feelings, over time, builds stronger awareness that allows people to know what they are feeling and make choices about how to respond that takes their emotions into account. Using this method, small business owner Brian realized that because he was usually in a more negative mood when reviewing error reports, it was not the best time for him to pick up customer calls.

## What Gets in the Way of Noticing?

Jordan, an engineering manager of a tech company, struggles with accountability. For one thing, he is someone who focuses on action and problem solving, while paying less attention to his own internal thoughts and feelings. Jordan is usually so busy with his own assignments that he does not make the time to check in with others on his team. He has said that he generally assumes that if people are having problems, they will come to him about them. Moreover, he doesn't want to be "that person." He explained that his company has a relaxed, friendly, supportive culture, and he was concerned that if he followed up and checked in on progress with his team, he might come across as negative, pestering, unfriendly, and not trusting them—in essence, counter to the culture of his company.

Noticing can be challenging for many reasons, as Jordan can relate. It requires a pause in action, focused reflection, and communication of observations. Some people view it as taking valuable time away from doing, which they consider to be the holy grail of productivity. Therefore, noticing can be undervalued and underutilized. Even when there is buy-in regarding the value of noticing, additional obstacles exist that have the potential to negatively affect the action of noticing. Based on our own observations, as well as conversations with many executives, here are three common barriers to noticing:

- **Overload.** When we are really busy and feeling overloaded, it can be difficult to pause for anything, making it hard to notice what is really happening with us, let alone anyone else.

- **Assumptions.** On the one hand, it is natural to make assumptions. At times they are useful in helping us move through life with efficiency, ease, and stability. But at other times, they can work against us. Jordan noted that he assumes that people will come to him if they are having problems, which may or may not be the case. So sometimes our assumptions lead us to overlook our own or other people's needs, feelings, and perspectives.

- **Resistance or avoidance.** This phenomenon has different names in different schools of thought within psychology. It refers to ways people protect themselves from thoughts and feelings they find troublesome, threatening, or upsetting. When people resist noticing, they may not notice at all, notice only infrequently, or only make cursory observations. As Jordan expressed, nobody wants to be "that person"—which may have been a disincentive for him to notice concerns or challenges. And some people, like Jordan, stay perpetually busy as a (typically unconscious) strategy to avoid reflecting what they really think or feel.

## Key Mindset: Compassionate Curiosity

To notice effectively, it is helpful to put yourself in the right frame of mind. The key mindset for noticing is compassionate curiosity. Being curious invokes questions rather than interpretations. It encourages wondering rather than concluding. You can be curious about yourself, as well as other people. This is conducive to expanding the scope of your thinking, bringing that which you may not be aware of into consciousness. And it allows for the gathering of deeper, broader, more nuanced information. Furthermore, being curious with compassion emphasizes the intention to be open and nonjudgmental, and to create psychological safety. It is not clinical, scientific, or detached curiosity. It is curiosity with care, and the sincere desire to make things better in some way. This type of approach is conducive to deepening relationships and elevating performance.

Compassionate curiosity also means keeping in mind that other people may have a different perspective than you and accepting that everyone's perspective—no matter how disparate it is from your own—is valid. Perspective is the result of many influences of both nature and nurture. We are each born with our own set of characteristics and preferences that shape how we see and move through the world. As we grow, learn, and have more lived experiences, these also affect our views on the world. Respecting and honoring each individual's perspective is key to noticing because it broadens your vision beyond yourself. By trying to understand a situation from someone else's perspective, from a place of compassionate curiosity, you expand the breadth of information that can inform your decisions.

## 3 Strategies for Noticing

Now that we have reviewed what we mean by noticing in the practice of conscious accountability, as well as its importance, common barriers, and helpful mindsets, let's put some action steps into this practice. We break down noticing into three strategies:

- Prepare.
- Become aware.
- Share.

### Prepare

Before you start taking note of how nailing it is going, it is imperative to prepare. Preparing includes four key actions: managing your mindset, checking your assumptions, knowing your motives, and owning your triggers.

## Manage Your Mindset

Our mindsets are affected by both internal and external factors. So even with the best intention to hold specific mindsets, such as compassionate curiosity, our ability to do so will vary based on the environment and our internal states. To address this, we suggest pausing and checking in with yourself internally. You can do this by simply asking, "What mood am I in?" "How is this mood impacting me?" Similarly, understanding how the environment impacts you is important. How might factors such as time of day, time of year, current setting, state of the world, or current workload influence your ability to be compassionately curious and take the perspective of others? If you are being affected by internal or environmental factors, take a moment to see if you can make adjustments that could mitigate their impact on your state of mind.

## Check Your Assumptions

Addressing your own assumptions is key to preparing to notice. Although we may think we are objective, no human being is. By attending to our thoughts and feelings with curious, nonevaluative compassion, we open up ourselves to consider how our personal perspectives are coming into play. A simple way to do this is by asking, "What are the facts about the situation?" Note only the behaviors—things said or done—and nothing else. Then ask, "What stories am I telling myself about the facts?" This will include your hunches, interpretations, assumptions, and biases. This process of highlighting and breaking down our assumptions can move us toward more accurate observations and an increased capacity to separate fact from story. Likewise, by noticing others' behaviors with compassionate curiosity, we open up ourselves to asking about others' experiences, which can result in greater clarity and understanding of the situation as well as deepen the bonds in the relationship.

## Know Your Motives

In any situation there are often various motives for our behavior. Some are obvious, others less so. We encourage you to try to understand what is guiding you in any situation. By improving your understanding of what is driving you, you can move forward with greater intentionality. For example, the three of us were engaged with a company that had experienced rapid and exponential growth. As a result, the executive leadership team had also grown to such a size that it was no longer effective. In working with the CEO, we wanted to understand what was driving the inclusion of so many people on the leadership team. It is typical to ask the question, "Why does this team exist?" to assist team leaders in clarifying the distinct purpose of a team. When Daryn flipped the question to ask the CEO what if this team didn't exist, the CEO had an "aha moment," where he understood that he was keeping people on the team to avoid hurt feelings, conflict, and ill will directed toward himself. Understanding his motives more fully allowed him to restructure the team according to its true purpose and led to a previously unconsidered solution.

### Own Your Triggers

The last, critical part of preparing to notice is to take responsibility for your triggers. Emotional triggers are anything—thoughts, memories, experiences, or events—that cause an emotional reaction, regardless of your current mood. Triggers are typically things that conjure up uncomfortable feelings related to past difficulties in a way that they affect your ability to stay focused in the present. Raising our own awareness of what triggers us can help us take responsibility for our reactions and help us begin to notice what's happening with less of our own internal chatter, noise, or reactivity getting in the way. We will discuss triggers further, as they relate to receiving feedback, in chapter 8.

## Become Aware

Once you have done the internal work to prepare to notice, you are ready to check in on the progress of the plan laid out during the practice of nailing it. Actively noticing requires looking at the process at different levels (individual, interpersonal, team, organization, and stakeholders) and across different dimensions (like thoughts, feelings, and behaviors). Use Figure 7-1 (presented earlier in this chapter) as a reminder of different places to notice. To increase your capacity to become aware, we recommend that you have a daily awareness routine in which you write down what you notice and decide what to do with that information.

## Have a Daily Practice

We suggest making time to briefly notice every day. Setting aside five to 10 minutes is all it takes. Sticking to a short daily routine will help make noticing a habit, which will become more natural over time.

A strong practice of noticing starts with the self. Use whatever method is comfortable for you to do this, such as going for a walk or just sitting quietly. Reflect with compassionate curiosity on what you are thinking and feeling, and your behavior with regard to your goal. Continue this process as you move the focus of attention from yourself outward to others and your relationships with them, as well as the group or team as a whole. Since we are not privy to anyone else's thoughts and feelings, see what behaviors you notice in others and then pay attention to your own thoughts and feelings about that behavior. Then you can consider how groups of people may be thinking, feeling, and behaving as a collective. Allow yourself to be curious about what may be influencing them and what they might need.

For example, Bob Motta, a clinical psychologist, Vietnam veteran, pilot, and beloved mentor of doctoral students, shared that his meditation practice helps him notice his own motives and be accountable. "I find that meditation is very helpful in terms of objectively viewing yourself," he explained. "Not putting a value on it, but just objectively viewing your behavior. That is part of accountability: Knowing yourself for others and knowing your own limitations."

With his dissertation students, Bob is often tempted, really tempted, to hold the person's hand and say, "OK, let's do this now, do this, and look over here." He's tempted to do that because he's nurturing. But by taking time to notice, he can stop and say to himself, "If you're being nurturing like that, you're doing something for yourself, you're making yourself feel good, you're making yourself feel like a nice caring papa." Then he asks himself, "Is this really beneficial to them?" And his thought is that what is beneficial for them is that they develop the ability to function independently.

This helps Bob sit on his desire to help his students directly, which allows them to grow more independent. "I really want them to succeed and do well, and that to me is accountability," he says. "I view that as my responsibility to the student—to get them to function to the best of their ability—and I'm not going to have that happen if I'm letting my desire to be paternalistic come out."

## Write Down What You Notice

While you are doing your daily practice, either during or afterward, take time to write down the things you are thinking, feeling, and noticing about yourself and others. Sometimes thoughts and ideas can pass through our heads fleetingly, and momentary awareness may not stick. The practice of journaling is a very good way to increase your capacity to notice and become more self-aware. It allows you to track your thoughts over time, which gives you an ongoing source of data to draw upon. You can then look at any patterns that occur in your noticing practice over time, which will give you information about whether you are persistently noticing the same things or varied things about yourself and others. In addition to greater self-awareness, the practice of journaling has been associated with other benefits, including reducing anxiety, depression, and stress, and improving mood and working memory (Ackerman 2021).

## Decide What to Do

After you have made some written notes on your observations, you can decide what, if anything, you would like to do with that awareness. You have a choice here about whether, what, and when to share with others. In this way, we build in a purposeful pause when we have an emotional reaction. Pausing to reflect on how we'd like to act leads to more intentional and better informed decisions about how and when to share what we have noticed.

If you are uncertain about what to share, imagine what it would be like for you to disclose what you notice with others. How do you picture that going? Perhaps you have some worries or concerns. Make note of those worries or concerns, or whatever thoughts you have about them. You may also wish to consider the risks of withholding your observations. Importantly, you are always the one who gets to decide what and how much of your observations you put out there.

## Share What You Notice

The last strategy is sharing the things you notice with others. For the purposes of creating conscious accountability, the value in noticing is not fully realized until it results in some kind of action. The purpose of sharing what you notice is to take some action to progress forward. That action could mean checking in, offering support, or promoting deeper dialogue about how you (and others) are doing and feeling as you work toward nailing it. This is different from sharing what you notice in the practice of exchanging feedback, which focuses on generating enhanced learning (as discussed in the next chapter). Consider these three things as you share what you notice:

- Establish times to share.
- Use the I-GROW model to structure conversations.
- Explore perspectives and options with open-ended questions.

### Establish Times to Share

For the people in your life with whom you are working toward a common goal, we suggest having noticing check-ins so you can stay aligned with and support each other along the way. In work contexts, this check-in could become part of an existing meeting. In personal relationships, it could become part of date night with your spouse or partner. Setting up expectations for these check-ins—why, when, and how you will do them— makes them easier to initiate because they eventually become standard practice for doing things well (rather than something you need to do only when there are problems to fix).

## Structure the Conversation

Having a reliable method for sharing what you've noticed will enhance your ease and effectiveness in doing so. While there could be many ways to approach this, we suggest using a common coaching conversation framework (based on Graham 2010), which you can remember using the acronym I-GROW, as shown in Table 7-2.

**Table 7-2.** Using the I-GROW Model for Noticing Conversations

| Intentions | Start by verbalizing your *intentions* for the conversation and seeking an *invitation* to share. For example, the meeting leader or facilitator might say: "Our intention today is to share without evaluation or judgment what we have all been noticing about ourselves, each other, and the team as a whole. Before we begin, let's check in to see if this is a good time for everyone and make sure we have permission to do so." This is also a time when you can ask for specific observations that you are curious about. |
|---|---|
| Goal | This involves first stating or asking about the *goal*. This means focusing everyone on their common objective for the conversation or for the issue that is being discussed. By orienting people to what they hold in common, it helps you help people stay focused on that, even in the presence of differences in experiences, ideas, or information. |
| Reality | In stating the current *reality*, people can share what they have seen during their daily practice of noticing. That could include their experiences of themselves, each other, the team, the project, or anything else that is relevant. The key is to share these observations without judgment or evaluation, and with the spirit of compassionate curiosity and interest in the perspectives of others. |
| Options | After everyone has shared their perspectives of the current reality, people identify *options*, or possible ways to deal with any problems, challenges, or opportunities that have been identified. This is a kind of brainstorming to generate potential course corrections. |
| Way forward | Finally, we look to the *way forward*. Here is when people narrow down the list of options and select the best way to proceed. If working in a team, we recommend a very brief round robin sharing key takeaways and actions steps. |

### Use Open-Ended Questions

In our work as leadership development coaches, each of us uses many open-ended questions to learn more about what our clients are thinking and experiencing. Open-ended questions generate richer information that increases insight into the respondent's perspectives.

Similarly, conscious accountability emphasizes the use of open-ended questions almost to the exclusion of closed-ended questions. This is because when people talk things through in more detail, increased clarity about next steps can emerge. Review the list of closed-ended questions and their open-ended counterparts in Table 7-3. Which questions do you find more thought-provoking and engaging?

**Table 7-3.** Examples of Closed-Ended Versus Open-Ended Questions

| Closed-Ended Version | Open-Ended Version |
| --- | --- |
| Did you complete the assignment? | Where are you in the process of completing the assignment? How is the assignment coming along? |
| Do you need help with that? | What might help you with that? |
| Are you worried about it? | How are you feeling about it? |
| Are you clear on the next steps? | What about the next steps might need more clarification? |

## Leadership by Example: Chris Duprey, Noticing the Impact of Emotions Without Judgment

Chris Duprey is a senior leader who has served in a number of executive roles within rapidly growing small businesses. Prior to his career in business, Chris served in the US Army as an officer who commanded a company of 80 soldiers and completed several tours of duty in Iraq and Afghanistan. Some years ago, Chris—a voracious reader—encountered some articles and books on meditation as a way to better manage stress. As he developed his own daily meditation practice, he began to see some changes in himself and in the way he leads others.

"One of the biggest changes was in the time it takes to go from 'flash to bang,'" Chris explains. "That means I have gotten better at noticing changes in my body that are signals to feelings, and not instantly reacting to whatever triggered those feelings. Instead of flying off the handle when there's bad news, I can slow down and choose a better response."

In the past, Chris would get visibly stressed and upset in response to mistakes and errors, or when problems popped up unexpectedly. While those things still bother him, he does not react to them like he used to, which has positively affected work practices and relationships. By creating a nonreactive space for the teams he works with, Chris learns about things that go wrong much sooner than before because no one is afraid to talk with him about what happened. And from a relationship standpoint, he has built more trust both with individuals and with teams. As Chris puts it, "People feel safe because they know I won't yell at them or belittle them; instead I will help them work toward a solution."

This practice of mindfulness has allowed Chris to interact with other people in a way that clearly indicates his own intentions and needs. He can engage other people with a focus on their mutual interests and objectives, and without any need to seek validation.

"All of this has happened because I am less clouded by my emotions, which I can watch arise momentarily and pass away without reacting to them," Chris explains. "As a leader, it manifests the best for me, because now I can see that 'shit happens' . . . so why blow your top? If you can be present and not show up with all of the judgment and react right away, you can then take compassionate action. Like 'Hey, I just noticed this, and I think we should talk about it because I might not be the only person noticing it.' In that way you aren't reacting to it, just calling attention to it, so you can have a conversation around it."

Finally, Chris pointed out that the practice of noticing without judgment creates greater efficiency with solving problems, because it reduces time and energy that is lost when people are in a state of emotional reactivity. "There's always something going wrong: sales are down, a person just quit, a client just left us. Then people freak out, and there's a storm within the organization," he observes. "If a CEO or manager freaks out and reacts, whoever reports to that person then goes into crisis mode as well, and then their reports do too. You end up spending the whole day fighting a fire, which probably wasn't actually a fire to begin with, just something that needed a conversation." So, noticing allows for course corrections to happen without the drama and creating unnecessary, fear-based negative energy.

Just like Chris, who developed his capacity to observe and respond to external situations and his own emotions differently, you too can get better at the practice of noticing. The two exercises that follow will help you begin to do just that.

## Exercise 1. A Noticing Self-Assessment

Use this brief self-assessment to reflect on your practice of noticing. Reflection allows for deeper learning and greater clarity about what is going well and where there are areas for improvement. This can help guide you in your development of noticing, targeting areas you might want to experiment with or build and expand upon.

**Figure 7-2.** Noticing Self-Assessment

| How Often . . . | Rarely/ Never | Sometimes | Often | Almost Always |
|---|---|---|---|---|
| Do I notice? | | | | |
| Am I self-aware? | | | | |
| Am I aware of others? | | | | |
| Am I curious about other people's perspectives? | | | | |
| Is my curiosity compassionate (not just intellectual)? | | | | |
| Am I taking into account my mood and the environment when I notice? | | | | |

**Figure 7-2.** Noticing Self-Assessment

| | | | | |
|---|---|---|---|---|
| Do I acknowledge that I am reacting based on my assumptions and triggers? | | | | |
| Do I check in with others and share my observations about myself and others? | | | | |
| Do I request permission before sharing what I notice? | | | | |
| Do I use open-ended questions? | | | | |

| What are the kinds of things that I tend to notice? |
|---|
| |

| How do I typically react to what I notice? |
|---|
| |

| What might I like to enhance about my practice of noticing? |
|---|
| |

## Exercise 2. Create Your Own Notice Map

Using Figure 7-1 as an example, create your own map to help keep track of who and what you want to notice. Your map could focus on work or home, or other groups of people you interact with. Because this chapter is noticing for the purpose of nailing it, we suggest you focus on the people with whom you are working toward a common goal. List the people involved, note the individual relationships between all the individuals, and consider the group as a whole as well as any other stakeholders or forces operating outside the group. Then, before you engage in your individual daily practice of noticing, you can glance at the map to remind you of all the things you could consider attending to.

## Summary: Noticing, the Great Catalyzer

In this chapter, we explored the practice of noticing. Noticing helps us nail it because it allows us to become aware of what is and is not working, and to open up conversations that allow for realignment and mutual support to happen. Importantly, noticing occurs without judgment. As Peter Boyd shared with us, "We all walk through life with an imperfect view of the whole system. Most people have something to teach you about it. Noticing without judgment opens you to a better view of the system you are trying to change."

We identified a number of common obstacles that make it harder to notice, including overload, assumptions, resistance, and miscommunication. But if you embrace a mindset of compassionate curiosity and follow the necessary strategies to prepare, be aware, and then share what you notice, you can set yourself and team up for success.

Noticing is vital for promoting conscious accountability because it enables greater awareness and intentionality, helps deepen relationships, and catalyzes growth and change. But, it goes beyond that too. Noticing also supports the basis of the practice we discuss in the next chapter, exchanging feedback.

# CHAPTER 8

# Exchanging Feedback

*There is no failure. Only feedback.*
ROBERT ALLEN

The youngest of six, Marianne grew up in a lively household. Conversation often flew across the kitchen table. She learned to jump in when she could to have her voice heard. She had no idea that she carried this habit into situations where it simply wasn't needed—until a friend gave her some feedback. They were having a conversation when all of sudden, the friend angrily exclaimed, "Stop doing that! You always do that! You cut me off and jump in when I am not done!" This took Marianne quite by surprise; it was clearly a blind spot. She took this feedback to heart, as she did not want to be a person who cut others off. Unfortunately, the manner in which the feedback was delivered also had an impact. The anger and hyperbolic language led to Marianne putting her guard up and withdrawing. Wanting to be a better listener and to avoid being on the end of another angry outburst, Marianne overcompensated and became reserved in conversation. It took time for her to find a balance. Now, it is not uncommon for others to remark about how well she listens. However, she still finds herself apologizing occasionally if she feels she might have stepped on someone's words, the reaction of her friend still in her memory.

This story clearly illustrates the power of feedback to help us recognize our blind spots and shift our behavior. However, it also illustrates that feedback delivered without consciousness may cause some unintended harm and potential overcorrection. Conscious accountability puts forth a practice of exchanging feedback that holds in mind both the behavior and the relationship. By raising our awareness of ourselves and others, we can exchange feedback in a manner that we hope has the intended impact and opens a space for all involved to be responsible for that impact.

Exchanging feedback entails providing feedback to others, receiving feedback from others, and soliciting feedback from others. We also see feedback loops and exchanges as a necessity for ongoing development, improved performance, and better relationships. Exchanging feedback is a skill that requires repeated practice over time. And it is something that many people—including seasoned leaders—struggle with.

In this chapter, we will consider the origins of the term *feedback*, why feedback is important for conscious accountability, the challenges associated with exchanging feedback, courage as a key mindset, strategies for exchanging feedback, and how we can create the conditions for feedback to occur more readily and easily.

## What Is Feedback and Why Does It Matter?

The word *feedback* hails from early 20th-century technical writings about electrical science, with the original definition being "a rumbling, whining, or whistling sound resulting from an amplified or broadcast signal (such as music or speech) that has been returned as input and retransmitted" (*Merriam-Webster* 2018). By 1952, the term was being used in the way we often think about it today, as "helpful information or criticism that is given to someone to say what can be done to improve a performance, product, etc." In the context of conscious accountability, we present our own interpretation of feedback as information that supports learning for the sake of improved performance and better relationships.

To appreciate the importance of feedback exchanges for conscious accountability, it is helpful to revisit our working definition: *Conscious accountability entails expanding awareness to create deliberate intentions, to take informed actions, and to be responsible for our impact.* First of all, feedback increases our awareness. As noted in the discussion of the Johari window in chapter 2, there are aspects of ourselves that we do not know or cannot easily observe. Everyone has these blind spots. One thing that we never fully know about ourselves is the impact that we have on other people. The only way we can get that information is through feedback. Feedback helps us be more responsible for our impact, because it lets us know what our impact actually is.

Second, the goal of conscious accountability is to improve performance while strengthening relationships, and feedback directly supports this goal. Feedback is essential to learning and growth. As we strive to develop skills and improve the quality of what we do—whether that is playing a sport or musical instrument, driving a car, learning a language, or managing a team—feedback is what provides information about the changes in our behavior or thought process that will help us perform more effectively. Feedback can also lead to stronger relationships. It can provide information about a variety of things that support relationships: what people want and don't want, what matters to them, and how they would like you to interact with them. If you respond to someone's feedback by changing something about how you interact with them, it conveys that you are listening and that the relationship really matters to you.

A few years ago, David was introducing a guest lecturer in his class—one of his close colleagues. The day after the class, David received an email from the colleague, who was miffed at what she experienced as a less-than-adequate formal introduction. David was surprised and saddened by this feedback, but very curious to learn what was lacking and how he could improve. When they spoke about it, his colleague explained that the way women get introduced has a big impact on how they are perceived by their audiences, especially for women of color. David's introduction had been too brief, too informal, and lacking in a sense of personal connection. David's operating perspective—that she was sort of a beloved celebrity in the department who needed little introduction—led him to underdo it. But for David, her feedback gave him the gift of greater awareness that created some powerful, memorable learning. His colleague expressed appreciation for how openly and nondefensively he received the feedback, and the two of them increased the level of trust in the strength of their relationship.

By contrast, without feedback, people's understanding of each other can become narrowed or distorted. Instead of working with fuller and more accurate information, it is natural to make up stories or assumptions in the absence of feedback. Maladaptive patterns can go on, unaddressed, leading to increased distance, superficiality, and resentments.

In sum, feedback helps us become more aware, and more *conscious*, of things that we might not readily see or know. Whether you are holding yourself or others accountable, feedback is helpful to ensure that they (or you) "got it right" and also to help increase learning and get better over time.

## Why Are Feedback Conversations So Difficult?

If feedback is so essential and important, why is it so hard to engage in these conversations? In our coaching and consulting work in business and healthcare, we have encountered several different reasons why people avoid giving, receiving, and soliciting feedback, many of which revolve in some way around fear:

- **Fear of becoming emotional or "triggered"**—fear of eliciting strong emotions in oneself or in others.
- **Fear of damage to relationships or reputation**—worry that feedback will make you look bad, make relationships worse, or result in repercussions or retribution.
- **Threats to self-esteem**—some people over-personalize and overgeneralize feedback in ways that affect how they perceive themselves.

- **Resignation or apathy**—feeling that giving feedback will not make a difference or bring about a change.
- **Lack of time or skill**—feedback is avoided because people don't prioritize it or don't feel equipped to do it well.
- **Culturally or socially discouraged**—not soliciting or giving feedback because it is (or was) not encouraged, perhaps not even permitted.

To the extent that these factors inhibit feedback exchanges from realizing their full potential (or from occurring at all), they impede the practice of conscious accountability. Whether in individual relationships or on teams, the fears described here can be stifling to relationships, which lead to lower agility, poorer adaptability, and slower progress.

## Key Mindset: Courage

With all of these fears and risk factors that discourage people from exchanging feedback, it is a wonder that it ever happens at all! Sometimes giving, receiving, or soliciting feedback can be difficult to do, but having the right mindset going into these exchanges can make a tremendous difference. And because it may mean having to face fears, we consider feedback exchanges to be courageous conversations. It takes courage to give feedback, to receive feedback, and to ask for feedback.

One of our colleagues is an incredible person who has spent time learning, thinking, and teaching about courage. Her name is Roz Savage, and she knows quite a bit about courage from her own experience. When she realized she was not leading the life she truly wanted to have, she gave up her job as a management consultant, her marriage, and her suburban home, and took up high-challenge sporting events. She ran two marathons and later decided to take up ocean rowing. She now holds four Guinness World Records, including being the first woman to row solo across three oceans: the Atlantic, Pacific, and Indian. She has connected these efforts to help raise environmental awareness around the world. Her formula for courage is simple: **C = P > F.** *Courage* exists when your *Passion* is greater than your *Fear*.

So, in stepping into courageous conversations, it is often helpful to think first about what you are passionate about and committed to. Why is this conversation important, worth having, and worth the potential risks in having it? Perhaps it is an intention for yourself and your own development, or perhaps it is something you are committed to for your relationship or for your team. Perhaps you are passionate about something that will benefit your organization, community, or the world at large. If you can get connected to what you are passionate about or are committed to, you can become grounded in a sense of deeper purpose that will help you overcome fears and reservations about feedback.

It can also be useful to consider the dangers or drawbacks of not exchanging feedback. What is at stake if feedback is not provided or received? One of our clients was an executive in his mid-50s, and as part of his executive coaching engagement, we administered a 360-degree exercise, in which he received feedback from his supervisor, peers, and direct reports. For him, this proved to be a humbling and eye-opening experience—people shared aspects of how he behaved that were interfering with his effectiveness and how he was perceived by others. He lamented, "If only they had told me about any of this sooner, I could have done something about it. Instead, I was passed up for several promotions. Think of where my career might have gone!" Denying feedback means lowering the possibility for positive changes in an individual, a relationship, a group, or a system.

## How to Create Better Feedback Exchanges

We have now explored what feedback is, why it is important for conscious accountability, why it is often difficult to engage in feedback, and a mindset to get past those hurdles. Now let us turn our attention to the matter of how to engage in feedback exchanges in a way that will promote conscious accountability. Before we explore the seven strategies for doing so, let's look at a framework to ground us further.

## Two Key Dimensions: Empathy and Data Quality

In describing what it means to create powerful feedback, our colleague Heidi Brooks (2019) highlighted two important dimensions to pay attention to: empathy and data quality. Powerful feedback occurs during exchanges that have high levels of both. In this context, conveying empathy means seeing the situation as the other person sees it—or being able to take on the perspectives of others, including how they think and feel; finding merit in their perspective, which means appreciating that a person's point of view has validity based on their own experiences; and expressing understanding of their perspective or validating that you get where they are coming from. Data quality refers to the clarity or specificity of the information being provided, as well as practical information that helps people improve over time.

In teaching feedback skills to hundreds of executives and other professionals, we often conduct an exercise in which we ask participants to recall the best feedback exchange they have been party to, as well as the worst feedback experience they have ever had. In both cases, we encourage them to think about what specifically made the exchange helpful or constructive (in the case of the best experience) as well as what made it not helpful or destructive (in the case of the worst experience). We have captured these ideas in Table 8-1.

Consistently, these two dimensions (empathy and data quality) are captured in how people describe their positive and negative feedback experiences. For example, in describing the positive experiences, people commonly used words like *caring, relatable, thoughtful, generous,* and *validating* (high in empathy), as well as words like *specific, direct, timely, practical,* and *actionable* (which refer to high data quality). And in describing their negative feedback experiences, people used words like *shaming, threatening, hostile,* and *condescending* (lack of empathy) and *delayed, lack of evidence, inaccurate, too broad,* or *too narrow* (poor data quality).

**Table 8-1.** Best and Worst Feedback Experiences, as Related to Empathy and Data Quality

|  | **Best** | **Worst** |
|---|---|---|
| **Empathy** | • Collaborative<br>• Supportive, caring, affirming<br>• Encouraging, motivating<br>• Balanced<br>• Transparent<br>• Genuine<br>• Desire to help | • Condescending<br>• Harsh, negative tone<br>• Hurtful<br>• Personal attack, retaliatory<br>• Too personal<br>• Blindsided<br>• Patronizing |
| **Data Quality** | • Specific<br>• Actionable<br>• Says how to improve<br>• Timely<br>• Clear<br>• Illustrative examples | • Vague, nonspecific<br>• No examples<br>• Not timely<br>• Unfounded, biased<br>• Inaccurate<br>• Meaningless<br>• Unclear, confusing, mixed messages |

## 7 Strategies for Exchanging Feedback

Now let's take a deeper look into seven specific strategies that are important whether you are giving, receiving, or soliciting feedback:

- Connect to your intention.
- Make it safe.
- Prepare.
- Listen actively and seek information.
- Manage triggers, emotions, and resistance.
- Express gratitude.
- Make a follow-up plan.

### Connect to Your Intention

The first step in preparing for a feedback conversation is to get clear on why this exchange matters to you. In considering both the relationships and performance goals, what are you committed to and what is at stake in the situation (for you and for the other person)?

In giving feedback, it is also important to clarify why you see the feedback as valuable for the other person or people—what are your hopes for them? If you can connect to what may be important to the feedback receiver, you are in a better position to build alignment with that person's goals or agenda. This is especially important when giving feedback to people who are not obligated to act on it.

In asking for feedback, it is helpful to let people know why you are soliciting feedback. Share your intention or your purpose for seeking it—"I am hoping to get better at managing people" or "I want to be a more supportive colleague, friend, or spouse." Along with sharing the purpose, it is also good to let people know what you will do with the information, or how you will (or won't) use it.

## Make It Safe

In their book *Crucial Conversations* (2012), Patterson and co-authors repeatedly stress the importance of safety when engaged in crucial conversations (or dialogue that feels high stakes, generates strong emotions, and in which people's opinions differ). Feedback conversations can feel loaded in these ways too. As such, it is imperative to consistently look out for signs—such as withdrawal or defensiveness—that someone in the conversation (yourself included!) is feeling unsafe. And if such ruptures to safety occur, they need to be addressed ASAP by observing the tension, apologizing when needed, and reestablishing the feedback conversation's shared purpose, which ideally should be your own or someone else's development.

When giving or asking for feedback it is helpful to go a bit overboard in an effort to make people feel safer. In soliciting feedback, you could consider telling people how much you would appreciate their candor and honesty, that you deeply value their perspective, and that their giving you feedback will in no way put them or your relationship at risk. You could also share that you are eager to receive feedback—even negative or constructive feedback—and hope that they will feel comfortable disclosing whatever they need to share. In addition, give the other person a choice about whether or not to provide feedback—that it is something you would like, but it is also OK for them to decline if doing so would make them feel very uncomfortable or unsafe in some way.

In our experience as coaches, we've found that when seeking feedback from people whose positions are subordinate to yours in the power structure, it can be a good idea to provide opportunities for that information to be given anonymously. Likewise, heightened sensitivity and transparency to power dynamics when giving feedback to direct reports can go a long way in helping to maintain psychological safety.

If you are receiving feedback, you can make yourself feel safer by reminding yourself that you get to decide what to do with it, that it is one data point, and that it reveals as much about the person giving it as it does about you. If you are giving feedback, you can make others feel safer by asking for permission to give feedback (if it is unexpected) and not giving negative feedback in front of others. You can also make it safer by conveying your regard for and support of the person.

### Prepare

In preparing to give feedback, it is helpful to focus on providing high-quality data. The Center for Creative Leadership has developed a simple yet effective way to encapsulate three critical focal points in delivering high quality feedback—Situation, Behavior, and Impact (SBI):

1. **Situation.** Provide information about the situation—what was happening at the time? This will help ensure that everyone is thinking about and recollecting the same set of circumstances, which sets a shared focus.

2. **Behavior.** Make sure you have specific examples of the behavior you wish to address. In doing so, it is best to stick with what you've observed directly about the behavior, and not inferences about or interpretations of those observations. For example, "I noticed you looked at your phone four or five times during that meeting" is more factual than "I noticed you were distracted, bored, or

disinterested during the meeting." After all, we can never really know another person's mental state.

3. **Impact.** Discuss the impact that the behavior had on relationships or work outcomes. How did the behavior make you feel or what did it make you think?

That said, you don't want to overprepare and end up waiting too long to give feedback. The closer in time feedback is to the occurrence of the behavior, the more likely it is that the details will be fresh and recalled correctly. If possible, choose a comfortable time and place for the conversation; in many cases, people prefer to receive feedback privately, not publicly. If feedback is unexpected, it is often advisable to ask permission first, or inquire about the extent to which the person is open to receiving it. If now is not a good time, you could work to schedule a meeting later. If appropriate, you can also frame the conversation as one of mutual feedback (inviting the other person to give feedback as well).

When asking for feedback, make sure you are specific in what you are asking about. When appropriate, we suggest making sure to ask for feedback about both relationships and tasks. The clearer you are about what kind of feedback you are looking for, the better data you are likely to elicit. For example, if you ask your spouse or partner, "How are we doing lately?" you may get a less specific response than a question like, "How did I do in supporting you when you were feeling down about what happened at work on Friday?"

## Listen Actively and Seek Information

Listening actively means engaging deeply with what someone is telling you in a way that allows for a fuller understanding of their perspective. In particular, it involves clarification—the act of making sure you comprehend what feedback is being given, by repeating or paraphrasing what you heard, and then checking for accuracy. For example: "So, Diane, let me see if I am understanding you correctly. You said that the way I explained the plan was confusing and, in the future, you'd prefer to see something in writing before we discuss it. Do I have that right?"

Clarifying the feedback you receive has a number of benefits:

- It helps ensure that you heard what the other person intended to communicate.
- It conveys to the speaker that you are listening and tracking what they are saying.
- It allows them to share any additional information that might make things even clearer.
- It also reflects back to the speaker how their words are landing, providing them with insight about their own impact too.

Another way to improve the quality of information you are receiving is to ask for additional information that will make the feedback more useful to you. This could mean requesting specific examples, asking for more context, inquiring about the impact that your behavior had on the person giving the feedback, asking about what matters to the other person, or anything else that might help you understand the person or the data they are giving you.

When seeking information, queries should be expressed nondefensively, with curiosity, and with the expressed intention of understanding (as opposed to coming across as a cross-examination or fact-finding mission to discredit the feedback or the person delivering it).

Clarifying and information seeking are also helpful when you are giving feedback. Once the conversion opens up, you can use these skills to make the conversation a dialogue that promotes mutual understanding.

### Manage Emotions and Resistance

It is very common for feedback to generate many different emotions. In the case of appreciative feedback, it can make us feel happy, seen, and valued. But in the case of more critical feedback, receiving it can make us feel vulnerable, angry, sad, or misunderstood.

Managing emotions is crucial because when we are feeling triggered or threatened, our brains process information differently. Our perceptual field narrows, with a diminished ability to think in more complex or nuanced ways. As a result, we can become more resistant to feedback and take in less information. In feedback situations, there are a number of ways we can get emotionally triggered. In *Thanks for the Feedback: The Science and Art of Receiving Feedback Well*, authors Douglas Stone and Sheila Heen (2014) articulated three ways that people often get triggered because of feedback:

- **The truth trigger** occurs when we perceive the feedback (or even some part of it) as not true. In fact, sometimes we may scan the feedback for any aspect that is not quite right and use that as a reason to minimize or dismiss it. For example, if you hear that you were 30 minutes late on three occasions, but believe you were 15 minutes late on only two occasions, you might be more likely to downplay the significance of the feedback or just say "that's not true" and reject it entirely.

- **The relationship trigger** happens when we are triggered not by the veracity of the information, but by the person who is giving the feedback. Sometimes that occurs because of how well the person giving feedback knows us; either because "you don't know me well enough to say that" or the opposite—"How could you say that? I thought you knew me." The relationship trigger could also be about perceived hypocrisy—"I can't believe you're telling me that my interrupting you is a problem, when you do that to me all the time!"

- **The identity trigger** is the most intense of all, because in this case the feedback is at odds with or calls into question some fundamental aspect of what we believe to be true about ourselves. A healthcare professional whom Daryn worked with was crestfallen to report a conversation he had with the head of his department, in which she voiced frustration at how blunt and unbending the doctor's demeanor could be during clinical case reviews. Because he considered himself to be a consummate team player—collaborative, collegial, and always respectful—the doctor was deeply shaken by his supervisor's words. Uncomfortably, he began to question whether he had an accurate read of himself and how he showed up for others.

Dealing with triggers effectively requires emotional intelligence (EI) skills. Managing emotions is one of the hallmarks of EI (Goleman,

Boyatzis, and McKee 2004; Salovey et al. 2003). In his book *Permission to Feel*, Marc Brackett (2019) described five research-supported EI skills that can help people deal with emotional triggers. They are easy to remember with the acronym RULER:

- **Recognizing emotions.** Being aware of when you are experiencing emotions through things like physical sensations in the body (racing heart or feeling warmer) and behavioral cues (pacing or raised voice).
- **Understanding the causes and consequences of emotions.** Being able to appreciate what triggered you and the influence your emotions may have on you or others.
- **Labeling emotions accurately.** Naming our emotions with specificity and nuance; for example, "I am feeling defensive, threatened, misunderstood, and vulnerable."
- **Expressing emotions appropriately.** Understanding how and when to communicate our feelings to others.
- **Regulating emotions.** Using strategies to shift and equalize emotional states. (Some of these strategies are similar to the noticing strategies from chapter 7.)

Later in this chapter, we offer an exercise to help you practice managing your emotions during feedback.

Sometimes managing emotions means helping *others* manage their emotions. Many people hope that if they frame the feedback just right, the other person will not become upset, defensive, or resistant to it. This might lead them to be more delicate or to tiptoe around the issue, perhaps at the cost of clarity and directness. But we think it is better to *expect* that the other person will exhibit some kind of defensiveness or resistance. By accepting the possibility of this kind of reaction, you can also prepare yourself to manage it.

There are a number of ways to address resistance, such as inquiring about how the other person is receiving or interpreting the feedback and clarifying what the feedback does (and does not) mean. You can also acknowledge and validate the person's feelings while maintaining your commitment to them and your intention in delivering the feedback. If someone is highly triggered, and thus cannot be open to taking in information, it is OK to take a break and come back to the conversation at a later time, after they have had a chance to allow their emotions to settle and think about the information.

## Express Gratitude

Remember to thank the person for the conversation, acknowledging the courage it took to provide, receive, or discuss the feedback. You can also thank the person for whatever additional insights the conversation brought to the surface. If you received feedback, recall that the person did not have to provide it and that this information could be valuable for your ongoing growth and development.

You can also appreciate feedback as something that can help grow your relationship. Indeed, when feedback exchanges go well, it can help build trust that the relationship can hold honest exchanges about what each person is doing that affects the other. When we positively reinforce others and ourselves for engaging in feedback, it makes it more likely that we will continue to have these exchanges in the future.

## Make a Follow-Up Plan

As Tara Mohr (2014) emphasizes in her book *Playing Big*, feedback ultimately says much more about the person giving it—their preferences, proclivities, and opinions—than about the person receiving it. In this way, feedback provides a double opportunity: the chance to learn more about the person offering it and for the receiver to objectively decide which pieces and parts of the feedback are useful and should be retained (versus those that do not resonate with their own needs and should be discarded).

So, after the exchange, spend time thinking about the feedback. If you received feedback, consider the potential value it has for you or how you might use it to improve your performance, how you are perceived by others, or the quality of your relationships. Remember, ultimately you get to decide what to do with the feedback. At the very least, it is a data point that may (or may not) be part of a larger trend or pattern.

If you decide to act on the feedback, it is helpful for your own account-ability to make a plan about how you will alter the way you think or behave. The plan may also involve following up and collecting additional information to assess how you are doing with integrating and using the feedback to adapt your behavior over time.

If you give feedback to someone else, it can be helpful to engage them in conversation about other ways they might operate in the future. Ideally, this would include information about what "better" or "more successful" would sound, look, and feel like.

## Building the Conditions for Exchange of Feedback

At its best, feedback is not merely a transactional exchange of information but an ongoing component of building and deepening longer term relation-ships. Feedback exchanges flow more freely and are experienced as benefi-cial when certain preconditions are met or created. Here are some of those important conditions:

- **Setting the terms.** How interpersonal exchanges unfold can be influenced by talking about various things that may come up over the course of your relationship. In our experience as coaches, we have these types of conversations at the beginning of coaching engagements. Here are some questions we might ask: "How do you like to receive feedback?" or "What do you need from me, as your coach, with regard to feedback?" or "How do you imagine it would be for you to give me direct feedback?" In asking similar questions and having these conversations with your teammates, you can create desired modes of behavior or aspirational norms for your relationship that can help prepare each of you for those conversations.

- **Making it routine.** To the extent that feedback occurs more frequently, it becomes standard operating procedure—over time, it gets more routine and less scary. If it only happens once in a while, people get less of an opportunity to practice and refine their skills around feedback. If feedback conversations occur with greater regularity, you and others will be more comfortable engaging in them. It allows you and them to develop a sense of trust and greater ease in the process.

- **Establishing (and re-establishing) trust.** Trust is a hugely important factor when it comes to feedback. Anecdotally, people we have worked with say over and over again that it is much easier for them to give and receive feedback in relationships with higher levels of mutual trust. That includes the sense that the people involved care about one another and have positive intentions in interacting with one another. Research on feedback and conflict in teams is consistent with the idea that when trust is lacking, negative feedback hurts relationships and performance (Petersen and Behfar 2003).

- **Maintaining psychological safety.** As discussed at length in chapter 5, psychological safety allows people to speak freely with less worry and fear about consequences, like lowered status or damaged reputation. When feedback is delivered with empathy and compassion, it can have a positive effect on psychological safety. And the presence of psychological safety makes it much easier for people to exchange feedback.

- **Holding a growth mindset.** Finally, having a growth mindset is a helpful condition to support feedback exchanges. When people are focused on learning and improvement, they are more likely to see feedback as supportive and helpful. By contrast, if they have a fixed mindset and are more committed to looking good and skirting failure at all costs, they are more likely to find feedback threatening and will tend to avoid it. We touch on growth mindset more in chapter 10 around the practice of trying again.

## Leadership by Example: Mary Carter, a CEO Soliciting Feedback With Openness

Mary Carter is the CEO of a company that manufactures small parts for solar panels. She recently worked with her leadership team to come up with an action plan for making their production process even more environmentally friendly. Mary observed that the team worked well to create this action plan, even if there were some hiccups along the way. After the plan was submitted, she sought direct feedback to learn more about how the process went and what she could do to lead the team more effectively in the future.

In a team meeting, Mary discussed why she was seeking the feedback. She stated that overall she was very pleased with the work the team had delivered. Mary also noted that she had been the CEO for seven months now, and that part of her job was to figure out how she could be most effective for this particular team. To do so, she thought she needed some honest feedback about their experiences of her leadership. She went on to add that she would not be offended by criticism, and asked them to be as specific and constructive as possible in their suggestions.

To help support that kind of honesty, Mary sent an anonymous survey to the team. In it, team members were asked to describe what went well and the strengths Mary showed, and what didn't work as well and how she might make adjustments. After the survey responses came in, Mary read through all of them carefully. Although she found herself feeling defensive about the criticisms at times, she reminded herself that well-intentioned behaviors can have unintended adverse impacts on other people. She then grouped the responses into specific themes or findings that she wanted to learn more about.

Survey results indicated that Mary was applauded for sticking to her stated intention of providing clear and thorough guidance to the team at the beginning of the project but for then stepping back to allow their work to unfold. She was further complimented on allowing the team to figure out its own process for calculating its carbon footprint and for writing up the report. In fact, several people noted that having more autonomy had enabled them to think through several novel ways of calculating the company's environmental impact. These novel formulations had then led to many interesting and important conversations across the leadership team as a whole about the company's overall environmental impact.

At the same time, Mary received some feedback about the drawbacks for team performance of her hands-off approach. A few people explained that they had assumed that Mary would provide more input on their written plan earlier in the process, perhaps at the midway point, rather than after she had received the plan in full. They noted that input from Mary might have prevented them from making several suggestions for reducing their environmental impact that they now understood did not ultimately fit in with the company's priorities. In addition, some team members had experienced Mary as busy and distracted at times and delayed in her response to their requests.

After reviewing the results, Mary sent an email to the team thanking them for the feedback, sharing the highlights, and inviting them to discuss the findings in more detail at their next team meetings. When they next came together, Mary once again thanked them for the feedback and sought some additional ideas about how she could adjust her approach in the future. She also listened and asked additional questions to clarify and deepen her understanding of the places she could improve. Based on everything she had learned, Mary made a plan to continue to give the team plenty of autonomy but check in with them more often after giving an assignment. In addition, she gave team members permission to tell her directly if she appeared distracted or less than attentive. This entire conversation was well received by the team.

In choosing to approach this feedback situation with openness and psychological safety in mind, Mary sought to elevate results while also deepening the relationships with her team. She made sure to check her emotions as she read the anonymous feedback and when she sought further information in the team meeting. This approach helped her see her role in the team's hiccups, rather than to simply brush them off and blame the team.

We can all improve our skill in approaching feedback exchanges. Here are two exercises to help you engage in courageous conversations.

## Exercise 1: Practice Giving Feedback

Think of a situation that would be challenging for you to give feedback. Some examples could be:

- You have a new work colleague—a peer—whom you do not know very well; perhaps you have only met on video conferences. Your direct reports have recently complained that this person is making demands on them that they do not have time for. Further, the demands are being delivered in an abrasive way.
- Your direct report is highly emotional and very defensive when receiving feedback. You need to bring up the fact that they have not made visible gains in areas identified for change last quarter.
- Your boss has a bad habit of interrupting other people. You and your teammates have commiserated in offline conversations about the negative effect of this on morale and performance. You all have decided you eventually need to let your boss know about his impact.

Choose one of these scenarios and role play the situation with a partner. Tell them the type of person you want them to play. Practice giving feedback and record a video of the conversation. If helpful, you can use the following script:

- **Intention.** The reason I wanted to have this conversation is . . . and my hope is that our talking about this will lead to . . .
- **Situation.** I was thinking about the time when . . . (*Describe the situation.*)
- **Behavior.** I noticed that . . . (*State the other person's behavior.*)
- **Impact.** The impact on me was . . . (*Describe your thoughts and feelings that followed from behavior.*)
- **Inquiry.** What was happening for you in that situation?
- **Request.** In the future I would prefer . . . (*State your request.*)

Ask the person who role played with you how they felt during the conversation; ask what you did that seemed effective or ineffective. Later, review the video and note which of this chapter's strategies you used. Notice your nonverbal behavior and body language. To what extent do they support or undermine your message? Make some notes on what worked well and what you want to continue to work on.

## Exercise 2: Practice Managing Emotions During Feedback

Imagine someone giving you feedback that would be difficult to hear and that you would find triggering in some way. It may help you to review the three different kinds of triggers and imagine what personal examples of each come to mind. Here are some possible scenarios to jump-start your thinking:

- Your client expresses strong disappointment in a project you delivered, which you thought went quite well.
- Your spouse says you are not doing enough to help with domestic tasks, yet you believe you do far more at home than your spouse does.
- You sit on a nonprofit board and have expressed concerns about a prospective new member's qualifications. Another board member questions whether you harbor a bias against young people.

Imagine having received this upsetting feedback and do the following:

- **Breathe.** Slower, deeper, diaphragmatic breathing can interrupt our sympathetic nervous response, and may be the fastest way to return our bodies and minds to a calmer state.
- **Check your narrative.** We are often very quick to interpret what's going on or make up a narrative that may not be true. *He's attacking me. She doesn't like me. They have a hidden agenda.* Slow down and distinguish the facts (what someone says or does) from the story (the meaning you assign to the facts).
- **Stay curious.** If we can encourage ourselves to stay curious about what the person is saying, it can help us suspend our defensive reaction and focus on learning more about their perspective. Ask yourself questions like: What does this person want? What is their concern really about? How are they viewing this? What are they feeling?
- **Connect to intention.** Remind yourself of your larger intention for this situation or relationship. Ask yourself: What is really important to me? How do I want to be present in this moment? A quick check-in on this can help you remain aware of your longer-term priorities, which can help you navigate your own reactions in the moment.

After doing these steps, notice your current state, and then practice what you would say in response to the other person. What would you want to clarify? What additional information would you seek?

## Summary: Effective Feedback Requires Courage and Practice

Management and leadership expert Ken Blanchard has been quoted as saying, "feedback is the breakfast of champions." It is something that people who strive for excellence seek out to continuously improve—and within the conscious accountability framework, the target of improvement is both performance and relationships.

And yet, when we speak with audiences about the practices of conscious accountability, engaging in effective feedback exchanges is what people say they struggle with most. To surmount these obstacles, we note that feedback exchanges require the mindset of courage. Further, we propose seven strategies that support effective feedback:

- Connect to your intention.
- Make it safe.
- Prepare.
- Listen actively and seek information.
- Manage triggers, emotions, and resistance.
- Express gratitude.
- Make a follow-up plan.

Cultivating the conditions for healthy feedback within the larger context of the relationship, team, or organization can go a long way toward building a culture where powerful feedback exchanges are the norm and part of the "secret sauce" that distinguishes the acceptable from the outstanding. Getting there is possible, with deliberate focus and commitment to practicing the mindset and skills.

# CHAPTER 9

# Claiming It

*It's only when you take responsibility for your life, that you discover how powerful you truly are.*

ALLANAH HUNT

Objectively looking at results, owning what happened, and accepting responsibility to improve can catalyze the effectiveness of any team. No place is this practice better illustrated than in the US military, where stakes are exceptionally high and the commitment to improvement is relentless.

Back in the 1970s, the US Army created the After Action Review (AAR) methodology to strategically look at results to learn and improve (Garvin 2000). In his 2018 book, *The Culture Code*, Daniel Coyle highlights the Navy SEALs' use of structured AARs immediately following training or actual missions. The missions of the Navy SEALs are incredibly complex, with the team working together quickly to solve emergent problems and issues. Under these conditions, it is essential for the group to be tightly coordinated and have a shared understanding of how to act, even when overt communication is not always possible. Having a shared mental model based on team learning from prior missions enables the SEALs to work together seamlessly under incredible stress.

The goal of an AAR is not to cast blame or to pat themselves on the back; rather, it is to get to the deep, root cause of any failures or missteps, and, more fundamentally, to understand how each person's actions affect the group as a whole. The open acknowledgment that processes can always be improved helps to strengthen SEALs' recognition of the necessity of AARs, and therefore their commitment to doing them often.

During an AAR, SEALs share their candid perspectives on what went well and what did not, and how everyone contributed, in detail, to the outcome. As one former SEAL put it, "We leave rank and emotion at the door. We engage in respectful conflict, transparency, and honesty. We have little time for games or politics" (Gleeson 2019). People need to trust that the feedback they are getting and the vulnerability they are showing in admitting mistakes will be handled in a sensitive, deliberate, and authentic way, all with the larger goal of improving the team's capacity to perform together with surgical precision and strength. The psychological safety required of the AARs, and the care with which this process is handled, helps the team deepen their trust and sense of belonging.

Even if the missions and projects in your life do not feel as high stakes or life or death as those of the Navy SEALs, reviewing your actions is a necessary activity for making improvements. These reviews occur in many industries and go by different names, including debriefs, retrospectives, and postmortems. We contend that in addition to reviewing your actions, *owning your results* is equally important for the practice of conscious accountability, and differentiates average from extraordinary teamwork.

In this chapter, we will define what claiming it means and why that is pivotal for the practice of conscious accountability. After sharing a few of the common obstacles that get in the way of this process, we will show you how to claim it, presenting the mindsets and strategies to take you through it step by step.

## What Is Claiming It and Why Does It Matter?

Very simply, *claiming it* means being willing to carry responsibility for the consequences of your actions or inactions, both with regard to the things you are working to achieve and the relationships involved. Claiming it is an essential practice for conscious accountability, because it is all about taking responsibility in the service of improvement. People who take responsibility for their impact are frequently viewed as great leaders, and their willingness to own the results inspires others to do the same (Gibori 2017; Zenger 2015).

Similar to the process used by the Navy SEALs, the purpose of claiming it is ultimately future focused: By reflecting on past performance, we can engage in actionable learning that can be used to improve relationships and outcomes going forward. Within our framework, data could be drawn from observations that came up when we took time to notice how everyone was doing, or any information that was generated through the process of giving and receiving feedback. Claiming it allows us to reflect and bring together this information and to take ownership of it.

## What Gets in the Way of Claiming It?

Can you think of a leader or someone you know who has trouble with claiming it? Maybe someone who avoids taking responsibility by deflecting criticism or redirecting the conversation? Or maybe someone who never accepts ownership of work done well and instead minimizes their contributions to the team? Or perhaps a person who attempts to spin the facts in such a way that they always portray themselves in a positive light? Recall from chapter 1 how CEO Josh Hudson, after being confronted about his behavior by members of his team, blew up and was unable to take any responsibility for the impact of his actions. He was unable to acknowledge the feedback he received from his cousins or to accept that his actions had affected others negatively.

Josh is not alone in his struggle to openly and fully claim his impact. While owning results and communicating responsibility may seem straightforward, there are quite a few things that hold people back from doing this effectively. Here are a few examples:

- **Lack of clarity on the outcome.** If there was no clear understanding of what the end goal was supposed to be or what the desired relationship outcomes were, it is harder to understand whether the results of our actions were positive or negative. Likewise, even if you know what the end goal was supposed to be, but you don't adequately measure performance, it can be hard to say whether the goal was actually attained.
- **Low commitment or sense of ownership.** When people feel less committed to goals or relationships, or when they experience themselves as unable to exert influence on achieving the goal, they are more likely to shrug their shoulders and feel less ownership and responsibility.
- **Fear.** Harboring fears of looking bad, losing esteem in the eyes of oneself or others, and incurring negative consequences if mistakes, errors, or shortcomings are exposed can all be barriers to claiming it. This can be especially true when the stakes are high, such as in high-pressure military, law enforcement, healthcare, or other life-or-death situations.
- **Ego.** When people over-personalize things that happen, they are more inclined to experience shame or personal failure when things don't go well. Under these conditions, people often act to preserve their self-image and reputation, which frequently shows up as avoiding responsibility. Another casualty of being overly self-focused is forgetting to appreciate and recognize the contributions of others. When someone tries to claim more than their fair share of impact (such as taking full credit for a team project that went well), this can also alienate others and damage relationships.

These barriers all undermine conscious accountability. They reduce people's capacity to hold themselves or others accountable, and they also make it harder to have informed, productive conversations about what happened, who contributed to the outcomes, and how to improve. Holding the mindsets of objectivity and acceptance can help overcome these obstacles as they emerge.

## Key Mindsets: Objectivity and Acceptance

In chapter 7, we described compassionate curiosity as a mindset that supports noticing the *process*. Here, the first mindset that supports claiming it is objectivity when looking at *results*. That means being able to look at and evaluate what you've done in a way that is rational, impartial, and emotionally neutral. It involves looking at the data as if you were a scientist, with the goal of seeing things dispassionately and as they actually are.

It takes some deliberate effort to be aware of your own wants, hopes, feelings, and beliefs about what you think the results should have been. This is not easy to do, because it is difficult (if not impossible) to be impartial or unemotional when it comes to yourself or things you care about. When it comes to ourselves, we all have biases that are difficult to recognize. For example, we often attribute our own behavior to situational causes, but view others' behavior as related to their character (also known as *the fundamental attribution error*; Miller 1984). We can see the impact of biases that others have but fail to recognize our own biases (also known as *the blind spot bias*; Pronin, Lin, and Ross 2002). While these challenges are universal, we can become more aware of how we are not great at being objective and make conscious efforts to limit the effects of bias, which can help create more honest relationships and better outcomes.

After you acknowledge how you think or feel about your results or impact, you can strive for more objectivity by suspending the thoughts and feelings (even temporarily) to focus on understanding the data and how it can be of value. Objectivity can be even easier to embrace when it becomes a team norm. If everyone is actively working on objectivity about themselves and others, then any corresponding feelings of vulnerability are shared and normalized as "the way that we do things around here." If you remember Kendra Curtis from the introduction, she intentionally modeled vulnerable sharing and baked in a regular weekly process for everyone to engage in objectively reviewing progress using three simple questions: What is the progress you have made? What are the problems? And, what is your plan?

The second mindset that supports claiming it is acceptance. In his work on mindful leadership, Marc Lesser (2013) described a key paradox that can guide us toward effective action: "Fight for change, accept what is." In claiming it, we try to accept with honesty how we did and what our successes and challenges were, and attempt to set realistic goals for how we can do better next time.

We can think about acceptance in three ways:

- **Accepting things as they are.** The results are the results—we can either deny them or accept them. Accepting them empowers us to improve upon them.

- **Accepting ourselves (and others) for who we are.** That means holding ourselves (and others) with kindness and compassion in all of our humanity, complete with weaknesses and shortcomings. When we distinguish our *selves* from our *results*, we can look at our results without our ego or sense of self-esteem being on the line. Similarly, when we accept others for who they are, we can help them feel secure enough to take responsibility for their actions.

- **Accepting ownership of our own power to shape results.** That means having a deep sense of personal responsibility, pride in ownership, and sense of stewardship (or caring for the things and people that have been entrusted to us), all of which embolden us to take steps forward in a new direction as needed.

It is through this process of honestly accepting ourselves and our work in its completeness that we are able to then fight for change, passionately incorporating all of our knowledge, setting realistic goals based on the realities of our circumstances, and working constructively to improve ourselves, support others, and strive for new results.

In 2012, Daryn was at a major career crossroads. She had spent the bulk of the past decade in training, learning a great deal about how to conduct psychological research. In graduate school, she investigated how early childhood relationships influence psychological well-being into adulthood. In her postdoctoral training, she shifted her focus to developing and evaluating parenting supports for mothers experiencing homelessness and/or diagnosed with mental health concerns. She was engaging in promising collaborations with research colleagues, publishing the results of their studies, and successfully applying for grants to continue her work.

By one set of metrics, it seemed that Daryn was well on her way to a solid research career. But when she paused and allowed herself to consider another data stream—how she felt about what she was doing—Daryn had to acknowledge that she was not fulfilled by spending most of her time conducting research. In her heart, she knew that other things—learning about new fields of knowledge, helping others grow and develop, and teaching in the university setting—spoke more deeply to her. But she also was uncomfortable fully owning and accepting this somewhat inconvenient fact.

With so much time and effort already invested in her research career, the possibility of moving away from it felt very scary. Daryn worried about letting down those people—her advisors, her sponsors, and her collaborators—who had invested time, money, and care into her training. She felt uncomfortable, even ashamed of her privilege, in having received excellent research training and now choosing to abandon it. And Daryn was concerned about how she would build another career now that she was slowly ruling out research as her main avenue of work.

Despite this discomfort, Daryn knew that she would not be happy in the long run unless she came to accept the objective fruits of her soul searching. And, ultimately, this acceptance freed her to take an important next step. As she owned the truth of her situation, Daryn began to seek out broader career guidance and advice from her mentors and other advisors. She also began to explore alternative career options, accepting a fellowship at the National Institutes of Health, where she was surrounded by new role models, including psychologists and other social scientists who were pushing forward cutting-edge science policy and programming. Daryn also reached back out to her wider professional network, including David, who had been a clinical supervisor in graduate school, and reconnected with her former advisor, who was now working to foster leadership development efforts within academic medicine.

These connections and conversations opened Daryn's eyes to the leadership development needs of clinicians and researchers doing vital work in academic medicine. With a new sense of excitement and purpose, Daryn began to parlay the listening and supportive skills she had gained in her clinical training into her emerging work as a leadership development coach. She harnessed her love of learning and teaching to help residents, trainees, and junior faculty develop their abilities to communicate effectively with others, work together on teams, and set leadership vision and direction in their own careers. She also began to build a small psychotherapy practice focused on the work-life balance needs of professional women. Over the course of several years, the pieces have come together into a career that Daryn finds highly enjoyable, engaging, and exciting, which she feels extremely grateful to pursue. This path ultimately came to fruition because she was willing to objectively evaluate her path and accept how she did—and did not—want to proceed.

## 4 Strategies for Claiming It

We will now break down the practice of claiming it into four strategies that will help you do this more methodically and effectively. Our suggestions derive from our review of the literature on AARs and our own experience in working with leaders and teams. The strategies include answering four questions (inspired by Mahal 2018):

- What were the actual results (versus the expected results)?
- What caused those results?
- How can we respond effectively to the results and what we learned from them?
- How can we apply this learning next time?

### What Were the Actual Results?

The first strategy in claiming it involves assessing what your results are, and how they compare to what was expected. To do this successfully, you need to have a specific understanding of what you wanted to happen. If, earlier on, you engaged in the practices of creating clarity, noticing, and meeting challenges when nailing it, you have already articulated the desired end state with enough specificity so you can gauge whether or not you are there. In going through those steps, you likely settled upon ways you plan to measure the outcomes. For some goals that lend themselves to being quantified or measured, this is easier (such as revenue goals, number of participants, customer satisfaction scores, accident rates, or percentage of on-time deliveries).

But other things—for example, in the interpersonal realm—can be harder to quantify. Fortunately, scholars who have studied high-quality relationships at work have identified a number of factors that can influence the quality of relationships (Dutton and Heaphy 2003; Brueller and Carmelli 2011). Consider asking yourself or others questions like these to evaluate relationship quality:

- How much vitality and aliveness did we experience in our relationship?
- How much openness was there to new ideas?
- To what extent did we experience a strong sense of positive regard?
- How engaged were we? How much did everyone actively participate?
- How well did we handle and recover from moments of strain, conflict, or distress?
- How much room is there in the relationship to express a range of feelings—positive, negative, and vulnerable?
- How much closeness, trust, or respect did we experience for one another?

And as captured in the last chapter, understanding how we actually did versus what was expected, especially with regard to interpersonal outcomes, necessitates the exchange of feedback. Feedback provides some of the important data around our results and our relationships. Notably, different people may have different perceptions about what the results were (especially with regard to more interpersonal outcomes), so there needs to be room in the conversation for sharing and listening to those perspectives.

## What Caused These Results?

The second strategy in claiming it is understanding the root causes for the results. At its core, this involves reflection and stepping back to look at the underlying factors that led you and your team to a given endpoint. This process of reflection can unlock new knowledge or awareness of the deeper results of the experience you just had. Having the right questions for reflection is the key. Here are some of our favorites:

- Why did we get the results we did?
- What were all the factors (including physical, human, and organizational or environmental) that determined our results?
- Which factors were the most critical underlying causes of what happened?
- What was the sequence of how these crucial factors interacted with one another to get to the results?
- What did we learn about what supports (or does not support) both our relationships and how we create success?

Typically, the process of capturing learning happens at the end of a project or endeavor, which represents a natural place to stop and reflect. But attending to learning continually while working on the project can also be useful, even as a way to collect data for further reflection later on. It requires developing a discipline of pausing periodically and asking the question: "What am I learning here?" One strategy for developing this habit is to keep track of learning insights in a personal journal. This is similar to the practice of noticing, except it is for the sake of generating learning, rather than checking in with others or making mid-course corrections.

For people who are more used to doing things than reflecting on them, this process of thinking about what was learned from the doing may not be easy, intuitive, or comfortable at first. But the psychological safety you worked to establish through the practice opening up engagement in chapter 5 will serve your team very well here. Now you will need to engage vulnerably and honestly about how the team performed on the task at hand and what was learned. The more that people feel safe and able to speak their minds, the more open (and useful) the conversation will be. This openness, in turn, will allow for a higher degree of sharing and learning. Also, having a growth mindset (which we discuss more in chapter 10) helps you stay focused on learning and getting better as the primary focus.

## How Can We Respond Effectively?

Once you've explored what happened and why, the next strategy to claiming it is owning the results and responding to them. In the conscious accountability sense, our responses are thoughtful and deliberate *actions*, as opposed to reflexive or impulsive *reactions*. They may include things like taking corrective measures and restructuring work, as well as appreciating or recognizing others. However, a very important aspect of the response is how you communicate about the review process and what was discovered.

This step is important for a few reasons. First, if you are working on a team, not everyone who is affected by the team's mission may be present during the review process (such as other employees, vendors, or customers). Being deliberate about communicating means thinking through what stakeholders would benefit from hearing about and contributing to the learning. Second, for leaders it is an important moment in which to convey through example what it means to lead with conscious accountability—that is, demonstrating awareness of others and being responsible for your impact. Finally, responding also represents an opportunity to raise morale, commitment, and a sense of ownership in others.

Researchers Shmuel Ellis and Inbar Davidi (2005) found that reviews that celebrate successes in addition to highlighting failures were associated with soldiers' improved subsequent performance. As we have previously discussed, people tend to respond more favorably to positive reinforcement than to punishment. Employee recognition is a powerful motivator that drives engagement and lowers turnover (Wickham 2021). The degree to which a review process allows for celebrating the positives and valuing individual contributions, in addition to framing the negative as an opportunity for change, can help determine people's openness to claiming responsibility and believing that they can actually make improvements. Ideally, there can be a healthy balance that neither glosses over problems nor misses the strengths, conveying all the results and their causes with realism and appreciation.

## How Can We Apply This Learning Next Time?

The last strategy involves answering an important question: Now what? Learning for learning's sake is fine, but for the purpose of conscious accountability, learning has the added importance of directing future action and supporting further commitment to taking that action. The process of making learning actionable starts with focusing on the most important takeaways. It is difficult to make many changes at once, so choose the areas of change that hold the most potential for making the biggest difference.

Start by listing all of the possible actions that flow from the learning points. These actions can be assigned to one of three categories:

- What do we need to continue doing?
- What should we stop doing?
- What should we start doing?

Once the actions have been categorized, decide on the top three that will make the biggest difference both in terms of task performance and relationship development. What changes will be most likely to move the needle in the desired direction? (And what is that desired direction?) Sometimes it is clear, but other times it is not so obvious. Answering these questions might require getting some input from team members and other stakeholders before making a plan for applying what you've learned. And it may also require going back to your intentions and deciding what you want *now*.

## Leadership by Example:
## Wanjiru Mukoma, Turning Crisis Into Opportunity

Wanjiru Mukoma, an organizational leader, researcher, and advocate, spent much of her career working to improve health and well-being in sub-Saharan Africa. For many years, she served as the executive director of LVCT Health, a Kenyan NGO that delivers programs to address HIV prevention and gender-based violence. The organization's mission was to increase access to health services, especially among those segments of the population that often had difficulty accessing services (such as people with disabilities, sexual minorities, and young people). One important donor-funded initiative involved bringing both prevention and curative services closer to the community across many different locations.

Before starting, Wanjiru's team identified particular targets that they needed to reach (such as the number of people served from various segments of the population). They were well into the implementation, and the team thought they were executing the initiative quite competently. "We were considered one of the best organizations in terms of implementing this kind of program," she explained. "Every month we did performance and progress reviews, and everything seemed great because whenever we saw that we weren't doing something well, we immediately put in strategies to rectify that."

But one day the funder conducted a site visit and did their own independent assessments. Much to everyone's shock, Wanjiru and her team were told that there were major gaps and they were grossly underperforming.

"We were caught completely off guard," she recalled. "At first we were in denial, and we initially disputed the findings, because as far as we knew we were doing well. We thought things like, 'This can't be true,' 'They didn't do the right assessment,' and 'Maybe they just don't like us!'—all the emotional things you go through when you are told you are not good enough."

But after the shock wore off, the leadership team decided to investigate what was really going on. After putting people on the ground and auditing what was happening at the implementation sites, they confirmed the funder's findings were right: They were underperforming in multiple areas, with process errors that ranged from honest mistakes to more serious individual and team issues tantamount to gross misconduct.

At that moment, Wanjiru had a crucial insight. She realized she could single out the individuals or teams that were not doing well or frame this as a problem across the entire organization. Ultimately, she determined that the best path forward was to approach this as an organization-wide issue. She needed to get the team to harbor and maintain a positive mentality.

"Within the leadership team, I kept reminding them we cannot get stuck in the mess of blame and negativity," explained Wanjiru. "We have to be the people that pull the team out of apportioning blame. And we do that firstly by taking responsibility ourselves, because this happened under our watch. We also have to take responsibility for providing the leadership to help everyone in the organization move forward. When I addressed the organization, I remember a lot of my language was: 'We are where we are. We are in this together, and we have to get out of it together. We are not going to spend time on who did what, how they did it, or what they ought to have done. That will drain our energy. Let's spend our energy on moving forward.'"

At the same time, behind the scenes, the leaders took disciplinary actions against the individuals who violated company policies. But they didn't bring that discussion to the rest of the organization, because they didn't want anyone who was not being disciplined to think they were not part of the problem or solution.

Next, they developed a strategy for how to turn things around over the remaining three years of the program and went to the donor with a plan that included both short-term and long-term corrective actions. They began tracking and monitoring progress very closely and sharing information on a real-time basis. The leaders started telling teams, "If your site is doing well and the site 20 kilometers away is doing poorly, there is no reason for you to celebrate."

"We are in a country where there's high unemployment, so people want to keep their jobs," Wanjiru explained. "If their jobs are threatened by somebody else's performance, what we saw starting to happen was people started holding each other accountable rather than blaming each other. Instead of saying 'You didn't do ABCD, and you should have done it,' they asked, 'How can we help you?' or 'Can we share with you what we have tried, because we think it is working?' So it started to create that kind of sharing and organization-wide ownership for the problem, including those who were not part of the problem."

As different groups shared in the progress, the positive attitude grew stronger; the more people saw what was being achieved, the better things became.

Wanjiru observed that this process of change was very rough and painful for the organization. "Nobody likes to be told they are a failure, especially when you have been a star performer. But we got through it by making everyone part of the solution." In looking back on this situation, Wanjiru saw it as a major learning point for her as a leader. "I remember very clearly being very distressed about the situation and thinking, 'What do I do?' And then I thought, 'This is the opportunity to create organization-wide cohesiveness. Use this opportunity.'"

In steering LVCT Health through a turbulent time, Wanjiru demonstrated how to claim it. First, she deployed the mindsets of objectivity and acceptance. She sought objective verification about the funder's assessment of the organization's actual performance and then accepted the reality that they were underperforming. In the process, they identified root causes. Rather than apportion blame on select individuals, she encouraged a broader organization-wide ownership and responsibility for performance, starting with the leadership team. She also did not allow ego, fear of reprisal, or the discomfort of the necessary review process derail her commitment to the larger goal: bringing about positive, iterative change for the organization, so that she and her teammates could work together more effectively and provide the care and services their stakeholders required. Finally, Wanjiru helped drive necessary change by building an environment of learning and collective sharing of best practices.

## Exercise: Conduct Your Own Claiming It Process

To help you practice conducting your own review process, we have developed the following exercise. Start by thinking about something you did recently that involved other people that you'd like to figure out how to get better at. In thinking about the situation and how you did, see if you can call forth the mindsets of acceptance and objectivity. Then reflect on the questions in Table 10-1 to generate some important learning for yourself. If you are working in a group or team, you can also present these questions to other team members to get their perspectives as well.

**Table 10-1.** Claiming It Reflection Exercise

| Steps for Claiming It | Task Performance | Relationships, Team and Interpersonal Process |
|---|---|---|
| What were the results (vs. expectations)? | • What was the actual outcome?<br>• What did I want or expect to happen? | • What happened with the other people involved?<br>• What did I think or hope would happen? |
| What caused the results? | • What were the top two factors that drove the outcomes and results? | • What were the top two factors that affected relationships? |
| How can I respond effectively to the results and their causes? | • What actions or changes are needed in response to the results?<br>• Where do I think others may need to own up too? | • What do I need to own up to when I speak with others?<br>• Who do I need to thank, appreciate, or recognize? |
| How could I apply the learning next time? | • What will I sustain?<br>• What will I change? | • What will I sustain?<br>• What will I change? |

## Summary: Steps to Claiming It

As the stories of the Navy SEALs and Wanjiru Mukoma demonstrate, the way that leaders claim it can make a huge difference for how organizations deal with crises and respond to failures.

Claiming it means owning your results and taking full responsibility for what happens, but in a way that generates learning that can be applied to future situations. It is an essential practice for conscious accountability, because accountability at its core is all about being responsible for one's impact and remaining committed to making change when this is necessary.

Claiming it may sound simple, but there are several things that make it hard to do, including not being clear on desired outcomes, low commitment, fear, excessive ego, and overlooking others in the process. But having the mindsets of objectivity and acceptance can make it considerably easier.

Drawing from the concept of AARs, we suggest specific strategies for claiming it, which involve answering four questions:

• What were the actual results (versus the expected results)?

- What caused those results?
- How can we respond effectively to the results and what we learned from them?
- How can we apply this learning next time?

Like every other practice in this book, you can improve at claiming it by setting aside time to reflect and become more aware of learning opportunities that arise from everyday situations around you. This effort can pay enormous dividends and put you in the best possible position for trying again—the final practice of conscious accountability, which we will explore next.

# CHAPTER 10

# Trying Again

*If we want to have a fighting chance at changing everything for the better, it's important we always remember to take care of one another. It's important that we keep showing up, offering solutions, and simply keep trying.*

COREY WHEELAND

People who achieve astounding successes of one kind or another often do so after having failed—sometimes after many, many painful setbacks. One person whose life exemplifies this is Abraham Lincoln. Prior to becoming one of the most renowned presidents in US history, Lincoln suffered numerous defeats, disappointments, and tragedies:

- His mother died when he was nine, and the older sister who subsequently helped raise him died 10 years later.
- His first business endeavor (a general store) was unsuccessful.
- Ann Rutledge, his first serious romantic interest, died of typhoid fever.
- Across his political career, he lost numerous nominations and elections, including for state legislature, House speaker, Congress, Senate, and the nomination for vice president.

- He experienced the loss of two of his four sons—one at age three and the other at age 11.

Lincoln saw the learning value in failure. He once said, "I find quite as much material for a lecture in those points wherein I have failed, as in those wherein I have been moderately successful" (as cited in Basler, Pratt, and Dunlap 1953). In our opinion, Lincoln rose to become an incredible leader, able to claim many accomplishments and successes because, even in the wake of many losses and setbacks, he kept trying. So have many other successful, well-known people who have made notable impacts on the world. To achieve success, one must accept failure as an inevitable part of the deal.

As the co-founder of a digital health startup, Marianne and her colleagues submitted an application to the National Institutes of Health for seed funding to develop and test a new product through a Small Business Innovation Research (SBIR) grant. As you might guess, these grants are highly competitive. The co-founders knew their chances were slim, with only 3-8 percent of submissions receiving funding (Flavin 2018). After spending six months writing the grant and waiting another four months to hear the result, they found out they did not get it. However, they received critiques from the reviewers and an invitation to resubmit. In other words, to try again. Marianne and team set out to do just that.

First, the team had to prepare themselves for going through the whole arduous process again. They took some time away from working on the new proposal to rest and recharge, then they recommitted to resubmitting. Part of this recommitment included sharing why the project was important to each of them. As the product was geared toward helping people with addiction issues, the team shared stories of how addiction had touched their own lives. This more intimate understanding of one another helped strengthen their alignment and firm up their dedication to be part of the solution. Next, the team reviewed the grant critiques with the intention of finding the opportunities for improving the proposal. This enabled them to draft a new proposal with increased clarity, and address the feedback from the reviewers.

Six months later, they were thrilled to hear that they were awarded the grant, which would give them the opportunity to further develop their product. In fact, the new proposal was viewed as so promising that they were also invited to participate in a startup boot camp program to further refine their product and business plan.

As you engage in the practice of exchanging feedback, you can generate some important learning. When you claim it, you begin to consolidate that information and take responsibility for how you can use it in supporting your relationships and results. From these practices you should emerge with a clearer picture of what happened, what went well, what did not go well, and what changes you would like to make. This positions you well to try again. In this chapter, we first consider why trying again is of vital importance and what can impede us from trying again. We then explore why having a growth mindset can enable you to refuel, recommit, and rerun your effort.

## What Is Trying Again and Why Does It Matter?

Trying again is, perhaps, the practice that most fosters growth and excellence, because it requires a full commitment to the lifelong learning journey. It acknowledges that there will be wavering commitments, miscommunications, breakdowns, fumbles, missed opportunities, actions unnoticed, and disappointments along the way. But even in all of these (often difficult) moments, there is potent learning available.

So what does it mean to try again, in the context of conscious accountability? Recall that part of our definition of conscious accountability involves being responsible for your impact. That does not just refer to the impact that occurred from your previous actions, but also means being cognizant of the potential impact of your future actions as well. In this light, trying again means taking new actions that are informed by previous learning from your experience—regardless of whether it is based on success or failure.

The practice of trying again can separate average outcomes from extraordinary ones. Let's look at why it is such a vital practice:

- **Trying again elevates results and drives innovation.** We need to try again to get better results and new solutions. Conscious accountability emphasizes the ongoing practice of continuous improvement, which is not about achieving perfection or avoiding failure, but about generating learning and gradual improvement over time. This kind of learning is not about striving for success once, but rather a developmental process that leads to deeper knowledge, wisdom, and sustained progress. Coming back from failure is a necessary component of this type of growth. Basketball legend Michael Jordan famously intoned in a Nike commercial titled "Failure": "I've missed more than 9,000 shots in my career. I've lost almost 300 games. Twenty-six times, I've been trusted to take the game winning shot and missed. I've failed over and over and over again in my life. And that is why I succeed." Similarly, the great inventor Thomas Edison, who held more than 1,000 patents and developed breakthrough technology including electric power generation, mass communication, sound recording, and motion pictures, clearly believed in the importance of trying again. He was quoted as saying, "I have not failed. I have just generated 10,000 ways that won't work," and "Many of life's failures are people who did not realize how close they were to success when they gave up."

- **Trying again can deepen relationships.** The ability to try again opens the way to repairing, strengthening, and transforming relationships, as opposed to halting or stymieing their development. After studying thousands of romantic relationships, couples researcher John Gottman found that what matters for relationship health and longevity is not what you fight about, but how you come back and repair after tensions flare. Couples that are able to talk about regrettable incidents and past hurts tend to build stronger relationships over time (Gottman 1994). Being willing to try again after interpersonal tensions occur makes these better outcomes possible.

- **Trying again is necessary to solve difficult problems.** Complex, intractable problems, by their very nature, do not get solved right away. Instead, they require multiple successive attempts, over years, decades, or even generations. In our day, these deeply vexing problems are all around us: climate change and environmental threats, disparities in wealth and access to resources, global health threats, systemic racism, and gender-based violence and oppression, to name a few. Many of these issues have deep social, historical, and cultural roots that are not easy to change, and therefore require repeated, persistent efforts. Similarly, there are many factors that complicate human efforts to work effectively together, such as power differentials and differences in culture, personality, and lived experiences. When these factors impede our progress, strain our relationships, and detract from our results, we can feel frustrated and demoralized. Trying again involves possessing the persistence and tenacity to keep coming back to understanding one another with renewed energy and enthusiasm.
- **Trying again builds character, resilience, and grit.** The Japanese proverb "Fall down seven times, stand up eight" captures the idea that although failing repeatedly is unfortunate, it is the getting up that really matters. And the repeated practice of getting up builds muscle around our ability to do it time and time again, whatever life hands to us. If we want to develop the strength to pursue our dreams and have the kind of results and impact that we aspire to, trying again is an essential component of the workout plan for getting there.

## Why Do People Not Try Again?

There are many great reasons to try again, yet many people choose not to. Why not? What stops them? Three of the most common challenges are:

- Painful emotions
- Lack of commitment
- A short-term approach

## Painful Emotions

The experience of a failure—whether it is an academic failure, a business or work-related failure, or a failed relationship—can be devastatingly painful. It is typical for people to feel some measure of disappointment when things go wrong. But we can magnify the pain by how we think about failure. For example, if we overgeneralize the failure, over-personalize it, or dwell on it, failure can make us feel more helpless, less capable, and more fearful of taking risks in the future (Winch 2003). There is also some evidence that experiences of failure impede future performance, perhaps because people are distracted by fears about future failure or because they end up applying less effort (Beaton 2016). If we focus on blaming ourselves for failures, it can make us more self-critical and ashamed.

When we experience things that are intensely painful, we have a natural tendency to want to avoid them (or to make decisions that will minimize the chance of us experiencing that pain again). So, while giving up or moving on is a normal (and understandable) instinct in the face of failure, the cost of doing so may be moving further away from something that we could accomplish if we tried again.

## Diminished Commitment

Sometimes people do not try again because they realize that they are not as committed to whatever they were trying to do in the first place. When David was an undergraduate, he planned to go to medical school to become a psychiatrist. One of the first courses he needed to take was inorganic chemistry. David had struggled through high school chemistry, and college chemistry was even more challenging for him. Despite his best efforts, he earned a C in the course. The following semester, he continued with organic chemistry, which he found equally difficult and even more unpleasant.

One day, after performing poorly on a quiz, he decided to drop the class and pre-med altogether. He realized that he did not enjoy chemistry and, likely, wouldn't enjoy any of the other science courses he would need to take to apply to medical school. He also began to see that what he really wanted—his true goal—was not to be a medical doctor, but to be able to help other people with their problems. David realized that becoming a clinical psychologist was an equally viable path toward that goal, and so he made the choice to pivot and move on. When people choose not to try again, it might be because what they are most deeply committed to and the goals they had been pursuing are not entirely aligned.

## Shorter-Term Approach

Sometimes people do not try again because they are working under short-term constraints. Under these circumstances, there is a greater emphasis on quick wins than longer-term learning or solutions. For example, when faced with loss or failure, some might change strategy and move on to a different project right away, not wanting to invest the time and effort it takes to really learn about how something (or someone) works.

Another example is a venture capital-backed organization in which the principals were focused on getting acquired by a larger company within the next three years. They produced great financial results on paper, but their turnover rate for entry-level positions was high, and their employee engagement scores were rather low. The organization made some initial efforts to improve this situation, by giving a slight increase in wages and adding some benefits, but turnover and engagement remained problematic. Rather than try once more to improve the employee situation, they instead decided to forge ahead, maintain profitability, and focus on their exit strategy with less attention to raising employee satisfaction.

There is a bit of a paradox here that is worth mentioning. On the one hand, trying again can be seen as an indicator of resilience and perseverance that is needed for achieving goals and other things of significance. However, not trying again does not have to be a sign of weakness or lack of resilience. The decision not to try again can also be understood as a valid choice, informed by your own experience, self-knowledge, and a realistic assessment of what you are willing and able to do in a given situation. Making the intentional choice not to try again can become a pivot to trying something else or could be a result of having learned something important from past experience.

For example, after being bitten by the entrepreneurial bug, Marianne started the journey of creating a tech startup to improve women's health by using a fitness-tracker bracelet that incorporated behavioral psychology techniques to motivate them to walk. She created a prototype through crowd-funding, won an award, participated in a startup incubator, pitched at events, and met with investors. It was a challenging, inspiring roller-coaster ride, and she eventually found herself at a crossroads: Try again to secure funding or pivot? Major companies were also launching wearable health products, and the Apple Watch has just been announced. These were formidable competitors, and Marianne wanted to be realistic about her chances of success. After conversations with her partner, advisors, and peers, she made the painful decision to pivot instead of seeking more investments. Full of uncertainty, struggling with embarrassment, and laden with guilt for letting her supporters down, little did she know that this pivot would put her on the path of a different digital health startup that would lead to the successful grant funding you read about at the beginning of this chapter.

From a conscious accountability standpoint, when trying (or not trying) again comes as a result of conscious awareness and choice (as opposed to something that is reactive, impulsive, or automatic), it is a productive way to move forward in greater alignment with what you want and who you are.

## Key Mindset: Growth Mindset

In order to try again, we suggest cultivating a growth mindset, an idea developed by Stanford psychologist Carol Dweck, who has also studied implicit theories of intelligence (or how people think about where their ability comes from). In researching children's learning, Dweck observed an interesting range in how people think about themselves and their learning process. On one end of the spectrum were kids who held a fixed mindset. They viewed intelligence and ability as static traits; you only have a set amount that does not change. Fixed mindsets also entail a greater desire to look smart, avoid challenges, give up more easily in the face of obstacles, view effort as useless, and reject negative feedback. On the other end of the spectrum were kids who had a growth mindset. They believed intelligence and ability could be developed, and therefore focused less on looking smart and more on learning. These children tended to embrace challenges, persisted in the face of obstacles, viewed effort as the path to improvement and mastery, and used criticism as a learning opportunity (Dweck 2006).

Fixed and growth mindsets also have relevance for how we think about our relationships. For example, if you are having problems with your colleague Jack, a fixed mindset understanding of this might sound like, "I'll never be able to get along with Jack at work." Contrast that with a growth mindset about the relationship: "I haven't gotten along very well with Jack so far, but I'm committed to figuring out how to develop a stronger relationship with him." Growth and fixed mindsets can also influence how teams realize their potential. When team members believe in the possibility of improving their collaboration, they may be more willing to stick together as they navigate challenges. This stands in contrast to the sense of deflation that could result from seeing team dynamics as binary and immutable (either good or bad).

Fixed and growth mindsets are not static themselves but are dynamic and changeable. You might have a fixed mindset about one area of your life (like your mathematical ability) and a growth mindset about your relationship skills. Or you might start off having a fixed mindset about something but be able to shift into a growth mindset.

For example, Kerry is a management consultant who was working with a sales team to help them improve their results. After a group meeting that she believed went quite well, she received an email from the team leader telling her that she missed the mark in a few ways. Initially, she was very upset by the email, and even felt like firing the client. She thought things like, "If they can't appreciate the value of what I am contributing, maybe it's not a good fit." But after talking with her coach about it the next day, she was able to shift to more of a growth mindset. Rather than feeling threatened by the feedback, she became curious about it and replied to the team leader, asking for some clarification about his comments. She was able to see that the points he raised were valid and things that she could consider modifying for next time. In her next meeting with the team, Kerry adapted her plan based on the feedback. Not only were the results better, but the team leader was appreciative of how flexibly she adjusted her approach.

As you consider whether to try again and set out to do so, checking your mindset and seeing whether there is an opportunity to view things from more of a growth perspective can make a huge difference. One of the easiest ways to do this, advocates Carol Dweck, is by simply incorporating the word *yet* into your language. In Kerry's case, this would include reframing feedback as, "I have not hit the mark, yet."

## 3 Strategies for Trying Again

Holding a growth mindset about your ability to engage your work relation-ships, tasks, and other aspects of your life is a terrific start for building a practice of trying again. Next, we suggest three practical strategies for mov-ing past the obstacles and getting into action on trying again:

- Refuel.
- Recommit.
- Rerun the experiment.

### Refuel

Before you are ready to try again, you may need to take some time to put gas back in your tank. Whatever it was that you just did likely required sus-tained energy and effort over time, which can leave you feeling physically, mentally, emotionally, or spiritually depleted. And, if you have experienced some degree of failure, you may need some extra measures to help you move through the thoughts and feelings that are getting you down.

Here are some different ways to refuel:

- **Ensure you are getting enough sleep.** Sleep loss is related to reduced focus, increased errors, slower reaction times, and greater likelihood of feeling irritability and reacting with anger (Newsom 2021).
- **Eat healthy food.** Adequate nutrition is needed to optimize your brain's functioning, and undernourishment can negatively affect efficiency and performance (Stahl 2019).
- **Do things that bring you joy.** When you are feeling emotionally depleted, allowing yourself time to do things that feel good and make you happy can help you recover.
- **Connect with people who lift you up.** If you are down on yourself because things did not turn out as you hoped, surrounding yourself with people who love and support you—rain or shine—can remind you of who you are, regardless of disappointing circumstances.
- **Allow yourself some mental downtime.** Give your brain a chance to relax and operate along different wavelengths. Some people refuel by disconnecting and being alone, others by listening to music or being social. You know yourself best, so do whatever helps you refuel; there is no one way to do it.

## Recommit

Another important component of trying again involves recommitting yourself to whatever you are trying to do, or whomever you are doing it with. This means getting connected (or perhaps reconnected) to the core motives for your activities and relationships. In the process of recommitting, you may wish to ask yourself some of these questions:

- What are the reasons why I might try again? (List as many as possible). Of all these reasons, which ones are the most compelling?
- What are the reasons why I might *not* try again? How do these compare to my reasons to try again?
- If I did not try again, how would I feel about that in the future? What, if anything, would cause me to feel regret? What, if anything, would cause me to feel relief?

- Why might I do this *at this time*? What is important to me now?
- How does trying again align with my values?
- If or when I try again . . .
  - What do I want to commit to doing?
  - What do I want to commit to not doing?
  - What do I want to stand for?

If you are trying again with a group or team, variants of these questions can be the source of group reflection and discussions, which can help get the team recommitted and realigned in a common purpose. After you have renewed your sense of purpose and commitment, you are ready to move to the last strategy for trying again: rerunning the experiment.

## Rerun the Experiment

Framing what you are doing as an experiment allows you to approach it with a sense of curiosity and possibility. Imagine yourself as a scientist, pushing the boundaries of what you can learn (and what knowledge you can generate) through multiple attempts and iterations. This approach means having the willingness to be surprised, to look at things from a different angle, and to discover new outcomes that you did not expect. It also invites you to create intentions for your experimentation:

- What do I want to do differently?
- What previous learning do I want to expand on or deepen this round?
- What new idea or approach do I want to road test?
- What do I hope to learn from success?
- What can I learn from failure?

These questions can be adapted for use with groups and teams as well. Here are some other questions teams can use to guide their reflection and preparation:

- Based on our previous experiences together, what have we learned about our teamwork (both in terms of the process and outcomes of how we work together)?

- In this next endeavor (or next sprint, cycle, project, quarter, and so forth), what do we want to make sure we do? What do we want to make sure we do not do?
- Where do we want to direct the focus of our learning together in this next go-around?

This process of deliberation before you rerun the experiment brings the cycle of conscious accountability full circle, as it brings you back to the first practice of creating clarity around your intentions.

## Leadership by Example:
## Simidele Adeagbo, Trailblazing Olympian

Simidele Adeagbo made Olympic history at the 2018 Winter Games, becoming the first Nigerian Winter Olympian and the first African and Black woman to compete in skeleton at the Olympics. But her inspiring journey to becoming an Olympian was not easy, and along the way she developed an incredible capacity to try again.

Simi had tried out twice for the Summer Olympics in triple jump but was just inches short of qualifying. "The second time was particularly heartbreaking because I felt that I had dedicated everything to becoming an Olympian," she recounted. "I relocated and I was training six to eight hours per day with the world's best coaches at the Olympic training center. I dedicated my life to triple jump and that goal, so it was devastating when I didn't make it. That could have been the end of my Olympic dream."

But the dream persisted, and subsequently she had the opportunity to try out for the Nigerian bobsled team, which is when she was introduced to skeleton. "My goal was always to be a Summer Olympian, but why not try again in a way that looks very different from what I thought it would look like?" she said. "I was open to that and took decisive action and said 'I am going to try this and see what happens.'" A hundred days later, Simi qualified for the Winter Olympics.

When we spoke with Simi, she was in the midst of trying again—this time to qualify for her second Winter Olympics. An important part of her trying again was reconnecting to her sense of purpose, and interestingly, she discovered that her core purpose had changed since her first time in the Olympics. When she first qualified for skeleton, in addition to pursuing her Olympic dream, she found deep meaning in the idea of helping people see Nigeria and Africa differently. "The idea that somebody that comes from Nigeria could be at the Winter Olympics for the first time ever," she explained, "that was something that helped me get up every day in cold climates and hurl myself headfirst down an icy hill at 80 miles per hour."

But in trying for her second Winter Olympics, she discovered that her sense of purpose had shifted. Although the idea of changing the narrative about Africa was still important to her, this time she knew she wanted to unlock her full potential as an athlete. "The sport I do is so extreme and crazy," she explained. "There are so many reasons not to do it: It's cold, it's expensive, you crash at high speeds, you sustain concussions, and it can be life threatening. But when I am clear on my why, it gives me all the reasons I need to try again."

Simi shared that as she trains, trying again has become almost a daily practice for her. While training on a particularly challenging track in Germany, she attempted about 24 different runs in the span of two weeks and crashed on 60 percent of those runs. The people there started calling her "crash girl." Simi recalled, "It could have been really discouraging. But I had a very clear goal. I needed to just complete a race as part of the qualification process for the Olympics. So even though I was crashing, each time I crashed it came with learning—even if the learning was small, I took it and kept building. And eventually I completed the race and even came in ahead of another person." Simi concluded by noting that trying again is not linear and it is not always pretty, but it will lead to progress when you continue to show up and do your part.

Simi's story contains some powerful lessons about trying again. First, trying again does not mean doing the exact same thing over again. Sometimes the way you try again to reach a goal or aspiration may take a different form from what you previously envisioned. And that's OK. What you have learned in the past will inform what you try again, how you try again, and with whom you try again. You may also find that your deeper reasons for trying again have shifted. Second, each time you try again presents a valuable learning opportunity and a source of incremental progress—whatever the result. And third, trying again can be hard, painful, and there is not always a linear relationship between trying again and visible progress. But having the fortitude to try again will pay off if you keep learning and stay with it.

## Exercise: Run a 3-Day Experiment of Trying Again

Choose something you are working on and want to get better at. Here are some examples:

- Making healthier food choices
- Being kinder to and less critical of yourself
- Meditating and being more self-aware
- Being a better listener to your friends
- Communicating more clearly with your team members
- Limiting when you use your cell phone
- Being more present and patient with those close to you

The purpose of this experiment is to practice trying again within the framework of conscious accountability. You will be engaging the part of you that is "doing" and the part of you that is "observing."

The observer part is particularly important. As the preeminent educational scholar and philosopher John Dewey famously said, "We do not learn from experience . . . we learn from reflecting on experience." It is easy to get swept up in repeatedly doing, and in fact we often think of trying again as simply meaning doing it again. Here, we are emphasizing a more conscious, intentional approach to trying again with the deliberate act of observing and reflecting on the process.

In this framework, there are two main components to trying again:

- Taking new action that is informed by your previous experience
- Observing your experience around trying again.

Start by listing the behavior you are working on and writing down the daily goal you have for that behavior. Next, write down why getting better at this behavior is important to you. This is critical because it represents your commitment to the behavior change you are working to bring about or strengthen.

## Day 1

Ask yourself these questions as you reflect on day 1 of doing:

- What did you do?
- On a scale of one (did not meet my goal) to 10 (fully met my goal), how would you rate how you did?
- What about that worked well and what could be improved?
- Note how you are feeling overall about your first effort.
- What modifications would you like to make tomorrow (if any)?

## Day 2

This is your first opportunity to try again. Ask yourself these questions as you prepare for day 2:

- How are you feeling about trying again today? If you need a motivational boost, revisit your reasons for why this behavior is important to you.
- What actions did you take as part of trying again?
- On a scale of one (did not meet my goal) to 10 (fully met my goal), how would you rate how you did?
- What about that worked well and what could be improved?
- Note how you are feeling overall about your second effort.
- What modifications would you like to make tomorrow (if any)?

## Day 3

Here is your second chance to practice trying again. Ask yourself these questions as you prepare for day 3:

- How are you feeling about trying again today? If you need a motivational boost, revisit your reasons for why this behavior is important to you.

- What actions did you take as part of trying again?
- On a scale of one (did not meet my goal) to 10 (fully met my goal), how would you rate how you did?
- What about that worked well and what could be improved?
- Note how you are feeling overall about your third effort.
- What modifications would you like to make in the future (if any)?

**Reflection Questions**

Ask yourself these questions to reflect on your three-day experiment and what you learned:
- What did you observe about how it felt to try again?
- What thoughts or actions helped keep you motivated to try again?
- If you experienced frustration or disappointment, how did you manage that?
- How, in the future, would you like to approach your practice of trying again?

## Summary: Coming Full Circle by Trying Again

Throughout the practice of conscious accountability, there is powerful learning available. In this chapter, we explored what it means to try again: taking new actions that are informed by what you learned from previous experience, regardless of whether it is based on success or failure. Trying again is important for conscious accountability, because it helps us be responsible for generating the impact that we want to have going forward: deeper relationships, elevated results, and movement toward solving difficult problems. However, we do not always try again for a number of different reasons, including the emotional pain of confronting failure, diminished commitment to the goal, or having a more short-term outlook. As in the case of Simidele Adeago's extraordinary Olympic journeys, trying again is not always what you think it will be, and it is not easy, but it does yield progress.

To engage in the practice of trying again, a growth mindset is extremely valuable. Three strategies to try again involve refueling yourself, recommitting to your goal, and rerunning the experiment with a fresh perspective and an eye toward what can be learned this time around. Thus, trying again brings the cycle of accountability full circle, as it brings you and those you work with back to the beginning of creating clarity about your intentions.

Next, in part 3, we will bring it all together and offer some ideas for implementing conscious accountability.

# PART 3
## Implementing Conscious Accountability in Real Time

# CHAPTER 11

# Putting It All Together

> *As you start to walk on the way, the way appears.*
>
> RUMI

As you are nearing the end of this book, we hope you feel like you are at the beginning of a bright new future of accountability. When humans reimagine traditional approaches to the ways we have always done or thought of things, incredible possibilities open up.

Marianne had a watershed moment when she first heard the term *social entrepreneurship*, while listening to a talk given by Jessica Jackley, the founder of Kiva, the world's first person-to-person microlending website. Kiva successfully reimagined the way lending and charity has always been done to create an inclusive financial world where everyone can access life-changing loans. Kiva crowdfunds loans from lenders in small increments to people who are financially excluded or are making a social impact in their communities. Repayments can then be recycled back into the system to fund new loans. At the time of this writing, Kiva had lent $1.6 billion to mostly women (81 percent) across 71 countries, with a repayment rate of approximately 97 percent.

Hearing Jessica share the origin story of Kiva enabled Marianne to realize she had been having a failure of imagination about how to have a positive impact in the world. The aha moment was becoming aware of businesses—social enterprises—that existed with a double bottom line of both profit and social impact. People were working hard using market forces to help solve pressing social issues.

This opened up a whole new world to Marianne about how she might find meaningful work and create a positive impact. It was also the beginning of her expansion from the world of clinical psychology into business psychology.

In much the same way that social enterprises have a double bottom line, we hope you see that accountability too can have a double bottom line. We no longer have to envision accountability as focused on the single outcome of results. Rather, we can add a second bottom line of interpersonal relationships. We have the opportunity to use the activity of work to help us connect and deepen relationships. And we can elevate our results by leveraging our relationships. We believe the CONNECT framework and its seven practices are a tool that can help you achieve this goal. This section will provide strategies for how you might implement the practices in real time, tips on how to press through challenges, and encouragement to settle into a vitality-giving adventure.

Throughout this book, our intention has been to provide you with a variety of mindsets, behaviors, and tools that can greatly enhance how you work with others and improve the quality of results that you can generate through these partnerships. Figure 11-1 recaps the mindsets and behaviors of the seven practices, first introduced through the CONNECT model presented in chapter 3 and elaborated throughout part 2.

Together, these seven CONNECT practices create a comprehensive and robust approach to enhancing accountability into a transformational practice that builds connections and improves outcomes. At its core, conscious accountability is a sophisticated practice of harnessing personal responsibility, a growth mindset, and a huge amount of open, authentic communication to unleash dynamic interdependence and teamwork. And just like any practice, the more we flex our muscles and keep at it, the more adept we become.

**Figure 11-1.** Summary of the CONNECT Model of Conscious Accountability

| Practice | Mindsets | Strategies |
|---|---|---|
| Creating Clarity | Humility and Patience | • Clarify your intention.<br>• Consider your audience.<br>• Communicate the message.<br>• Check for understanding. |
| Opening Up Engagement | All In | • Align values.<br>• Honor individual needs.<br>• Model vulnerable learning.<br>• Be inclusive. |
| Nailing It | Grit and Grace | • Activate knowledge of self and others.<br>• Organize for task completion.<br>• Stay together. |
| Noticing | Compassionate Curiosity | • Prepare.<br>• Be aware.<br>• Share. |
| Exchanging Feedback | Courage | • Connect to your intentions.<br>• Make it safer.<br>• Prepare.<br>• Listen actively and seek information.<br>• Manage emotions and resistance.<br>• Express gratitude.<br>• Make a follow-up plan. |
| Claiming It | Objectivity and Acceptance | • Identify what the actual results were. (versus the expected results).<br>• Determine the root cause of the results.<br>• Respond to the results and what was learned from them.<br>• Consider how to apply this learning next time. |
| Trying Again | Growth | • Refuel.<br>• Recommit.<br>• Rerun the experiment. |

## How to Implement

So, how would *you* like to use all that you have learned through reading this book? As you begin to implement the CONNECT practices, what will work best for you, your relationships, your teams, or your organization? Here we outline three possible approaches:

- Focus on a single relationship.
- Concentrate on a single practice
- Take a more comprehensive approach using the whole model.

Of course, you can also choose a middle-ground approach and land on whatever number of practices you would like to use. Choose the approach that will best foster your own learning and development.

Whichever options you try, it is helpful to frame your attempts to implement the practices of conscious accountability as an experiment with the aim of generating data. This data is then useful in formulating your subsequent attempts. With this perspective—similar to what we have endorsed in the try again practice of the CONNECT model—all outcomes are positive in that they hold the power to promote your learning and growth. It may be tempting to view attempts that did not pan out as you hoped as failures. However, analyzing this type of process in a simple binary way (pass or fail) leaves rich information on the table and can be demotivating.

Instead, we advocate for more of an experiential learning approach in which the learning happens continuously by doing and is not strictly judged by whether the intended outcome was achieved (Kolb 1984). It can be boiled down to three simple steps: *do, reflect, apply*. *Do*, in this case, is picking a practice to try, deciding on a strategy, and taking an action. *Reflect* happens after you have taken the action and involves thinking about what happened and identifying the critical points of learning—the aha moments. *Apply* comes next, and this entails using such moments to refine the next experiment (the next "do"). As you can see, there is no predetermined end to this type of learning, no pressure to arrive at a specific level of mastery. Rather, this approach opens up a path for continuous lifelong development.

## Try It With a Single Relationship or Stakeholder

The first way to implement the model is to consider which relationships in your life might benefit from a higher level of conscious accountability. Start by making a list of some of the people in your life who matter to you, or the ones whom you need to rely on the most to get things done. This could include your boss, your partner, a direct report, a friend, or a teammate. Then for each person you list, write down the most important expectations you have of this person, and what expectations you believe that they have of you.

Next, think about these key questions, and rate your answers on a scale of one to 10 (one is lowest and 10 is highest):

- To what degree have I been accountable to meeting this person's expectations of me?
- To what degree have I held this person accountable for meeting my expectations?
- How satisfied am I with the overall level of accountability in our relationship?
- How important is this relationship to me?

From there, you can choose a relationship to work on building better accountability—for example, one that is very important to you and where accountability needs attention. Once you identify the person with whom you want to improve accountability, you can go on to explore which practice or practices—if improved—would make the biggest difference for accountability in your relationship. You can focus on a single practice, multiple practices, or the whole model. It is up to you. But in the spirit of conscious accountability being a shared endeavor, we suggest that you have a conversation with the other person to share your thoughts and enlist them in identifying what is going well with regard to conscious accountability, as well as how it might be improved.

## Try a Single Practice

Another way to start using these practices is to ask yourself a simple set of questions, beginning with, "What might be my next step to implement conscious accountability?" The good news is that you do not have to try everything all at once. Plus, there is no prescribed order in which to apply the practices. So you can test the waters with the practice of your choosing.

To pick which practice and potential plan, you might find it helpful to reflect on the questions we pose when we present this model in workshops. We ask participants to think about these three key questions:

- Which practice holds the most room for improvement at present?
- What are two possible strategies you could use to address this area?
- What is one action you are willing to commit to in order to improve your practice of conscious accountability?

These questions allow you to ascertain, on an individual level, the areas in which you would like to improve, and they encourage you to make a plan for doing so. Use them when first introducing the model to a team, or at various moments in the team's development. You may find that an individual's sense of their strengths in one area of the model may change over time or as they interact with different people or stakeholders. Another option is to reflect on other dimensions that you find more motivating, such as:

- Which practice would be the most fun to try next?
- Which practice would be the easiest for me to try next?
- Which practice do I find most interesting?
- Which practice would have the most impact at work or in my life?

## Try the Whole Model

It is also possible to implement the conscious accountability model using a more comprehensive approach that includes all of the practices. To assist you, we have put together a Conscious Accountability Action Guide (Table 11-2). This guide provides some suggested prompts to help think through how you might experiment with conscious accountability. We hope it will open up some possibilities for how you use this framework in your particular context. It is by no means a strict road map. Think of it as a way to spark your own process and modify it as you see fit. The road map consists of two sections: an action plan and an action review. You can use this template for yourself and for your team.

**Table 11-2.** Conscious Accountability Action Guide

| Action Plan | | Action Review | |
|---|---|---|---|
| **Goal** | **Options** | **What Happened?** | **Performance** |
| • What do I/we want to happen by using this practice? <br> • Why is this important to me/us? | • Looking at the mindsets and key behaviors of [*insert practice*], how might I/we try to put this practice in place? <br> • Who can help me/us? | • How did I/we try to [*insert practice*]? | • How well did I/we adhere to the mindsets and behaviors of [*insert practice*]? <br> • What was the impact? |
| **Expectations** | **Commitments** | **Learning** | **Next Time** |
| • How do I/we think this will go? <br> • What do I think will go well? What challenges am I anticipating? <br> • What is my/our plan to address the challenges? | • What is one action I/we will commit to do? <br> • What do I/we commit to not doing? | • What did I/we learn? <br> • What may I/we have missed in my/our efforts? <br> • What am I aware of now that I was not aware of before? [*Fill in the blanks: I used to think _____, now I think _____.*] | • How can I/we improve my/our efforts to [*insert practice*] going forward? |

*Use this space to answer each question in the action guide.*

| | | Action Plan | Action Review |
|---|---|---|---|
| C | Creating Clarity | | |
| O | Opening Up Engagement | | |
| N | Nailing It | | |
| N | Noticing | | |
| E | Exchanging Feedback | | |
| C | Claiming It | | |
| T | Trying Again | | |

The action plan provides questions for you to reflect upon when planning your implementation of conscious accountability. The template will help you create deliberate intentions for attempting this approach and help you delineate why that specific practice is important to you and your team. It will also help you be proactive about potential obstacles, identify people who can support you, and specify your next step.

There are four parts to the action plan:

- **Goal** is about establishing the outcome you want to attain by implementing this practice. The idea here is to home in on the results you hope to achieve in the specific situation where you are applying conscious accountability and why those results are important.
- **Options** allows you to brainstorm potential actions you might take to implement the practice.
- **Expectations** encourages you to be proactive by anticipating what will be the easier pieces and what roadblocks may emerge.
- **Commitments** is where you decide specifically on your next action step. This piece is best actualized by including both an action you will take and actions you will not take because they may hinder or sabotage your goal.

The action review, which reviews adherence to the mindsets and behaviors of conscious accountability, calls your attention to the areas where you are doing well and to those that could benefit from a bit more investment of your time and energy. It also consists of four parts:

- **What happened** is an opportunity to review the facts of what unfolded and the attempts that were made at implementing the practice.
- **Performance** is when you can review how well you did at fulfilling your intentions of the action plan and the impact your behavior had on yourself, others, and the work.
- **Learning** involves uncovering insights gained and opportunities missed.
- **Next time** is where you can synthesize the information from the other three components to help plan your next attempt.

To conduct an action review, reflect upon and answer the prompts for each of the components.

As an example, let's consider the first practice, creating clarity. The purpose of this practice is to establish clear, mutually held goals and expectations of yourself and others on a given project. As we reviewed in chapter 4, there are a number of different behaviors (for example, considering your audience) and mindsets (such as humility) that you can adopt to optimize your capacity to be clear. Our aim in the Conscious Accountability Action Guide is to see how well each person adopted these behaviors and mindsets, to what degree clarity was achieved, and how clarity could be made even more complete in our next iteration of teamwork. Questions intended to help with this analysis, as well as with the evaluation of adherence to the other six practices of the conscious accountability model, are presented in the action guide.

## Summary: Implementing the Practices of Conscious Accountability

Having learned about each of the seven practices in the CONNECT framework, you are now ready to begin to implement conscious accountability. There are a number of ways you can do this: You can focus on a single relationship, you can take on a single practice, or you can implement the full model. There is no right or wrong way to go. You are fully in the driver's seat for which practices you try, and in what aspects of your life you try them. And you get to set the pace for your efforts and monitor your own progress. Whichever way you try to implement conscious accountability, we invite you to practice using an experiential learning framework. That means creating an intention for your practice, trying some new mindsets and behaviors, observing how that works for you, noting your learning, and then allowing that learning to inform your future efforts to practice. Be aware that this might not go perfectly, and that is to be expected. In chapter 12, we describe a few of the challenges you might run into and how to approach them.

# Challenges to Implementation

*There are no great people in this world, only great*
*challenges that ordinary people rise to meet.*

WILLIAM FREDERICK HELSEY JR.

Our aspiration in this book was to rethink accountability in a way that would promote growth, risk taking, creativity, and meaning to unleash results we may have never dreamed attainable. We know that humans at their deepest core are social and emotional beings and that our drive to connect is operating constantly, whether we are aware of it or not. We believe that by bringing this drive front and center, by honoring how central relationships are for how we behave, feel, and engage, we can acknowledge the importance of interpersonal connections and then leverage these to make accountability safer and more collaborative.

So then, why can this feel so dang hard? While frameworks can be extremely useful for helping formulate our approaches to working with complexity, no model can account for everything. Actualizing these practices is not always easy, even on a good day under "normal" circumstances. And even during times when you believe you are implementing all seven practices, the desired outcomes are not always evident.

There may be circumstances or forces operating that make practicing conscious accountability more nuanced and challenging. These can include effectively harnessing diversity in the workplace, navigating remote work arrangements, and building the right organizational culture, all of which add a level of complexity that influences your attempts at implementing the practices of conscious accountability. In this chapter, we discuss each of these challenges and offer some suggestions about how to tackle them. And finally, we will share a process to uncover what is going on when conscious accountability efforts get stuck or stalled.

## Harnessing Diversity

It is not unusual to be drawn to people who think and behave as you do. Most humans do not naturally organize in a diverse way; in fact, the opposite is true. Social scientists and other scholars refer to this as *affinity bias*—an unconscious preference for people who we perceive as similar to ourselves (Russell, Brock, and Rudisill 2019). Therefore, many people end up surrounding themselves with people who look and act like they do. This may feel more comfortable and easy, but it can also result in individuals, groups, or organizations getting stuck in their ways of thinking and behaving, failing to be innovative, and having more sizable areas of unawareness.

In the healthcare space, greater racial and ethnic workforce diversity is associated with enhanced access to care and satisfaction with clinical encounters among patients from minority backgrounds (Institutes of Medicine 2004). The presence of diversity can also have a positive impact on group and organizational performance in the business world. Professor of sociology and public policy Cedric Herring (2009) found that racial and gender diversity was positively associated with a number of indicators of financial performance, including increased sales revenue, more customers, greater market share, and greater relative profits. Similarly, Deloitte (2013) reported higher profitability for gender diverse and ethnically diverse teams and ethnically diverse boards. McKinsey (2018) found that gender diverse and racially diverse executive teams outperform their less diverse counterparts by 21 percent and 33 percent, respectively. However, the mere presence of diversity does not guarantee better results. Some literature reviews suggest the evidence is "mixed," with diversity also leading to increased conflict and communication problems (Jayne and Dipboye 2004).

Let's review several situations that illustrate the challenges in implementing different conscious accountability practices when there are issues of human diversity in play:

- **Creating clarity.** The Parent Teacher Association (PTA) of an urban K-8 school has nine positions, which are held a parent representative from each grade. The group is highly diverse by race, ethnicity, gender, family type, socioeconomic status, and religion. The PTA president is concerned about how to get this group to work together harmoniously. How can she help co-create clear shared goals, expectations, and working norms for a group that may have many different needs, values, motives, and concerns?

- **Opening up engagement and exchanging feedback.** Samantha is the corporate counsel for a large electrical engineering firm, and the only woman on the executive team. She believes that the firm is cutting some corners for the sake of efficiency, which may be putting them at greater risk. But when she expresses her views, they are frequently downplayed; she gets the sense that she is being perceived as too negative or overly cautious. She begins to worry that an implicit gender bias may be operating in the way the team sees and relates to her. How can the electrical engineering firm's executive team create more psychological safety in the way they interact, so Samantha feels less self-conscious about giving important feedback?

- **Nailing it.** The leadership team of a family-owned manufacturing firm has eight members—six are family employees who have never worked anywhere else and two are longtime nonfamily employees. The team is very agreeable, but they are all concerned about the fact that profitability has flatlined over the past three years. How can this leadership team create the most value for their company, when their ways of thinking may be limited in ways they cannot even see?

- **Noticing.** The board of a community health center is composed mainly of upper middle-class white men and women, while the center's client base is primarily people of color from low-income backgrounds. This pattern is mirrored in the clinical and administrative staff: Most of the higher-power positions are occupied by older white men, while the paraprofessionals and aides are mainly younger women of color. How can the board fully serve their organization when they may not be attuned to the structural issues that are affecting access to seats of power and influence for people of color?

- **Claiming it.** Reverend Harper is the pastor of a Christian church in a rural area on the outskirts of a small town. Over the past six months, three or four people who attended a few services stopped coming because "they didn't feel comfortable" or thought it was not a good fit for them. Reverend Harper suspects that all the people who left identified as LGBTQIA+. When Revered Harper asked the head of the parish council about this pattern, she seemed unconcerned. How can Reverend Harper take responsibility for the ways he has (perhaps inadvertently) contributed to the culture of this congregation that is inhospitable to LGBTQIA+ people?

The presence or absence of diversity in groups and organizations can bring with it challenges that make conscious accountability more difficult to practice and, therefore, to fully realize. Next, we will explore possible strategies to use in situations in which there is too little diversity, and in situations where there is considerable diversity.

## Dealing With Low Diversity

Groups or organizations with lower levels of diversity in certain demographic areas or social identities might struggle on their journey to become aware of this state of affairs and address the structural reasons behind it. Here are some ideas about how to begin to change that.

### Listen to Underrepresented Minorities

Leadership expert Heidi Brooks (2020) explains the connection between organizational dynamics and the experiences of employees from underrepresented groups: "The power and dynamics of the organization and culture often show earliest at the margins, with people who are least protected and buffered in the organizational system. Which is often underrepresented minorities—which in many organizations includes women of all ethnicities. It's not that those populations have unique problems, exactly. It's that they are the place . . . where you see the largest disparities. So one of the ways that you can understand organizational dynamics is actually to look and see what's happening with underrepresented people."

The perspectives underrepresented people share can raise awareness about opportunities for improving conditions in the organization more broadly, as well as ways to attract and retain talent from underrepresented groups. However, organizations and leaders should not place an undue burden on their minority groups to have all the answers.

### Obtain High-Level Support by Linking Diversity to Strategy

Too often, efforts to increase diversity are viewed as a human resources issue, and therefore do not get robust attention from all senior leaders. Such efforts are more likely to be successful if they have full support and authentic participation from the top of the organization. This signals to the organization the importance of diversity-related initiatives.

In helping people at the top appreciate the value of diversity for the organization, it is important to articulate the ways that having a diverse leadership team connects to the organization's strategy. This means deep reflection about "diversity for the sake of what?" Or specifically, what kind of diversity is needed, and how exactly will that further the objectives of the organization? This thought exercise is also a good practice when forming teams: What mix of technical skills, teaming skills, experiences, perspectives, and areas of expertise are needed for this team to fully meet its objectives?

### Conduct an Opportunity Audit

Take a step back and review the organization, paying attention to the challenges and opportunities that exist for improving possibilities for underrepresented groups. This could mean re-examining recruiting practices and talent pipelines, changing candidate screening and hiring practices, providing clear opportunities for mentorship and sponsorship, or helping underrepresented employees broaden their networks. It may also be useful to provide opportunities for members of majority groups to educate themselves about the histories and experiences of underrepresented groups so they can be more aware of how their behaviors at work could have a positive (or negative) impact.

Another option could be providing inclusion coaching, which helps grow awareness around how unconscious biases and privilege can inhibit the development of an inclusive workplace. By enhancing everyone's understanding of behaviors and actions, we can more fully open the door to greater collaboration and commitment to inclusion across the organization (Harris 2019).

## Optimizing High Diversity

As groups, teams, and organizations become more diverse, here are some ideas for increasing the likelihood that diversity will have a positive effect on performance.

### Promote Equity and Inclusion

Diversity encompasses all the ways people are different from one another and includes:

- **Separation diversity**—within-group differences along a horizontal axis, like opinions, time zones, or locations

- **Variety diversity**—categorical group differences like gender, race, sexual orientation, or type of expertise
- **Disparity diversity**—within group differences along a vertical axis, like power, status, or pay (Harrison and Klein 2007).

But diversity without equity and inclusion is unlikely to yield positive results. *Equity* refers to the fair treatment, access, opportunity, and advancement for all people, while acknowledging that not everyone is starting from the same point. *Inclusion* goes beyond differences to describe an environment in which any individual or group feels welcomed, respected, and valued. Verna Myers (2012), an inclusion strategist and thought leader, put it simply: "Diversity is being asked to the party. Inclusion is being asked to dance." In other words, it is not enough to have a diverse workforce—what is needed is a diverse workforce that receives equitable opportunities and feels fully included in the life of the organization.

## Learn to Embrace Discomfort

The presence of diversity means there are likely to be lots of different ideas and perspectives in the mix. That is a good thing for creating better products, services, and results. A number of studies show that, compared to homogeneous teams, diverse teams are more successful—in part because they focus more on facts and process the facts more carefully, making fewer factual errors (Rock and Grant 2016). However, diverse groups often feel less comfortable with group members than do homogeneous groups.

NeuroLeadership Institute co-founder David Rock and his colleagues argue that this discomfort is part of what makes diverse groups more successful, because members are more "on point" or cognitively vigilant. They also note that people tend to overestimate the amount of conflict diverse teams actually have. To optimize high diversity, teams need to develop the capacity to experience and work through disagreements, instead of seeking to minimize differences and avoid discomfort.

Harvard Business School professor Linda Hill coined the term "creative abrasion" to describe the ability to generate ideas through discourse and debate. According to Hill and colleagues (2014), innovation in organizations is fueled by diversity in perspectives and healthy intellectual conflict. This is where psychological safety and open communication can play an important role.

### Focus on Common Goals, Purpose, and Values

Professor of management at the Stanford Graduate School of Business Margaret Neale and her colleagues made a useful distinction between three types of diversity:

- **Informational diversity**—differences with respect to knowledge bases, perspectives, education, and experience
- **Social category diversity**—differences based on demographic identities, like race, gender, and ethnicity
- **Value diversity**—differences in the members' beliefs about the group's real task, goal, target or mission

Based on their research, they concluded that informational diversity was generally helpful for group performance, and that value-based diversity was likely to have detrimental effects on performance and morale. Therefore, helping ensure that team members are similar with regard to their understanding of the task and mission—which relates to the conscious accountability practice of creating clarity—is a critical strategy for preventing destructive conflict from arising.

Interestingly, social category diversity was linked to greater conflict, while it was also associated with increased group morale, especially when the team's work was interdependent and when the group performed well (Mannix and Neale 2005). These findings add more nuance to the story of diversity in work groups, suggesting that the kinds of diversity that make or break a group are actually harder to spot than social demographics.

## Navigating Remote Work

The global lockdown resulting from the COVID-19 pandemic forced many workplaces to examine the question, "Are we able to work remotely?" The experiences of this grand experiment tell us that, yes, remote work is very possible in many industries, and that, very likely, remote work is here to stay. However, spending less time physically in the same space as co-workers poses many challenges to work, as well as to the implementation of conscious accountability.

Alex Kharlamov, senior director of engineering at Yieldstreet, a fintech company, has bumped up against several complications due to remote work. He shared that onboarding new employees, burnout, emotional distress, and miscommunication have been particularly challenging. As a result, Alex has had to be increasingly deliberate about setting clear intentions and adjusting how he manages his teams. He also had to revisit his process of onboarding new employees because new hires were being placed on teams where they had never met their teammates in person. To help these new connections take hold remotely, Alex created a detailed onboarding plan that included one-on-one video chats, time for social chats called "donut buddy chats," virtual happy hours, and he would ask icebreaker questions at the beginning of sessions to scaffold the "getting to know each other" process that does not happen as naturally in virtual settings. The plan also made sure everyone was set up for success at home, providing a budget for equipment, allowing flexibility with regard to scheduling and other family commitments, minimizing off-hours messaging, and encouraging clear work boundaries, frequent breaks, and getting outside.

To combat overwork and emotional distress, managers received training to recognize signs of burnout, everyone was required to take time off, and frequent communications encouraging employees to take care of themselves and others became a norm. To help with miscommunication and potential subsequent conflict, there was no back and forth via messaging through email or other channels, such as Slack. If a miscommunication arose, it was handled exclusively on a video call.

All the potential strains remote work can put on our relationships and work suggest its potentially negative influence on implementing each of the seven practices of conscious accountability. Clear communication, engagement, nailing the work, noticing the process, sharing feedback, claiming results, and trying again all are potentially harder when we are not gathered together in person in the same space.

On the other hand, with its emphasis on creating deliberate intentions and awareness, perhaps conscious accountability is just what the remote work environment needs. Let us look at each practice in the context of remote work and see how it may be affected and also how a recommitment to the principles of conscious accountability may help you to mitigate the complications.

## Creating Clarity

Creating clarity in a remote work world is challenging because we lose so much information when we are virtual. The diminished physical and social cues from others that usually help us "read" a person and what they are saying lessen our ability to fully communicate and understand, making it difficult to get an accurate take on exactly what people mean when they speak. In a group of directors and managers that Marianne facilitates, individuals repeatedly shared how they were missing a ton of information about the productivity and well-being of their teams because they were unable to simply look over to see, catch the vibe, or casually check in. For example, they lost all the information about how people were getting along that they would usually pick up through body language, or if someone was struggling, by how late they were staying at work.

Supercharging our efforts to gain clarity may be what is in order. Even higher levels of patience and humility will be needed to cope with the extra rounds of communication necessary to ensure everyone understands expectations and is on the same page. Aileen, the division section chief of vascular medicine at a regional hospital, routinely states at the outset of every virtual meeting that, as messy and imperfect as communication is in the best of circumstances, it is even messier over Zoom. And that the team's job is to clean it up. In a word, this requires "overcommunicating"—restating, repeating, and reclarifying to create as much clarity as possible. This requires acknowledging that communication is affected by remote meetings, accepting that the team needs to supercharge its conscious accountability efforts to create greater clarity, and having the discipline to put this heightened level of effort into practice.

## Opening Up Engagement

Engaging people, building commitment, and creating psychological safety are likely to be harder without the intimacy of being in person as well. In person you can do things like have lunch, go for a walk, share a snack, bring someone a cup of coffee, or shake hands. These activities build history, familiarity, closeness, and trust. These moments of connection happen naturally in the face-to-face environment. Remote work affords us fewer opportunities to engage. Therefore, we need to be more deliberate about taking action to build connection, safety, and commitment. Some organizations sponsor activities to help people remain connected, such as online cooking classes, escape rooms, and mystery solving parties. The all-in mindset is more important than ever because it will help you keep all individuals in mind as you stay engaged to honor their needs and be inclusive.

## Nailing It

Nailing it might also prove challenging, perhaps because of diminished mental capacity. The phenomenon of feeling tired, fatigued, and burned out after a day of videoconferencing has become commonly known as "Zoom fatigue." Some companies are combating this by having a dedicated no-meeting day, such as "No Meeting Mondays." This protects workers' time and energy so they can devote their mental capacity to completing their work. Nailing it might also be arduous for people who find themselves more productive when they are in the company of other individuals at work. Focusmate, a virtual co-working website, is one potential answer to this problem. The site allows you to sign up for blocks of time to meet with an accountability partner via video.

## Noticing

Noticing is perhaps the practice that will suffer the most in a remote work environment. After all, there is much less opportunity to notice. However, you can be more deliberate and elevate your level of compassion and curiosity. You might consider inviting noticing by initiating your own observations first. For example, Jess shared with their co-worker, Sam, that they are much more productive when they put their shoes on and followed up with asking Sam about what helps her productivity. There is also an opportunity to notice aspects of individuals that might have previously been unavailable, such as pets, children, family, home offices, backyards, and hobbies. Noticing done in the spirit of conscious accountability, even remotely, is likely to assist in helping your work process and building bonds.

### Exchanging Feedback

Exchanging feedback is an interesting practice that actually might be easier for some to do through the buffer of a screen. The extra distance and being in one's home environment might create a sense of increased safety and allow people to be more willing to receive and give feedback. Conversely, others may feel less inhibited with the distance created by interacting virtually and be less sensitive in their delivery of feedback. Regardless of the impact, exchanging feedback remotely will likely require an extra dose of courage. Misunderstandings will inevitably occur, and feelings may be hurt. Slowing down the interaction and returning to creating clarity might ease potential friction.

For example, a group of colleagues were on a Zoom call, when Matt took the opportunity to offer feedback to his co-worker, Nick. He noticed Nick was working on a shared document while Sue was relating information from a critical phone call with a client. Matt held his hands up in a T shape to indicate he was requesting a time out and then briefly said, "Nick, I want to make a request. I am distracted by seeing you work on the document. Would you mind pausing until Sue is finished?" Matt wanted Nick to pause from working, but he also wanted the team to build the habit of regularly sharing even minor feedback so that it would become a normal part of how they worked together remotely.

## Claiming It and Trying Again

Claiming it and trying again might require some extra effort because the key behaviors involved in these practices typically go better when people are together and able to share and build ideas off of one another. An energy usually emerges in a room that can set off a chain reaction of ideas and insights. There are online tools that allow teams to brainstorm and whiteboard, which can facilitate activities for reviewing results and planning to try again (Jamboard, Miro, and Mural, to name just a few). Setting timers, having people "pass" to someone after they have contributed, and using hand signals and virtual reactions are some additional ways to help energize learning and planning.

# Building the Right Organizational Culture

Organizational culture has been described as "all that invisible stuff that glues organizations together" (Merchant 2011). It encompasses the collective assumptions, values, and norms that guide how people in an organization think and behave and informs the more visible aspects of that culture—how people interact and work together. Organizational culture has a big impact—positive or negative—on how the organization gets things done as well as how it feels to be a part of that organization. But because culture is often hard to see or quantify, it can be difficult to figure out how to address or manage it.

Organizational culture can present many challenges for the implementation of conscious accountability. One is when the organization's culture runs counter to goals or practices of conscious accountability. Another is when there are different kinds of cultural "misfits." For example, there might be a poor fit between a key individual and the organization's culture; a poor fit between the culture of a team or division and the larger organization's culture; or a mismatch between the organization's strategy and their culture. Let's look at some examples.

- A human resources executive at a leading financial institution is trying to build a culture of learning, but his efforts are hampered because the organization does not feel psychologically safe enough to admit mistakes or support the exchange of feedback. There is a history of leaders who criticize their subordinates harshly and sometimes publicly, which has led to a culture of fear and anxiety.

- A finance manager from a law firm joins a nonprofit board but is frustrated by an apparent willingness to tolerate what she considers to be lackluster performance. Longstanding members of the organization enjoy having work-life balance and support for self and family care. While they aspire to perform well, they do not normally set aggressive stretch goals.

- A highly creative team of designers has worked for years with a great deal of flexibility and informality, which they believe helps them be more innovative in their work. But they feel squelched after their design firm is acquired by a larger branding company that implements stricter policies on when and where work can take place.

- A young, idealistic leader is appointed to run a government human services agency. She develops a well-formulated strategic plan to raise efficiency and customer satisfaction scores, but her efforts do not get the traction she hoped for, particularly among the employees with long-standing contracts.

The common thread among all of these examples is that, when people from different organizational cultures interact, there are often underlying differences in assumptions, values, and norms that different parties hold. Because culture is largely invisible and usually not fully conscious, differences in culture can be difficult to identify and discuss easily or comfortably.

What could be done to handle organizational culture clashes that impact accountability? How might they be addressed through the framework of conscious accountability, such that everyone could move forward, ideally together, and in a more productive way (both in terms of relationships and performance)? Here are some suggestions of ways to increase your consciousness about what might be operating out of awareness, so you can respond to organizational cultural challenges in a more informed and thoughtful way:

- Learn more about organizational culture and values.
- Allow time for acculturation and adaptation to change.
- Find common ground.
- Lean into clarity and noticing.

## Learn More About Organizational Culture and Values

One important solution for dealing with organizational culture challenges is to become more aware of the critical dimensions that drive variations in organizational culture. There exists a vast literature on these different dimensions, with numerous scholars and researchers who have described different models for dimensions of culture in a general sense, as well as organizational cultures more specifically. Table 12-1 shows some examples of the important dimensions of culture (Ferraro and Briody 2016; Meyer 2014). Familiarity with these dimensions can help provide perspective on culture, which is sometimes difficult to see or appreciate.

Once you become aware of these different dimensions of culture, the next step is to see if you can make your own organization's culture more visible to you. What are your assumptions and values, and how do they influence the way you think, behave, and expect others to behave? How do you think you came to hold these values? There are different assessments that can also be useful in this regard. For example, the Motives Values and Preferences Inventory (MVPI) helps leaders examine where they stand on nine different values, the implications of these values for the kinds of organizational environments they are likely to prefer, what kinds of environments they create as leaders, and how these values may result in certain unconscious biases (Hogan 1999).

**Table 12-1.** Dimensions That Influence Organizational Culture

| Dimension | Perspective 1 | Perspective 2 |
|---|---|---|
| **Individual vs. Collective** Should people's focus be on themselves or a larger group? | **Individual** People identify first as individuals. | **Collective** People identify first as members of a group. |
| **Power Distance** How do people with different levels of power or status interact? | **Egalitarian** Status differences are downplayed. | **Hierarchical** Status differences are highlighted and maintained. |
| **Change Orientation** To what extent are people comfortable with ambiguity and uncertainty? | **Change Embracing** There is high tolerance for uncertainty and risk, and greater ease with change. | **Change Fearing** There is anxiety about the future, resistance to change, and low risk tolerance. |
| **Time Orientation** How do people deal with time? | **Precise Reckoning of Time** Time is seen as scarce, with rigid schedules and emphasis on punctuality. | **Loose Reckoning of Time** Time is seen as plentiful, with loose schedules and punctuality de-emphasized. |
| **Disagreement** What is the best way to handle disagreements? | **Confrontational** Disagreements are taken on directly. | **Avoidance** Disagreements are avoided or handled indirectly. |

## Allow Time for Acculturation and Adaptation to Change

In situations where you are working with organizational culture differences, allow for a period of adaptation in which you actively work to come up to speed on how best to navigate within that cultural context. It can be very useful to have a trusted person who can help raise your awareness about how that organizational culture functions, and how to be more successful within it or when interacting with it.

If you are leading a change effort and encounter resistance, remember that organizational change is a process that evokes many different emotions. It takes time to work through these feelings, to get to a better place in terms of both outlook and performance. The Kubler-Ross Organizational Change Curve, depicted in Figure 12-2, demonstrates how organizations or teams going through change experience a decline in morale and productivity as they work through stages of shock, denial, frustration, and depression (Goodman and Loh 2011). But over time, these feelings shift as individuals accept and adapt to the changes in question. Awareness of the natural challenges that come with change can help you better understand and adapt, which will help you engage with and respond to others more effectively.

**Figure 12-2.** The Kubler-Ross Change Curve

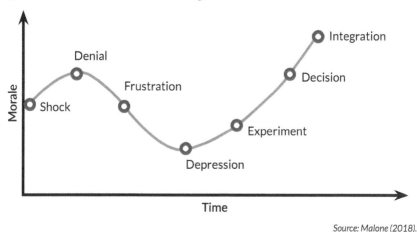

Source: Malone (2018).

## Find Common Ground

Take time to find the basis of your commonalities and establish mutual understanding. That might happen by discovering similar kinds of work or life experiences or identifying congruous values. Sometimes that shared territory exists within the purpose of your connection. Focusing on the common task or the overarching goals can help groups think together about the things that join them, as opposed to the things that separate them. Finding common ground relies on communicating effectively across organizational cultures. This capacity involves other skills, mindsets, and behaviors, including:

- Genuine curiosity, interest, and openness to others

- Patience with the process of understanding others and making oneself understood
- Listening deeply and observing carefully
- Humility and acknowledgment that your way of doing things is your way, but not necessarily the best way or the only way
- Managing ambiguity and tolerating not knowing
- Practicing all of the above to reach a higher level of comfort and competence

## Lean Into Clarity and Noticing

When we encounter differences between individuals or teams and the dominant organizational culture, some of those differences are in attitudes and behaviors that relate directly to the practices of conscious accountability: communicating, decision making, task completion, and giving feedback, just to name a few. Two of the most important practices to focus on are creating clarity and noticing. Clarity is key, not just in negotiating the desired outcomes, but also in establishing the processes that will be used to reach those outcomes. Ensuring mutual understanding and articulating desired norms and metrics can take additional time, but doing so is especially crucial to prevent problems later. Even with the best of intentions and time invested in creating clarity, misunderstandings are inevitable. This is where noticing is also important—to be especially alert to places where there may be misalignment and to be proactive about checking in to identify and resolve any differences before they snowball.

Organizational culture may be intangible and hard to shift, but an important thing to remember is that organizational cultures are not completely static. Rather, they are dynamic and can evolve based on how people behave with one another on a day-to-day basis. As such, when we choose our responses wisely, we can introduce the possibility for cultural change.

The following story is an inspiring illustration of how an individual can gradually influence an organization's culture through their everyday decisions. Here, a young junior manager positively influenced the evolution of his organization's culture.

During the early years of John's career, one of his greatest challenges was the hierarchical and bureaucratic culture at work. When he first joined the corporate finance team, the overall culture was very authoritative—practically top-down—with little cross-team collaboration.

One day in his third year on the job, John received a phone call from the senior manager of the global sales team. Her team leader was asking her to make vendor payments because the person in charge was taking a few personal days. Since the payment was due and it was her first time using the financial accounting data management system, John offered to help her in person.

Upon hearing about this, John's supervisor rebuked him sharply. "Are you a sales clerk?" he snapped, insisting that John just send the manual and let the global sales team take care of it themselves. However, after explaining the unique situation to his supervisor, John was given reluctant permission to help the manager in person.

A couple of days later, John's supervisor cautioned that this voluntary attitude would only increase his workload and that of other team members. While he considered this advice, John firmly believed that the company's culture and the way they worked needed to change. So, he maintained his way of doing things, but did so without calling attention to his efforts.

As a result of John's continued supportive behaviors, the people he helped shared the know-how with their co-workers. Moreover, his team's need for field response was significantly streamlined. Thanks to John's repeated attempts to make small changes, the perception that the work culture needed to be changed increased, and the overall working atmosphere gradually became more people oriented.

In the process of overcoming that challenge, John learned that it was possible to influence culture from the bottom up. Although it may take more time and effort, he saw it as an important opportunity for him as a junior manager. He realized that it would not only make things better for himself but also for the rest of the organization.

## An Uncovering Process

Life is full of complexity and challenge. So when you are facing any number of challenges to implementing conscious accountability, please, do not despair. Do not let them derail you. It is possible to work through the challenges, especially when you raise your awareness of relationships and results and reframe such challenges as opportunities to learn even more than you imagined. Let's review a process that can help you figure out what is going on.

### Step 1. Check Psychological Safety and Commitment

You have to dig a little deeper to uncover the barriers that might be impeding your practice of conscious accountability. Therefore, it is important to check the psychological safety and commitment level of all involved. You can do this using one of the assessments presented in chapter 5. If safety and commitment are not at sufficient levels, this may be the underlying cause of current challenges. Returning to the practice of opening up engagement would be your next step. If safety and commitment are at sufficient levels, it is still a good idea to reaffirm the importance of safety, identify exactly what is making everyone feel safe, and restate commitments before proceeding to step 2.

### Step 2. Ask Powerful Questions

Following are some questions that may prove useful to uncovering challenges that have yet to be identified. You may use these questions for self-reflection or as a team exercise. In addition, you can tackle these questions through contemplation, writing, or conversation, on your own, with a partner, as a small group, or in a larger team. In our opinion, putting pen to paper proves to be a powerful tool to get at issues that may not be accessible otherwise. Therefore, we recommend writing your responses by hand. Ask:

- What is not being said?
- What am I afraid to say?
- What needs to be said?
- What is not being done?
- What am I afraid to do?
- What needs to be done?
- What is getting in the way?
- What am I not seeing?
- What am I afraid to see or acknowledge?
- What needs to be seen or acknowledged?

## Refine Your Goal

After reflecting on these questions, you will most likely have some hypotheses about what is getting in the way of your success. With these in mind, you can return to the practice of creating clarity to refine your goal, or any of the other conscious accountability practices. Of course, another possible outcome of reflection and refinement may involve changing direction entirely.

Through deep consideration of next steps, you might uncover some illuminating or even upsetting responses. That is OK and to be expected, especially when dealing with interpersonal relationships. Deepening of relationships does not always result in moving toward one another. Rather, it may manifest as an increased understanding, which allows for more intentionality and discernment about whether a team is a good fit.

As an example, upon reviewing their recent efforts and interests, some team members in an architecture firm found they no longer wanted to work together on a portion of the firm's portfolio. Instead, several members whose values were more aligned with developing residential properties, rather than commercial ones, wanted to move in a new direction. After bringing their preferences to the firm's partners, the original team disbanded, and the partners moved the interested employees to the residential team, which was currently short staffed.

It is not a failure if teams that engage in conscious accountability choose to part ways. It is in fact, an excellent example of our definition of conscious accountability: expanded awareness to create deliberate intentions, take informed actions, and be responsible for our impact.

No matter how challenging or uncomfortable the issues that arise, if they are addressed with the spirit of conscious accountability, they will benefit the dynamics and productivity of your team. The conscious awareness is the key to transforming our relationships and results by enabling us to make more informed decisions.

## Concluding Invitation: Embrace the Journey

Accountability is deceptively complex. It sounds simple enough—do what you say you are going to do, deliver on your promises, and make good on your word. However, this type of thinking is limited because it encourages a primarily self-focused (if not self-interested) perspective. All too often we see people putting their hands in the air and saying, "I did my part, I'm out." And we hear a litany of phrases defending one's position as accountable: "That's not what you said. I did do that. You said not to do that. We already talked about that." Who wants to work in an atmosphere like that? Who wants to be part of a culture of keeping your guard up, defending your work, keeping a paper trail, all to make sure you are viewed as doing your job and being accountable?

Conscious accountability aspires to change this more traditional perspective of accountability into a transformational process by expanding our awareness of the multitude of influences affecting our relationships and work efforts. Leveraging this awareness results in greater intentionality, more informed decisions, and the ability to more readily see and take responsibility for our actions. In this way, accountability evolves from reacting to the past behavior of individuals to find out who is to blame and punish, into creatively harnessing the compassion and wisdom of the team and promoting perseverance and learning.

The journey toward awareness is a life's work. If you choose to engage in this work, we encourage you to remain humble and curious. Humility helps us acknowledge that no one has all the answers, we are all muddling through at some point or another, and there is an ocean of unknowns. Curiosity lights the desire to explore and venture into territories that are currently hidden or unknown and fuels us along this never-ending endeavor. The payoff is that by doing the work to be more conscious, we can become fuller versions of ourselves. And by becoming more conscious in terms of accountability, we can become the reliable and responsive person who people feel safe approaching, colleagues love to have on their team, and ups everyone's game. We invite you to embrace the journey and use the seven practices we detailed in this book to help guide you in connecting more deeply with yourself, others, and the world. It is our hope that the creation of connections will elevate the results you seek and contribute to your life being well lived.

## Summary: Meeting the Challenges of Conscious Accountability

Implementing the practices of conscious accountability can be challenging, especially in the context of certain conditions in our lives and organizations today. In this chapter, we reviewed three areas of challenge: effectively harnessing diversity, navigating remote work, and building the right organizational culture. We also shared an uncovering process to help you figure out what is going on when your efforts to implement conscious accountability are stuck or stalled. Finally, we encourage you to see the process of developing conscious accountability as a journey—sometimes painful and challenging, but also rich and rewarding. And one that promises to make transformational differences in your life, in your workplace, and—as we will discuss in chapter 13—in the world.

# A World of Conscious Accountability

> *I am no longer accepting the things I cannot change.*
> *I am changing the things I cannot accept.*
>
> ANGELA BASSETT

Throughout this book, we have described what conscious accountability is and how to practice it, both as an individual and within the context of interpersonal relationships and teams. It is our hope that you are now ready to practice the model in ways that work effectively for you. And it is our belief that as more people like you begin to incorporate the model into their work and other parts of life, the effects of conscious accountability can ripple outward, influencing our world more broadly and fully.

As we become more aware of ourselves and our interconnectedness with others, how might this growing awareness change us? What choices will we make? Will we remain disconnected bystanders, witnessing events around us in a way that leaves us feeling indifferent at worst, or sympathetic but powerless at best? Or will we embrace ourselves and others as important parts of a larger whole, with the ability and responsibility to do what we can to make some kind of difference? And when we choose to respond, how would we like to discern what kind of actions to take, particularly around the "wicked problems" of the world?

To these questions, we offer two ideas. The first is captured by the adage "think globally, act locally." We encourage you to think broadly and deeply about systemic issues, but then take action within your local communities and spheres of influence. We think about this as a three-step process that we refer to as connect, reflect, and effect:

1. **Connect.** Start by connecting to what is happening. That means becoming informed of what is happening—in the world, in your country, region, community, or organization. As system-level dynamics are not always obvious, this means becoming a keen observer and cultivating an active curiosity and learning orientation. (In this day and age, you only need to go as far as your web browser to learn about nearly anything!) It might mean ingesting news sources from different places or points of view. It might mean soliciting stories about other people's experiences. Or it might mean listening to people who have very different views and values from you.

2. **Reflect.** The next step is to reflect on what you learn. This reflection is meant to allow you to take in the information and make it personal to you in some way. It can help foster a sense of empathy for other people involved in this situation. Consider how the people involved might be just like you. If you are considering a larger social issue, reflect on how the phenomenon affects your world; how does it relate to you? In what ways might you contribute to the problem or the solution?

3. **Effect.** In this step, the idea is to take some action, no matter how small, that represents your attempt to effect some kind of change. It could mean making a change in yourself (such as learning more about an issue or problem or changing a behavior). It might mean sharing what you learn or talking with other people about it. It might mean donating time, talent, money, or goods to local organizations that in some way relate to the larger issue. It might mean contacting your local, state, or national representatives and letting them know

about your concerns. Maybe it means organizing with other people or in your circle of influence. But the idea is to take some action that represents your response to the issue to bring about change.

Here is a personal illustration: David was deeply saddened by the heartbreaking stories of migrants who leave their countries—often due to violence or oppression—in search of a better life. These news stories led him to seek out further information about trends in human migration. As he reflected on what he learned, he recalled stories from his grandparents, about his ancestors who had left Ireland during the Great Famine, and others who had emigrated from Italy at the turn of the century. They left everything and everyone behind in search of a better life. David realized that whatever success he experienced was in no small part due to their courage and sacrifice. In considering how he wanted to help migrants now, David connected with a local organization that cares for immigrants and refugees, helping them establish new lives in the New Haven community. He has donated money and goods as a way to respond to the larger issue of global migration, and to honor his ancestors who were once in the same position.

The three steps of connect, reflect, and effect represent a broader, holistic approach to conscious accountability. They ask us to broaden our awareness and appreciate how we are in some way connected to others—even to people we do not know and will never meet. They then challenge us to choose to take responsibility for contributing to the solution in some way, no matter how large or small.

The second idea we would like to offer is to never underestimate what one ordinary person—someone just like each of us, and like you—can do to make a difference or to bring about change. Consider these real-world examples:

- Marie Rose Belding was a high school student in a small Iowa town when she first thought of an idea: creating an online database to match businesses with excess food with charities that serve the hungry. While working at her church's food pantry, she was distressed when a large shipment of food went unused and had to be discarded. She knew that she wanted to address this problem, and she had a hunch that an online database would help, but she did not have the computer skills needed to develop the software. So she teamed up with a law student named Grant Nelson, who provided the coding acumen for their project. Together, they launched a nonprofit organization called MEANS (Matching Excess And Need for Stability). Now run largely by high school and college students, MEANS has about 3,000 community partners across the US and has assisted with the redistribution of more than 1.8 million pounds of food since 2015 (Toner 2018).

- Musician Marika Shaw was inspired to make a difference in the world by two role models: her mother, who worked to preserve and pass on native languages within indigenous communities, and Dr. Paul Farmer, a medical anthropologist and physician who founded Partners in Health, a global nonprofit organization that serves people who are sick and living in poverty. Marika and her bandmates in Arcade Fire saw an opportunity to create positive change, both in their industry and in the world. By adding $1 to each ticket sold, the band and their fans raised $2 million to build healthcare infrastructure in Haiti. And so the fundraising organization, Plus 1, was born. Over time, they partnered with others, and their impact grew even greater. As of this writing, Plus 1 has raised more than $10 million from 3,500 shows involving 150 artists, festivals, and events worldwide. All funds have been granted to more than 300 high-impact organizations. Shaw put it this way: "Plus 1 is the bridge, the connective tissue between the energy that exists on one side to do good, and the capabilities that exist on the other to actually make the change happen."

- In 2015, Dadarao Bilhore lost his 16-year-old son to a pothole-related accident in India, where thousands of such deaths occur each year. The personal tragedy compelled Dadarao to do something directly. Inspired by his son's memory, he began filling the potholes himself. To date, he and others who have volunteered alongside him have filled more than 1,330 potholes by hand, saving an untold number of lives. He has also told his story to help raise awareness about the danger and to encourage others to take action. His example reminds us that we need not wait for the government or some "bigger" power to solve urgent challenges. We have what we need to make the change ourselves and inspire others in the process.

In all of these examples, people were motivated to respond to problems they saw in their communities or elsewhere in the world. Are they just good people who are especially compassionate? Perhaps. In each of their stories, though, we see inklings of conscious accountability: the expanded awareness they each embraced concerning a larger problem. The deliberate intentions set and actions taken to address it. The enhanced engagement with others as part of the solution. All while taking responsibility for impact and outcome.

What if more people shifted their thinking from "someone should do something about that" to "I can do something about that"? What if more people embraced the possibility of change by embracing and leveraging interpersonal connections, while also collectively striving for optimal results? What other good might manifest by unleashing, simultaneously, the power of our relationships and our capacity to get things done?

We imagine a world where people harness the strengths of our diversity and privilege. We envision a world where people help one another to live and thrive. We imagine a world where the practice of conscious accountability helps us drive progress and bring about positive change.

# Acknowledgments

This book and the ideas we share in it represent the culmination of many years of work. We could not have made this project happen without several different groups of people who have inspired and supported us in various ways throughout the process.

- **Our students:** We have had the privilege of interacting with some of the best and brightest students and adult learners anywhere. Your engagement, questions, experiences, and feedback, as well as your willingness to learn by challenging yourselves and us, have consistently inspired and helped us to push our ideas further.
- **Our clients:** We honor the many clients we have had the incredible privilege to serve and walk beside. You are out in the world making wonderful things happen and leading change. Thank you for your energy, for the trust you placed in us, and for the courage to rise and face the challenges of self-development, working with others, and choosing to lead.

- **Our colleagues:** We are blessed to be surrounded by colleagues who are in equal parts brilliant, accomplished, compassionate, and generous. Thanks to our colleagues at Yale (the Schools of Management, Medicine, and Global Affairs, and the Faculty of Arts and Sciences), other universities, the federal government, 6 Team Conditions, Venwise, and Ei World.
- **Our influencers:** We are grateful for the people whose work has captured our attention and imagination. Your thinking, writing, and speaking have been a continual source of inspiration to us: Brené Brown, Dan Coyle, Amy Edmondson, Edward Deci, Richard Ryan, Marshall Goldsmith, Peter Hawkins, Celeste Headlee, Kerry Patterson and colleagues, Doug Stone, Sheila Heen, Mark Lesser, Fred Tsao, Chris Laszlo, Tara Mohr, Michael Pirson, Daniel Pink, Carol Dweck, Richard Hackman, and Ruth Wageman. Thank you for the ways your ideas have had a positive impact on us and on the world.
- **Our storytellers:** We have also been inspired by a number of incredible leaders whom we have had the good fortune to know. Their courage, dignity, and resilience have inspired us and hopefully you too: Simidele Adeagbo, Peter Boyd, Ji woo Choi, Kendra Curtis, Chris Duprey, Kevin Jackson, Sonja LaBarbera, Alex Kharlamov, Robert Motta, Wanjiru Mukoma, Kate Rebernak, and Erik Schreter. Thanks for your examples and for your generosity in sharing your stories with us.
- **Our publisher:** The team at ATD has been absolutely wonderful to work with. Ryan Changcoco, Jack Harlow, Kay Hechler, Suzy Felchlin, and Melissa Jones—your kindness, patience, advice, professionalism, competence, and belief in the value of this book have kept the wind in our sails and helped us remain on course, even when the seas were choppy!
- **Our team:** Thanks for jumping in, rolling up your sleeves, and answering our calls for help to manage lots of details, big and small: Reese Adams, Susan Bugden, Toniann Butler, Sam Cassidy, Karen

Collins, and Stacey Laureanos—thanks for your valued efforts on our behalf.

- **Our friends:** Writing a book is a marathon, not a sprint. Our friends have been cheerleaders, supporters, and, yes, accountability partners, who have kept us moving forward. Heidi Brooks, Teresa Chahine, Zoe Chance, Stephanie Dunson, Aileen Gariepy, Tracey Gilhuly and Bob Huebner, Suzanne Glaser, Derrick Gordon, David Marcotte, Mary Frances McGuiness, and Julia Pimsleur—thanks for being there for us in so many ways.

- **Our families:** You have been in the at times unenviable position of getting to see how this book was birthed! We appreciate your love for us, your belief in us, your encouragement, your sacrifices, and your willingness to pick up the slack as we labored to bring this book to fruition. Your love and support mean everything and give untold fulfillment to our lives.

To all those who have supported this work, we offer our sincere thanks, deep appreciation, and profound gratitude for the ways you have contributed to this work and enriched our lives.

# References

Ackerman, C.E. 2021. "83 Benefits of Journaling for Depression, Anxiety, and Stress." *Positive Psychology* blog, July 15. positivepsychology.com /benefits-of-journaling.

Alexander, G. 2010. "Behavioural coaching—the GROW model." In *Excellence in Coaching: The Industry Guide*, 2nd ed., edited by J. Passmore. Philadelphia: Kogan Page, 83–93.

AECF (Annie E. Casey Foundation). 2021. "Generation Z and Mental Health." Annie E. Casey Foundation, October 16. aecf.org/blog/generation-z-and -mental-health.

Bandura, A. 1998. "Health Promotion From the Perspective of Social Cognitive Theory." *Psychology and Health* 13(4): 623–649.

Barnfield, H., and M.M. Lombardo. 2014. *FYI: For Your Improvement—Competencies Development Guide*, 6th ed. Los Angeles: Korn Ferry.

Basler, R.P., M.D. Pratt, and L.A. Dunlap. 1953. *Lincoln, Abraham, 1809-1865, Collected works*. The Abraham Lincoln Association, Springfield, IL. New Brunswick, NJ: Rutgers University Press.

Bass, B.M. 1985. *Leadership and Performance.* New York: Free Press.

Beaton, C. 2016. "This Is What Happens to Your Brain When You Fail (and How to Fix It)." *Forbes*, April 7. forbes.com/sites/carolinebeaton/2016 /04/07/this-is-what-happens-to-your-brain-when-you-fail-and -how-to-fix-it.

Bersin, J. 2016. "New Research Shows Why Focus on Teams, Not Just Leaders, Is Key to Business Performance." Forbes, March 3. forbes.com/sites /joshbersin/2016/03/03/why-a-focus-on-teams-not-just-leaders-is -the-secret-to-business-performance/#2b6adff924d5.

Bethune, S. 2019. "Generation Z More Likely to Report Mental Health Concerns." *APA Monitor* 50(1). apa.org/monitor/2019/01/gen-z.

Biden, J. 2008. "Biden's Remarks on McCain's Policies." *New York Times*, September 15. nytimes.com/2008/09/15/us/politics/15text-biden.html.

Bouffard-Bouchard, T. 1990. "Influence of Self-Efficacy on Performance in a Cognitive Task." *The Journal of Social Psychology* 130(3): 353–363.

Bourke, J., and A. Titus. 2020. "The Key to Inclusive Leadership." *Harvard Business Review*, March 6. hbr.org/2020/03/the-key-to-inclusive-leadership.

Brackett, M. 2019. *Permission to Feel*. New York: Quercus Publishing.

Brooks, H. 2019. "Receiving and Giving Powerful Feedback." Yale Case 18-021, Yale School of Management, revised September 4.

Brooks, H. 2020. "How to Start Making Real Change in Your Organization." Yale Insights, Faculty Viewpoints, June 11. insights.som.yale.edu /insights/how-to-start-making-real-change-in-your-organization.

Brown, B. 2017. *Braving the Wilderness*. New York: Random House.

Brown, B. 2018. *Dare to Lead*. New York: Random House.

Brueller, D., and A. Carmelli. 2011. "Linking Capacities of High-Quality Relationships to Team Learning and Performance in Service Organizations." *Human Resource Management* 50(4): 455–477.

Bui, K-V.T., L.A. Peplau, and C.T. Hill. 1996. "Testing the Rusbult Model of Relationship Commitment and Stability in a 15-Year Study of Heterosexual Couples." *Personality and Social Psychology Bulletin* 22(12): 1,244–1,257.

Burns, J.M. 1978. *Leadership*. New York: Harper and Row.

Carucci, R. 2017. "Executives Fail to Execute Strategy Because They're Too Internally Focused." *Harvard Business Review,* November 13.

Cho, Y.J., and Perry, J.L. 2012. "Intrinsic Motivation and Employee Attitudes: Role of Managerial Trustworthiness, Goal Directedness, and Extrinsic Reward Expectancy." *Review of Public Personnel Administration* 32(4): 382–406.

Covey, S. 1989. *The 7 Habits of Highly Effective People: Powerful Lessons in Personal Change*. New York: Free Press.

Covey, S. 2008. *The Speed of Trust: The One Thing That Changes Everything*. New York: Free Press.

Coyle, D. 2018. *The Culture Code: The Secrets of Highly Successful Groups*. New York: Bantam Books.

Deci, E.L., and R.M. Ryan. 1985. *Intrinsic Motivation and Self-Determination in Human Behavior*. New York: Plenum.

Deloitte and Victorian Equal Opportunity & Human Rights Commission. 2013. *Waiter, Is That Inclusion In My Soup? A New Recipe to Improve Business Performance*. Sydney: Deloitte. deloitte.com/content/dam/Deloitte/au /Documents/human-capital/deloitte-au-hc-diversity-inclusion-soup -0513.pdf.

Duhigg, C. 2016. "What Google Learned From Its Quest to Build the Perfect Team." The Work Issue, *New York Times Magazine*, February 25. nytimes .com/2016/02/28/magazine/what-google-learned-from-its-quest-to -build-the-perfect-team.html.

Dutton, J., and E.D. Heaphy. 2003. "The Power of High-Quality Connections at Work." In *Positive Organizational Scholarship*, edited by K. Cameron, J.E. Dutton, and R.E. Quinn. San Francisco, CA: Berrett-Koehler, 263–278.

Duval, S., and R. Wicklund. 1972. *A Theory of Objective Self-Awareness*. Oxford, UK: Oxford University Press.

Dweck, C.S. 2006. *Mindset: The New Psychology of Success*. New York: Random House.

Dysvik, A., and B. Kuvaas. 2010. "Exploring the Relative and Combined Influence of Mastery-Approach Goals and Work Intrinsic Motivation on Employee Turnover Intention." *Personnel Review* 39(5): 622–638.

Edmondson, A. 2012. *Teaming: How Organizations Learn, Innovate and Compete in the Knowledge Economy*. San Francisco: Jossey-Bass.

Edmondson, A. 2014. "Building a Psychologically Safe Workplace." TEDx video, May 5, 2014. youtube.com/watch?v=LhoLuui9gX8.

Edmondson, A. 2018. *The Fearless Organization*. Hoboken, NJ: John Wiley & Sons.

Edmondson, A. 2019. "Creating Psychological Safety in the Workplace." HBR IdeaCast, episode 666, January 22. hbr.org/ideacast/2019/01/creating -psychological-safety-in-the-workplace.

Edwards, J.R., and D.M. Cable. 2009. "The Value of Value Congruence." *Journal of Applied Psychology* 94(3): 654–677.

Ellis, S., and I. Davidi. 2005. "After-Event Reviews: Drawing Lessons From Successful and Failed Experience." *Journal of Applied Psychology* 90(5): 857–871.

Etcheverry, P.E., and B. Le. 2005. "Thinking About Commitment: Accessibility of Commitment and Prediction of Relationship Persistence, Accommodation, and Willingness to Sacrifice." *Personal Relationships* 12(1): 103–123.

Ferraro, G.P., and E.K. Briody. 2016. *The Cultural Dimension of Global Businesses*, 7th ed. New York: Routledge.

Fishbein, M., and I. Ajzen. 1975. *Belief, Attitude, Intention, and Behavior: An Introduction to Theory and Research*. Reading, MA: Addison-Wesley.

Flavin, R. 2018. "Is Your Startup Right for Non-Diluting SBIR-STTR Government Grant Funding?" Founder Institute blog, September 10. fi.co/insight/is-your-startup-right-for-non-diluting-sbir-sttr -government-grant-funding.

Fox, K.C., S. Nijeboer, M.L. Dixon, J.L. Floman, M. Ellamil, S.P. Rumak, P. Sedlmeier, and K. Christoff. 2014. "Is Meditation Associated With Altered Brain Structure? A Systematic Review and Meta-Analysis of Morphometric Neuroimaging in Meditation Practitioners." *Neuroscience & Biobehavioral Reviews* 43:48–73.

Freud, S. 1915. "The Unconscious." *SE* 14:159–204.

Garvin, D.A. 2000. *Learning in Action: A Guide to Putting the Learning Organization to Work*. Boston: Harvard Business School Press.

GEM Report. 2007. "What Does Accountability Mean to You?" World Education Blog, April 24. gemreportunesco.wpcomstaging.com/2017/04/24 /what-does-accountability-mean-to-you.

Gibordi, R. 2017. "The 1 Think Greater Leaders Don't Do: Why Great Leaders Take the Blame and Pass on the Credit." *Inc*, October 2. inc.com/ron -gibori/great-leaders-take-blame-pass-along-credit.html.

Gleeson, B. 2019. "How Navy SEALs Plan, Lead and Learn." *Forbes*, August 27. forbes.com/sites/brentgleeson/2019/08/27/how-navy-seals-plan-lead -and-learn.

Goleman, D., R. Boyatzis, and A. McKee. 2004. *Primal Leadership: Learning to Lead With Emotional Intelligence*. Boston: Harvard Business School Press.

Gonçalves, A., A.C. Zuanazzi, A. Salvador, A. Jaloto, G. Pianowski, and L. De Francisco Carvalho. 2020. "Preliminary Findings on the Associations Between Mental Health Indicators and Social Isolation During the COVID-19 Pandemic." *Archives of Psychiatry and Psychotherapy* 2:10–19.

Goodman, E., and L. Loh. 2011. "Organizational Change: A Critical Challenge for Team Effectiveness." *Business Information Review* 28(4): 242–250.

Gottman, J.M. 1994. *What Predicts Divorce? The Relationship Between Marital Processes and Marital Outcomes*. Hillsdale, NJ: Lawrence Erlbaum Associates.

Grant, A.M., L. Curtayne, and G. Burton. 2009. "Executive Coaching Enhances Goal Attainment, Resilience and Workplace Well-Being: A Randomised Controlled Study." *The Journal of Positive Psychology* 4(5): 396–407.

Grossman, D. 2016. "The Costs of Poor Communications." Society for Human Resource Management blog, February 19. shrm.org/resourcesandtools /hr-topics/organizational-and-employee-development/pages/the-cost -of-poor-communication.aspx.

Hamilton, D. 2009. "Top Ten Email Blunders that Cost Companies Money." Creative Communications & Training. online.fliphtml5.com/eadm/btcd.

Harari, Y. 2018. *Sapiens: A Brief History of Humankind*. Toronto: McLelland & Stewart.

Harris, L. 2019. *Diversity Beyond Lip Service: A Coaching Guide for Challenging Bias*. Oakland, CA: Berrett-Koehler.

Harris, S.G., and K.W. Mossholder. 1996. "The Affective Implications of Perceived Congruence With Cultural Dimensions During Organizational Transformation." *Journal of Management* 22:527–547.

Harrison, D.A., and K.J. Klein. 2007. "What's the Difference? Diversity Constructs as Separation, Variety, or Disparity in Organizations." *Academy of Management Review* 32(4): 1,199–1,228.

Herring, C. 2009. "Does Diversity Pay? Race, Gender and the Business Case for Diversity." *American Sociological Review* 74(2): 208–224.

Hill, L.A., G. Brandeau, E. Truelove, and K. Lineback. 2014. "Collective Genius." *Harvard Business Review*, June.

Hogan, R., and J. Hogan. 1996. *Motives, Values, Preferences Inventory Manual*. Tulsa, OK: Hogan Assessment Systems.

Holt-Lunstad, J., T.B. Smith, and J.B. Layton. 2010. "Social Relationships and Mortality Risk: A Meta-Analytic Review." *PLoS Med* 7(7): e1000316.

Huang, C., and P. Jiang. 2012. "Exploring the Psychological Safety of R&D Teams: An Empirical Analysis in Taiwan." *Journal of Management & Optimization* 18(2): 175–192.

Hunt, V., L. Yee, S. Prince, and S. Dixon-Fyle. 2018. "Delivering Through Diversity." McKinsey & Company Report, January 18. mckinsey.com /business-functions/people-and-organizational-performance/our -insights/delivering-through-diversity.

Institute of Medicine (US) Committee on Institutional and Policy-Level Strategies for Increasing the Diversity of the U.S. Healthcare Workforce, B.D. Smedley, A. Stith Butler, and L.R. Bristow, eds. 2004. *In the Nation's Compelling Interest: Ensuring Diversity in the Health-Care Workforce*. Washington, DC: National Academies Press.

Jayne, M.E., R.L. Dipboye. 2004. "Leveraging Diversity to Improve Business Performance: Research Findings and Recommendations for Organizations." *Human Resource Management* 43(4): 409–424.

Jordan, M. 1997. "Michael Jordan—Failure." Nike Commercial. youtube.com /watch?v=GuXZFQKKF7A.

Kaba, F., A. Lewis, S. Glowa-Kollisch, J. Hadler, D. Lee, H. Alper, . . . and H. Venters. 2014. "Solitary Confinement and Risk of Self-Harm Among Jail Inmates." *American Journal of Public Health* 104(3): 442–447.

Kahneman, D., and A. Tversky. 1977. "Intuitive Prediction: Biases and Corrective Procedures." Decision Research Technical Report PTR-1042-77-6. Sponsored by Defense Advanced Research Projects Agency Contract N00014-76-C-0074. apps.dtic.mil/dtic/tr/fulltext/u2/a047747.pdf.

Klimecki, O.M., S. Leiberg, C. Lamm, and T. Singer. 2013. "Functional Neural Plasticity and Associated Changes in Positive Affect After Compassion Training." *Cerebral Cortex* 23(7): 1552–1561.

Koch, C. 2018. "What Is Consciousness?" *Scientific American*, June 1. scientificamerican.com/article/what-is-consciousness.

Kolb, D.A. 1984. *Experiential Learning: Experience as the Source of Learning and Development*. New Jersey: Prentice-Hall.

Kuvaas, B., R. Buch, A. Weibel, A. Dysvik, and C.G.L. Nerstad. 2017. "Do Intrinsic and Extrinsic Motivation Relate Differently to Employee Outcomes?" *Journal of Economic Psychology* 61(August): 244–258.

Lama XIV, D., and S. Stril-Rever. 2010. *My Spiritual Journey*. New York: Harper One.

Laskas, J.M. 2019. "The Mister Rogers No One Saw." *New York Times Magazine*, November 19. nytimes.com/2019/11/19/magazine/mr-rogers.html.

Leading Effectively Staff. 2020. "Use Situation-Behavior-Impact (SBI) to Understand Intent." Leading Effectively, Center for Creative Leadership, November 18. ccl.org/articles/leading-effectively-articles/closing-the -gap-between-intent-vs-impact-sbii.

Leigh-Hunt, N., D. Bagguley, K. Bash, V. Turner, S. Turnbull, N. Valtorta, and W. Caan. 2017. "An Overview of Systematic Reviews on the Public Health Consequences of Social Isolation and Loneliness." *Public Health* 152:157–171.

Lesser, M. 2013. *Know Yourself, Forget Yourself. Five Truths to Transform Your Work, Relationships, and Everyday Life*. Novato, CA: New World Library.

Lincoln, A. 2006. "Abraham Lincoln's Notes for a Law Lecture." In *Collected Works of Abraham Lincoln*, edited by R.P. Basler et al. abrahamlincolnonline.org/lincoln/speeches/lawlect.htm.

Liu, J. 2020. "Companies Are Speaking Out Against Racism, But Here's What It Really Looks Like to Lead an Anti-Racist Organization." CNBC, June 15. cnbc.com/2020/06/15/what-it-means-to-be-an-anti-racist-company.html.

Luft, J., and H. Ingham. 1955. "The Johari Window: A Graphic Model of Inter-personal Awareness." *Proceedings of the Western Training Laboratory in Group Development*. Los Angeles: University of California, Los Angeles.

Mahal, A. 2018. *After Action Review: Continuous Improvement Made Easy*. Basking Ridge, NJ: Technics Publications.

Malone, E. 2018. "The Kubler-Ross Change Curve and the Flipped Classroom: Moving Students Past the Pit of Despair." *Education in the Health Professions* 1(36).

Mannix, E., and M.A. Neale. 2005. "What Differences Make a Difference? The Promise and Reality of Diverse Teams in Organizations." *Psychological Science in the Public Interest* 6(2): 31–55.

Merchant, N. 2011. "Culture Trumps Strategy, Every Time." *Harvard Business Review*, March 22. hbr.org/2011/03/culture-trumps-strategy-every.

Mercurio, Z.A. 2015. "Affective Commitment as a Core Essence of Organizational Commitment: An Integrative Literature Review." *Human Resources Development Review* 14(4): 389–414.

*Merriam-Webster*. 2018. "Get Looped In on 'Feedback.'" World History, April 3. merriam-webster.com/words-at-play/the-history-of-feedback.

Meyer, E. 2014. *The Culture Map: Breaking Through the Invisible Boundaries of Global Business*. Philadelphia: Public Affairs.

Meyer, J.P., and N.J. Allen. 1991. "A Three-Component Conceptualization of Organizational Commitment." *Human Resources Management Review* 1(1): 61–89.

Meyer, J.P., and L. Herscovitch. 2001. "Commitment in the Workplace Toward a General Model." *Human Resources Management Review* 11:299–326.

Meyers, V.A. 2012. *Moving Diversity Forward: How to Go From Well-Meaning to Well-Doing*. Chicago: American Bar Association.

Miller, J.G. 1984. "Culture and the Development of Everyday Social Explanation." *Journal of Personality and Social Psychology* 46(5): 961–978.

Miller, W.R., and S. Rollnick. 2013. *Motivational Interviewing: Helping People Change*, 3rd ed. New York: Guilford Press.

Mitchell, R., B. Boyle, V. Parker, M. Giles, V. Chiang, and P. Joyce. 2015. "Managing Inclusiveness and Diversity in Teams: How Leader Inclusiveness Affects Performance through Status and Team Identity." *Human Resource Management* 54(2): 217–239.

Mohr, T. 2014. *Playing Big: Practical Wisdom for Women Who Want to Speak Up, Create, and Lead*. New York: Avery.

Monday, R.T., R.M. Steers, and L. Porter. 1979. "The Measurement of Organizational Commitment." *Journal of Vocational Behavior* 14:224–247.

Nawaz, S. 2016. "For Delegation to Work, It Has to Come With Coaching." *Harvard Business Review*, May 5.

Nembhard, I.M., and A.C. Edmondson. 2011. "Psychological Safety: A Foundation for Speaking Up, Collaboration, and Experimentation." In *The Oxford Handbook of Positive Organizational Scholarship*, edited by K.S. Cameron and G.M. Spreitzer. New York: Oxford University Press.

Newsom, R., and H. Wright. 2021. "The Link Between Sleep and Job Performance." Sleep Foundation, June 24. sleepfoundation.org/sleep-hygiene/good-sleep-and-job-performance.

Nin, A. 1961. *Seduction of Minotaur*. No. 5 of *Cities of the Interior*. Athens, OH: Swallow Press.

Ouellette, J., and W. Wood. 1998. "Habit and Intention in Everyday Life: The Multiple Processes by Which Past Behavior Predicts Future Behavior." *Psychological Bulletin* 124:54–74.

Pantalon, M.V. 2011. *Instant Influence: How to Get Anyone to Do Anything—Fast!* New York: Little, Brown & Company.

Patterson, K., J. Grenny, R. McMillan, and A. Switzler. 2012. *Crucial Conversations: Tools for Talking When Stakes Are High*, 2nd ed. New York: McGraw-Hill.

Petersen, R.S., and K.J. Behfar. 2003. "The Dynamic Relationship Between Performance Feedback, Trust, and Conflict in Groups: A Longitudinal Study." *Organizational Behavior and Human Decision Processes* 92(1–2): 102–112.

Pink, D. 2009. "The Puzzle of Motivation." TEDGlobal 2009, July. ted.com/talks/dan_pink_the_puzzle_of_motivation.

Pink, D. 2011. *Drive: The Surprising Truth About What Motivates Us*. New York: Riverhead Books.

Pronin, E., D.Y. Lin, L. Ross. 2002. "The Bias Blind Spot: Perceptions of Bias in Self Versus Others." *Personality and Social Psychology Bulletin* 28(3): 369-381.

Rock, D., and H. Grant. 2016. "Why Diverse Teams Are Smarter." *Harvard Business Review*, November 4. hbr.org/2016/11/why-diverse-teams-are-smarter.

Rothwell, D.J. 2004. *In the Company of Others: An Introduction to Communication*. New York: McGraw Hill.

Russell, J.A., S. Brock, and M.E. Rudisill. 2019. "Recognizing the Impact of Bias in Faculty Recruitment, Retention, and Advancement Process." *Kinesiology Review* 8:291–295.

Ryan, R.M., and E.L. Deci. 2000. "Self-Determination Theory and the Facilitation of Intrinsic Motivation, Social Development, and Well-Being." *American Psychologist* 55(1): 68–78.

Salovey, P., J.D. Mayer, D. Caruso, and P.N. Lopes. 2003. "Measuring Emotional Intelligence as a Set of Abilities With the Mayer-Salovey -Caruso Emotional Intelligence Test." In *Positive Psychology Assessment: A Handbook of Models and Measures*, edited by S.J. Lopez and C.R. Snyder. Washington, DC: American Psychological Association.

Savage, J., and L. Moore. 2004. *Interpreting Accountability. RCN Institute Research Report.* Oxford, UK: Royal College of Nursing.

Schaper, D. 2020. "Congressional Inquiry Faults Boeing and FAA Failures for Deadly 737 Max Plane Crashes." NPR, September 16. npr.org/2020 /09/16/913426448/congressional-inquiry-faults-boeing-and-faa-failures -for-deadly-737-max-plane-cr.

Schawbel, D. 2019. "The Top 10 Workplace Trends for 2020." LinkedIn, November 1. linkedin.com/pulse/top-10-workplace-trends-2020 -dan-schawbel.

Senge, P. 2006. *The Fifth Discipline: The Art and Practice of the Learning Organization.* New York: Currency.

Seppala, E. 2014. "Connectedness and Health: The Science of Social Connection." The Center for Compassion and Altruism Research and Education, May 8. ccare.stanford.edu/uncategorized/connectedness-health-the -science-of-social-connection-infographic.

Smarp. 2021. "8 Employee Engagement Statistics You Need to Know in 2021 [Infographic]." Smarp blog, Updated January 4. blog.smarp.com /employee-engagement-8-statistics-you-need-to-know.

Sparber, S. 2021. "At Least 57 People Died in the Texas Winter Storm, Mostly From Hypothermia." *Texas Tribune*, March 15. texastribune.org/2021/03 /15/texas-winter-storm-deaths.

Stahl, A. 2019. "3 Ways Your Diet Impacts Work Performance." *Forbes*, August 6. forbes.com/sites/ashleystahl/2019/08/06/3-ways-your-diet- impacts-work-performance.

Steward, J. 2021. "The Ultimate List of Remote Work Statistics for 2022." Findstack, September 21. findstack.com/remote-work-statistics.

Stone, D., and S. Heen. 2014. *Thanks for the Feedback: The Science and Art of Receiving Feedback Well.* New York: Viking.

Toner, K. 2018. "She Makes Sure Unwanted Food Gets to Hungry Americans." CNN Health, December 9. cnn.com/2018/07/19/health/cnnheroes-maria-rose-belding-means/index.html.

Tran, S., and J.A. Simpson. 2009. "Prorelationship Maintenance Behaviors: The Joint Roles of Attachment and Commitment." *Journal of Personality and Social Psychology* 97(4): 685-698.

Wageman, R., D.A. Nunes, J.A. Burruss, and J.R. Hackman. 2008. *Senior Leadership Teams: What It Takes to Make Them Great.* Boston: Harvard Business School Press.

Ward, P. 2021. "Is It True That 90% of Startups Fail?" NanoGlobals, June 29. nanoglobals.com/startup-failure-rate-myths-origin.

Wickham, N. 2021. "The Importance of Employee Recognition: Statistics and Research." Quantum Workplace, June 10. quantumworkplace.com/future-of-work/importance-of-employee-recognition.

Wieselquist, J., C.E. Rusbult, C.A. Foster, and C.R. Agnew. 1999. "Commitment, Pro-Relationship Behavior, and Trust in Close Relationships." *Journal of Personality and Social Psychology* 77(5): 942–966.

Winch, G. 2013. "The Essential Guide to Recovering From Failure." Psychology Today, July 16. psychologytoday.com/us/blog/the-squeaky-wheel/201307/the-essential-guide-recovering-failure.

Zenger, J. 2015. "Taking Responsibility Is the Highest Mark of Great Leaders." *Forbes*, July 16. forbes.com/sites/jackzenger/2015/07/16/taking-responsibility-is-the-highest-mark-of-great-leaders.

# Index

Page numbers followed by *f* and *t* refer to figures and tables, respectively.

# About the Authors

**David C. Tate** is a licensed clinical psychologist, professionally certified coach, and organizational consultant. He is a founder and CEO at Conscious Growth Partners, a boutique consultancy that focuses on helping organizations realize their potential through better relationships, leadership, and teamwork. David has worked with leaders and senior managers in healthcare, financial services, manufacturing, distribution, publishing, media and design, education, human services, technology, and construction.

David is an assistant clinical professor in psychiatry at Yale University, where he received the 2013 Distinguished Faculty Award. He is a lecturer at the Yale School of Management, where he teaches within both the graduate and executive education programs. He also coaches global leaders within the Yale Greenberg World Fellows Program. David is an author of *Sink or Swim: How Lessons From the Titanic Can Save Your Family Business*.

David received a BS from Cornell University and a PhD in clinical psychology from the University of Virginia. He completed pre- and post-doctoral fellowships at Yale University before joining the faculty. David also has a Certificate in Family Business Advising from the Family Firm Institute, where he is also a fellow. He is a graduate of the Executive Coaching Academy and has completed additional coaching certification through the Institute for Professional Excellence in Coaching.

David enjoys the daily adventures of being a husband and dad, cooking and laughing over dinner with friends, playing board games with his 15 nieces and nephews, traveling, spending time in the great outdoors, and participating in community theater.

**Marianne S. Pantalon** is a clinical and consulting psychologist and executive coach. She is a founder and chief strategy officer at Conscious Growth Partners, a mission-focused consulting firm dedicated to helping organizations improve both their results and relationships through improved awareness, intentionality, and skill development. Her specialties are interpersonal dynamics and team effectiveness. Marianne provides assessment, individual and team coaching, facilitation, skills training, leadership development, and culture change across a variety of settings including corporate, academic, and startups. In addition to her private consulting work, she serves as a senior facilitator at the Yale School of Management, where she helps students develop the skills needed to become powerful global leaders.

People who work with Marianne often describe her as compassionate, insightful, and exceptional at creating the safety needed for courageous conversations. Helping folks shed light on influences operating below the surface is where Marianne thrives and finds deep meaning and fulfillment in her work.

Social entrepreneurship is Marianne's passion. She is the primary investigator of an NIH Small Business Innovation Research grant to build a digital health tool to help individuals with opioid use disorder. She also volunteers as a mentor and judge at the Patricelli Center for Social Entrepreneurship at Wesleyan University.

A creative at heart, Marianne enjoys photography, graphic design, interior design, writing, and calligraphy. She began her academic studies as a film major at Binghamton University and went on to earn a PhD at Hofstra University, studying the impact of writing for her dissertation. You can get a glimpse of her fun-loving competitive nature during family games and at the gym. More often, she loves spending time outside, getting lost in views, and dawdling among the trees.

 **Daryn H. David** is a licensed clinical psychologist, educator, and leadership development coach. At the Yale School of Medicine, Daryn holds a faculty appointment at the Child Study Center and serves as associate director for leadership development in the Office of Academic & Professional Development and the Office of Diversity, Equity & Inclusion.

Through dynamic pedagogy, leadership development coaching, and innovative programming, Daryn leverages her expertise to help academics and healthcare providers actualize their fullest professional potential. She also promotes the broader educational mission of Yale University by coaching high-impact leaders through the Yale Greenberg World Fellowship and the Women's Leadership Program at the Yale School of Management.

In addition to her work in academia, Daryn maintains a psychotherapy and coaching practice devoted to supporting women professionals.

Daryn holds a bachelor of arts in social studies from Harvard University and a PhD in psychology from Yale University. She received postdoctoral training at the Yale School of Medicine, held a Science & Technology Policy fellowship from the American Association for the Advancement of Science at the National Institutes of Health, and has completed the Playing Big Facilitators Training with Tara Mohr.

Daryn enjoys hiking and swimming. She cherishes time with her beautiful family, as well as more solitary moments spent writing prose or knitting.